PROGRAMMING
BUSINESS
APPLICATIONS
FOR THE
ANDROID™ TABLET

JAMES C. SHEUSI

Course Technology PTR
A part of Cengage Learning

COURSE TECHNOLOGY
CENGAGE Learning®

Australia • Brazil • Japan • Korea • Mexico • Singapore • Spain • United Kingdom • United States

COURSE TECHNOLOGY
CENGAGE Learning

**Programming Business Applications
for the Android™ Tablet:**
James C. Sheusi

**Publisher and General Manager,
Course Technology PTR:**
Stacy L. Hiquet

Associate Director of Marketing:
Sarah Panella

Manager of Editorial Services:
Heather Talbot

Senior Marketing Manager:
Mark Hughes

Senior Acquisitions Editor:
Mitzi Koontz

Project/Copy Editor:
Karen A. Gill

Technical Reviewer:
Jeffrey Tagen

Interior Layout Tech:
MPS limited

Cover Designer:
Luke Fletcher

Indexer:
Kelly Talbot Editing Services

Proofreader:
Gene Redding

For product information and technology assistance, contact us at
Cengage Learning Customer & Sales Support, 1-800-354-9706.

For permission to use material from this text or product,
submit all requests online at
www.cengage.com/permissions.

Further permissions questions can be emailed to
permissionrequest@cengage.com.

Portions of the references used in this book are modifications based
on work created and shared by Google and used according to terms
described in the Creative Commons 3.0 Attribution License.
Complete references can be found at http://developer.google.com.

Android is a trademark of Google, Inc. Microsoft, Windows, and
Internet Explorer are either registered trademarks or trademarks of
Microsoft Corporation in the United States and/or other countries.

All other trademarks are the property of their respective owners.

All images © Cengage Learning unless otherwise noted.

Library of Congress Control Number: 2012945772

ISBN-13: 978-1-285-15999-7

ISBN-10: 1-285-15999-3

Course Technology, a part of Cengage Learning

20 Channel Center Street

Boston, MA 02210

USA

Cengage Learning is a leading provider of customized learning
solutions with office locations around the globe, including
Singapore, the United Kingdom, Australia, Mexico, Brazil, and
Japan. Locate your local office at: **international.cengage.com/region.**

Cengage Learning products are represented in Canada by Nelson
Education, Ltd.

For your lifelong learning solutions, visit **courseptr.com.**

Visit our corporate website at **cengage.com.**

Printed in the United States of America
1 2 3 4 5 6 7 14 13 12

For Helena, as always...

ACKNOWLEDGMENTS

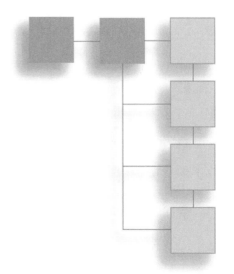

I would like to thank my family—Helena, Nicole, Nathan, Neal, and Dasher—for suffering through my preoccupation with another book for the better part of this year. I truly appreciate their patience. I would also like to thank the students who pioneered the first Android programming class at Johnson and Wales University, especially Wil Hall, Mike Rizzuto, and Owais Mughloo, for their enthusiasm and creativity; they inspired me to write this book. Finally, I would like to thank Mike Oliver at Claflin Medical Equipment in Rhode Island for bringing Android devices and their business application potential to my attention in the first place. I am indebted to you all.

ABOUT THE AUTHOR

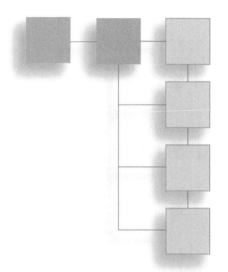

James C. Sheusi copyrighted and sold his first application for the real estate sales industry in 1984 and has developed applications for small businesses for more than 25 years. He is an associate professor and currently chair of the Department of Computer and Information Science in the School of Technology at Johnson and Wales University in Providence, Rhode Island. He is the author of another book, titled *Android Application Development for Java Programmers*. He resides with his wife in Bristol, Rhode Island.

Contents

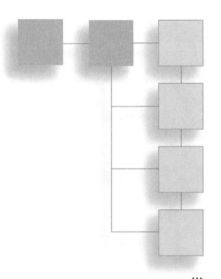

Preface. viii

Introduction x

Chapter 1   Installing Eclipse, Java, and the Android SDK. 1

    Configuring the Test Surface 6

    Summary of Key Concepts 11

    Suggested Projects 12

Chapter 2   Migrating to Android 3.0 and Above 13

    A Quick Eclipse Refresher 13

    The Action Bar 25

    Fragments 32

    Summary of Key Concepts 51

    Review Questions 52

    Suggested Projects 53

Chapter 3   Databases in the Application 55

    Bundling a Database 55

    Displaying the Table with a ListView 65

    Building a Table at Run-Time 75

    Summary of Key Concepts 87

    Review Questions 87

    Suggested Projects 88

Chapter 4   Forms and Graphics 89

    Forms with Pick-Lists 89

    Subclassing Controls 104

Extending the TextView with Graphics. 113
Summary of Key Concepts 127
Review Questions 127
Suggested Projects 128

Chapter 5   Content Providers. 129
Introduction 129
Calendars and Event Postings 130
Using the Contacts 138
Summary of Key Concepts 163
Review Questions 165
Suggested Projects 165

Chapter 6   Client-Server Applications 167
Connectionless Communications on the Internet 167
Connection-Oriented Client-Server Applications 179
Summary of Key Concepts 191
Review Questions 192
Suggested Projects 193

Chapter 7   Using External Data 195
Using XML and JSON with External Sources 213
Summary of Key Concepts 229
Review Questions 230
Suggested Projects 231

Chapter 8   The Camera as a Data Source. 233
Bar Codes and QR Codes 233
Photographs in Applications. 240
Summary of Key Concepts 253
Review Questions 253
Suggested Projects 254

Chapter 9   Deployment and Versioning. 255

Appendix A   Answers to Chapter Review Questions 265
Chapter 2. 265
Chapter 3. 266
Chapter 4. 267
Chapter 5. 269
Chapter 6. 271
Chapter 7. 272
Chapter 8. 273

Index 275

PREFACE

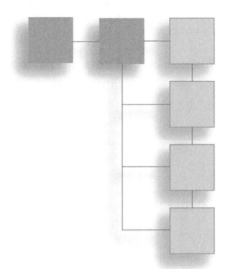

I was motivated to write this book because I believe the tablet platform is suitable and even ideal for those who need a mobile source of data in their everyday activities, from a quick update during a commute to the need to check inventory, quote prices, and place orders throughout the day. The platform is ideal as well for those who need an occasional source of information and correspondence but don't want the large footprint of a keyboard, mouse, and monitor taking up their desk space.

In October 2011, the Institute of Electrical and Electronics Engineers (IEEE) reported in its flagship publication, *The Spectrum*, that the Java programming language is by far the most popular applications programming language. Indeed, most surveys rate Java near or at the top in categories such as most discussed and web-searched, most books published, and most commonly used in open-source projects. Because there are so many resources available for Java applications programmers and there is such a range of choices and availability of Android-powered tablet devices, the Android platform puts business automation for mobile devices within reach of almost any size enterprise.

This book, like its predecessor *Android Application Development for Java Programmers*, is a tutorial for programming Android applications. The examples presented are created using the Eclipse integrated development environment (IDE) with the J2SE, Java Standard Edition, and the Android software development toolkit (SDK) added in.

Programming Business Applications for the Android Tablet is intended to be a quick, one-stop source of examples for the topics that are central to business application programming for mobile devices, particularly tablets. This book provides enough detail that a newcomer to Android programming can create a useful and, indeed, marketable application. However, each section covers only the surface of a topic; there is plenty of room for outside research. Java and Android are extremely well-covered topics on the Internet. You need only to search class names, method names, or key questions to receive further guidance. Simply add the word *tutorial* or *example* to your search query, and you will find plenty of what you are looking for.

This book is meant for programmers familiar with object-oriented programming (OOP) principles and preferably with Java programming experience. If you are familiar with C++ or C#, you will be able to follow the examples well enough to make the book a worthwhile read. Familiarity with the Eclipse IDE is ideal but not necessary. This book covers the basic install of the Java development toolkit (JDK), the Android SDK, and the Eclipse IDE. Configuration of the Eclipse environment is covered as the steps become necessary.

Although it is certainly preferable to have a tablet device to test and debug your applications, the Android SDK contains the necessary software to generate emulators for Android devices such as smart phones and tablets; you don't need to possess an actual device to develop and test an application. An emulator is a program that produces a screen display and the functionality of a handheld device on your development computer. Using the emulator, you can fine-tune the look of your application and test most of its features. Of course, the development experience will be much more rewarding if you can actually carry around your creations and use them as they are intended.

Each example in this book is functional and usable. You can copy the screen designs in the form of XML files from one application to others where the same configuration is appropriate. The same is true with subclasses found in examples—especially inline classes. The chapters are arranged so that you can use concepts introduced in the early chapters throughout the balance of the book. Gradually, built-in device features such as database management, file storage, and access to networks and the Internet are added to applications. Use your imagination as you read this book to convert the principles presented into useful, appealing applications. Be productive, and enjoy!

INTRODUCTION

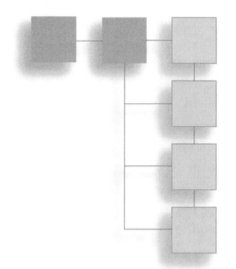

I have to admit that when I first saw the Apple iPad early in 2010, I thought, "Who would have the need for a giant iPhone…with no phone service!" In other words, all I saw was a giant iPod Touch. I am not an audiophile; I have no music on either my smart phone or my tablet devices (I have three), and I am not a particular fan of social networks or games, so I didn't see much in it for me. But after using an iPad for a few minutes, I discovered a feature that changed my whole opinion of the device: if I turned the tablet landscape, I could just about touch-type on it! Indeed, the keyboard was the same size as the keyboard on my HP—mini netbook. A keyboard was something I could relate to. In fact, this was the biggest shortcoming to smart phones like the iPhone in my opinion. With a usable keyboard, I could comfortably use the device for emailing or taking notes. I had to admit that the iPad was worth another look.

The sheer size of the device combined with WiFi would allow opportunities for tele-conferencing, give an acceptable and even enjoyable Internet experience, and offer an electronic reader platform that would rival devices such as the Amazon Kindle. And as much as I hate to mention games, the iPad made a better game platform than the smart phone. Like millions of others, I bought and became hooked on my iPad, but I missed writing my own applications.

Years before the release of the Apple iPod Touch, I began writing applications for the small platform with J2ME (Java 2 Platform, Micro Edition) on Palm devices. As an avid Java programmer (and a Sun-Certified programmer for Java 2), I quickly found a new application target when the Android-powered mobile phones hit the market.

I put my first application on the Android market early in 2011, before I even owned an Android device. I was happy to be able to use Java to create applications for platforms other than the desktop, just for the challenge of it. Mobility, combined with WiFi, cell communications, and GPS service, widens the range of opportunities for new and interesting applications for handheld devices.

When Android tablets began to hit the market in 2011, all the advantages of size that I enjoyed with the iPad combined with the ability to use Java to write applications. I turned my attention toward developing useful business applications for the Android-powered tablet devices.

The parallel evolution of cloud-based computing is providing a virtually unlimited source of back-end computing power for tablet devices. Large-scale applications and data no longer have to be stored on the device, which allows the tablet to serve as an "ultra-thin client." Nearly ubiquitous connectivity coupled with a truly lightweight manageable platform makes the mobile enterprise concept a reality. The only thing that needs to catch up to the possibilities is the app developer's imagination.

There isn't a single IT publication that hasn't spent a significant amount of time and space on mobile computing. In May 2011, Rieva Lesonsky posted an article on Networksolutions.com called "Tablet Computing Trends in Business." She made several observations worth noting. The first was that tablets (at the time, the iPad was essentially the only choice on the market) were cutting into the usage of traditional platforms such as desktop machines and laptops. Thirty-five percent of Nielsen survey respondents stated that since getting a tablet, they use their other computers less often or not at all. Second, Lesonsky cited a Gartner report that predicted that the iPad would dominate the tablet market through 2015, but in the same period predicted that Android's market share would rise to 39 percent. Ten months later, the market research firm International Data Corporation (IDC) predicted that Android-powered tablets would overtake the iPad by 2015. Finally, Lesonsky observed iPads being used to take orders and print receipts in a restaurant.

The term BYOD (bring your own device), a phrase that no one even used a couple of years ago, has become a hot IT topic. Big industry players such as IBM and Unisys, as well as leading publications such as *Networkworld*, *Computerworld*, and *Network Computing*, have weighed in on the topic of managing the BYOD phenomenon. Combined, the iPad and the various Android-powered tablets easily dominate the tablet market share. The May 21, 2012, edition of *NetworkWorld* magazine carried an article debating iOS versus Android use in business. On the Android side, Dennis Baliton credited Android's open-source nature and the large pool of developers that promotes, the large number of current Java programmers that already exists who can easily migrate to Android development, and the vast array of preexisting Java libraries that can be used in Android app development. At print time, those who voted favored Android 55 percent, with 45 percent favoring iOS.

In a paper released by Gartner in January 2012, author Stephen Kleyhans coined the phrase *personal cloud*, using it to describe how we are moving away from a hardware-centered view of technology toward using our favorite devices to channel the connected world's resources. Connectivity allows us to leave big jobs to big computers and big applications, while tiny low-cost or no-cost apps on one's favorite mobile device can manage specific everyday needs. A more tech-savvy population coupled with consumer-target virtual storage and services allows tiny devices to take on big tasks.

Let's not forget technological advances in hardware that today's smart phones and tablets bring to the consumer. Consider the touch screen itself. It is certainly not new technology, but its application-to-consumer devices have never been so pervasive. A tablet or smart phone essentially eliminates the need for a keyboard and mouse. Voice recognition technology hobbled along for years as an added PC feature but finds its niche on a handheld device as an ideal input option. Finally, the camera on most devices provides an input channel that has the potential to eliminate an immeasurable number of keystrokes when the right application utilizes it. All of these advanced input/output (I/O) features say nothing of the amazing processing power and storage capability of modern mobile devices compared to what personal computers offered not very long ago.

Whether you prefer the iOS or Android is irrelevant to the fact that tablet computing is becoming a popular alternative in the world of business computing. Consider the tablet device as a paper saver. Instead of receiving pages of briefing materials ahead of a meeting, you can prepare by reading them on a tablet. You can make changes and redistribute them instantly without reprinting. Not only are printing costs eliminated, but the whole distribution system can be sped up and decentralized. In the warehouse, the device's camera can scan bar codes to reveal information about particular items. Add a connection to a central database, and an employee filling orders can instantly update inventory information. With GPS capability, information can be not only time sensitive, but location sensitive. This offers a whole new dimension to information management. The possibilities for tablet apps are limited to the needs and the imagination of the developer. And that brings us to the purpose of this book.

My purpose in writing this book is to help the IT worker or entrepreneur who sees an opportunity for a business app but may need some insight into the mechanics of Android application development. I take 25 years of industry experience along with Java and database experience and build some simple business solutions, illustrating the code necessary to produce the app and apply the principles. The examples are heavily database laden and mix in some of the improvements to Android brought by Android 3.x and 4.x. I also make suggestions on user interface optimization and take advantage of some of the features on a typical Android tablet, including the camera and WiFi connectivity. For each feature or topic covered, I supply code for a fully functional sample application. In the sample applications, I point out some simple tricks for you to use, such as restricting the display to portrait or landscape orientation and using toast messages where appropriate. I also cover more advanced operations such as threads, fragments, and data-binding. My intent is not to present cutting-edge techniques, but to save you hours of research that might otherwise be needed to assemble an application. You will not find animation techniques, application of the accelerometer, or other things that may interest game developers. However, you will find use of graphics as a visual interpretation of data, as well as retrieval of GPS information from the device.

It is my hope that you will see how you can solve a problem or take advantage of an opportunity by customizing some of the examples to suit yourself. Feel free to use them as they are; I place no restrictions on the content. Where appropriate, I cite a source or point out some useful resources relevant to the topic at hand. Most examples are intended for the tablet platform but allow for any limitation caused by a minimum version of Android that might be required to use a particular feature; all would run on a handheld device as well.

May you find ways to free your target application audience from their PCs and laptop computers and help them find new uses for their mobile devices. Good luck, and happy coding.

CONVENTIONS USED IN THIS TUTORIAL

To make this book easier to read, special conventions are employed throughout.

Italic is used to indicate new terms.

`Monospace type` is used to indicate blocks of code, commands to be entered at a terminal screen, messages, menu paths, switches, controls, file and directory names, parameters, objects, classes, tags, methods, variables, and widgets.

WHAT YOU'LL FIND IN THIS BOOK

Here's what you'll find throughout the pages of this book:

- A guide to installing and configuring an Android development environment on your personal computer.

- A guide to configuring an Android device emulator on your personal computer and illustrations of running applications on the emulator.

- All the code necessary to create several simple applications to demonstrate the capabilities of an Android mobile device.

- A guide to publishing an Android mobile application.

- Explanations of the methodologies used in the examples, as well as descriptions of the classes and their methods used in the examples.

- Follow-up exercises and recommendations for further study as well as many outside references for clarification of principles and techniques used in the book.

WHO THIS BOOK IS FOR

I intend this book for on-staff, consulting, or freelancing applications programmers who are familiar with OOP, preferably in Java, and are interested or required to extend an enterprise's information processing to the mobile arena. This book concentrates on topics that complement and augment the common business uses of technology, such as database management, web-based user interfaces, and graphic representation of data. This book provides a quick start to prototyping applications on the mobile platform for the business applications programmer.

HOW THIS BOOK IS ORGANIZED

The book is organized in a logical, evolutionary manner starting with configuration of the development environment and ending with two comprehensive projects. The beginning chapters cover basic application components and configuration of the Android emulator and basic user interface design, whereas later chapters cover how to accomplish more involved areas such as use of GPS, graphics, networking, and databases. In most chapters, you will find the following:

- An introduction to the concept or technique to be covered

- A description of the example application presented to demonstrate the concept

- All the coding necessary to produce a running application to demonstrate the chapter's topic

- A recap of key points in the chapter
- A list of questions for review of key points in the chapter
- Several suggested projects to utilize the principles raised in the chapter

The appendix has the answers to the Chapter Review questions found at the end of Chapters 2 through 8.

CHAPTER 1

INSTALLING ECLIPSE, JAVA, AND THE ANDROID SDK

Because you have chosen this book, chances are that you are already developing or at least have attempted to develop some Android applications, and most likely for a handset such as a smart phone or small Android device such as the Galaxy Player 5 by Samsung. Android tablets are relatively new to the market, and most of them are running Android 3.x or higher. The primary purpose of the book is to develop tablet applications, so you may want to upgrade your development environment to be sure you can take advantage of the latest features. On the other hand, if you are starting from scratch, you need to download the Java software development toolkit (SDK), the Eclipse integrated development environment (IDE), and the Android SDK. Eclipse is available from www.eclipse.org, the Java development toolkit (JDK) is available from www.oracle.com/technetwork/java/javase/downloads/index.html, and the Android SDK is available from http://developer.android.com/sdk/index.html. All the sites include comprehensive documentation and installation guidelines, but I am including some basics and tips here.

It is better to download and install the JDK first. The current version at the time of this writing is version 7. After it installs, you will want to set its location in your computer system's PATH variable. You can consult references on how to do this on the Internet, but if you are using Windows 7 as I am, you can use the following steps.

1. Click the Start button, right-click on Computer on the right side of the Start menu, and choose Properties. You see a new window; the left side looks like Figure 1.1.

Figure 1.1
Computer Properties window.
Source: *Microsoft® Corporation.*

2. Choose Advanced System Settings. You see Figure 1.2.

3. If it isn't selected already, select the Advanced tab at the top, and then click the Environment Variables button at the bottom right. You see Figure 1.3.

4. In the bottom System Variables area, select Path from the list of variables, and then click the Edit button. At the end of that line, insert a semicolon (;), and then enter the path to your installed JDK's bin (short for binary files)

Figure 1.2
Advanced System Settings window.
Source: *Microsoft® Corporation.*

directory, probably a line similar to the following: `c:\program files\java\ jdk1.6.0_24\bin\`. You can check this by using a command prompt or the file manager on your development system. Move to the `Program Files` folder (directory) and look for an entry called `Java`. In that folder, check for the entry beginning with `jdk`; this is the folder you want to put in the path following the example. There will likely be another folder whose name starts with `jre`; don't use this one.

5. Finally, click OK and work your way out of the windows.

The next piece of your development system to install is Eclipse. You can download Eclipse at www.eclipse.org. The Eclipse website offers documentation to help you with the install, but it is pretty straightforward. What can be confusing, however, is the number and variety of Eclipse versions. The current version of the Android SDK requires Eclipse Helios version or later. The versions have nicknames that run in alphabetical order, so the Indigo version, newer than Helios, would work as well. For more details on which Eclipse version is appropriate, you can look at http://developer.

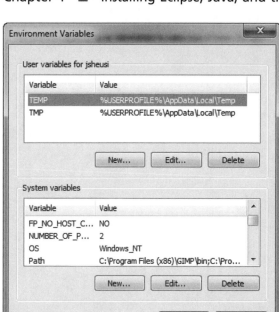

Figure 1.3
Environment Variables window.
Source: *Microsoft® Corporation.*

android.com/sdk/requirements.html. The Eclipse installation should use the system's PATH variable to find the JDK. The examples in this book were created with Helios.

If you can start Eclipse, select the New menu and choose Project, and see Java Project as a choice, so far so good. If that doesn't happen for you, go back and check documentation for the Eclipse and Java installations. Above all, be patient.

Finally, we can begin to install the Android SDK. There are actually two steps to configure Android. First you need the toolkit, and then you need to configure Eclipse. You can download the SDK at http://developer.android.com/sdk. Once you have it installed, you need to make another change to your PATH environment variable similar to what you did earlier. You will follow the same steps and add an entry similar to the following to the path: c:\program files (x86)\android\android-sdk\tools\. Don't forget to separate entries with a semicolon. If you currently have a version of the Android SDK installed, and you want to upgrade it, it can be a headache. If you are using Windows 7, choose All Programs from the Start menu, and find Android SDK Tools. In this group, look for Android SDK Manager. Instead of double-clicking it, right-click it and choose Run as Administrator. From inside Eclipse, you can choose Android SDK Manager under the Window menu, but if you didn't start Eclipse as administrator, you can't do that here. Of course, to start Eclipse as administrator, you can right-click the Eclipse shortcut icon and choose Run as Administrator.

Even when you're trying to upgrade Android as administrator, you may find error messages during the update process. Some posts on the Internet recommend reinstalling the whole Android SDK to take advantage of the latest features. At any rate, if you do encounter error messages during the upgrade, make a note of them and search them on your favorite search engine. If you are an Android fan, that is probably Google.

To configure the Eclipse plug-in for Android, start Eclipse and select Install New Software from the Help menu. You see Figure 1.4.

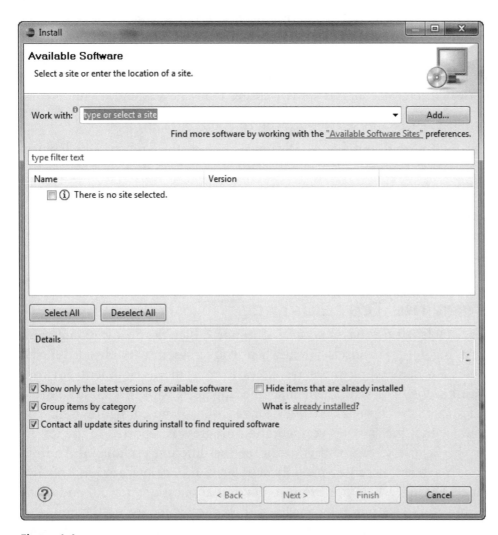

Figure 1.4
Eclipse Install New Software window.
Source: *The Eclipse Foundation.*

In the Work With field, enter the following website: http://dl-ssl.google.com/android/ eclipse/. Put a check in the box that appears in the screen under the Name column in the pick-list, click Next, and follow the prompts to the end of the process. You need to agree to all the licenses to get to the Finish button. Testing the Android installation is similar to testing the Java installation. Again, select the File menu on Eclipse, select New, Project, and you should see Android Project as a choice. If it is there, you should be good to go. If not, check your steps and look for some online troubleshooting help.

There is no lack of documentation on the Internet for Eclipse, Java, and Android. Just use your favorite search engine and use your problem as a keyword. I usually precede my issue with the keyword *android*. For example, *android upgrade will not install.* Indeed, if you ever run into a problem with part of a project you see in this tutorial or attempt on your own, you can rest assured that many other developers have run into the same problem and are more than likely to have posted solutions on the Internet. The list that follows contains some websites that I have found useful.

http://download.oracle.com/javase	Documentation on J2SE
http://developer.android.com	Documentation on the Android Development Toolkit
www.dreamincode.net	General programming help for many development languages
www.stackoverflow.com	Solutions to many common programming problems offered by other developers

CONFIGURING THE TEST SURFACE

Developing for a tablet device has a couple of minor difficulties to overcome compared to developing for a handset. First, when you cross into Android 3.0 and Android 4.0, you are demanding more resources from your development environment. Once you have your development machine upgraded with the latest Android SDK, you will notice that Eclipse takes a little longer to load and configure itself. You will probably notice that the start-up configuration progress is reported in the lower-right corner of the Eclipse screen, and you can see the different versions of Android being loaded and reported. Because you only start Eclipse once per session, this is a minor annoyance. Second, when you begin to develop applications for 3.0 and eventually 4.0, the emulators take much longer to load. Try to avoid closing the emulator during a session (if you are in fact using an emulator; more about this later); I prefer to minimize it between trial runs of an application project. Finally, you have to manage the size of the emulator on the screen. Because you will want to use a tablet emulator rather than a handset, be prepared to have the emulator cover most of the screen.

As a point of reference to the reader, I have developed on two machines: a laptop with a 2.5 gigahertz (GHz) Core i5 processor, Windows 7, and 4 gigabytes (GB) of RAM, and a desktop machine with a 2.8 GHz AMD Athlon processor with 2 GB of RAM, also running Windows 7. I configured an emulator for Android 3.2, 9 megabytes (MB) SD card, and WXGA skin (which is the default).

On the laptop, this emulator takes about 60 seconds to load, and the built-in apps are essentially unresponsive. On the desktop machine, the same emulator takes about 3 minutes to load, and the response from the built-in apps is about the same. The emulator defaults to a horizontal tablet configuration and takes up most of the screen. In fact, I find it useful to move the Windows toolbar from the bottom of the screen to the left side so it doesn't overlap with the emulator. Another tip to start the emulator is to open it from the AVD Manager under the Window menu in Eclipse. Once it's open, choose the emulator you want to use (if you have more than one), and click the Start button on the right. You see a dialog box, shown in Figure 1.5, that lets you reset the size of the emulator. (This dialog box isn't visible if you simply started the emulator from the Eclipse Java screen.) Check the Scale Display to Real Size check box and set the screen size you want. Finally, click the Launch button at the bottom. Once the emulator starts, just minimize it and go back to your code. Although this will take care of the size difficulties, it doesn't really do anything for the load speed and responsiveness of the emulator.

A desirable alternative to using an onscreen emulator is to connect an actual device to the development machine—preferably the device you are developing for if you are fortunate enough to be developing for a single deployment platform and you are able to get your hands on one. Aside from the obvious advantage of not having to wait for an emulator to "boot up," using an actual device essentially gives you an additional screen. With your app running on an attached device, you will have 100 percent of your development computer's screen to yourself. There will be no need to shuffle between Eclipse, or whichever IDE you are using, and the emulator.

I am using two devices to write this book: the Galaxy Player 5 by Samsung, and the Thrive 10-inch tablet by Toshiba. The former is running Android 2.3.5 Gingerbread, and the latter is running Android 3.2.1 Honeycomb. The Galaxy Player connects to the development machine via a micro-USB/USB cable, which is part of its charger hardware (the cord separates from the wall-socket plug), and the Thrive tablet connects with a mini-USB/USB cable through a port in the side. I chose the Thrive

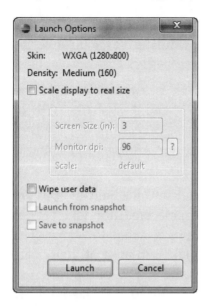

Figure 1.5
Eclipse Emulator Launch Options dialog.
Source: *The Eclipse Foundation.*

because it comes with a standard USB connector, a mini-USB connector, and an HDMI connector built in.

You can configure the development environment by connecting an actual hardware device with a cable and carrying out the following four steps. Each will be covered at length after the following list.

1. Install drivers for the device(s) on the development computer.

2. Set the device to allow debugging.

3. Check to see that the device is visible to the Eclipse IDE.

4. Set the manifest file in the application to allow debugging on the hardware device.

You can find the USB drivers for your devices by searching the Internet. With little difficulty, I found the drivers for both the Toshiba Thrive tablet and the Samsung Galaxy Player 5. Both of these drivers installed themselves, but I cannot guarantee that will always be the case. The Android Developers website at http://developer. android.com/sdk/oem-usb.html#Win7 offers a guide for installing drivers for different platforms, in this case Windows 7. The same web page also lists download locations for dozens of USB drivers for different devices. Before you start to use this guide, however, you should have your tablet or whatever device you are writing for wired up to your development machine. The procedure is a little different if you are using a development machine running Linux, but the steps for Linux are covered on the web pages as well.

You must carry out step 2 on the device itself. All Android devices have a Settings feature. If the device has a hardware menu button on the touch surface, you will find a Settings menu there. If not, there will be a Settings button in the Apps section or in the Shortcuts. Any way you can reach the settings, choose Applications, and then Development. Some devices may have a choice called Developer Options listed at the first menu level. You need to allow USB debugging by checking that option.

If you have done all this correctly and have your device wired up to the development machine, you can now check to see if your device is available to Eclipse (step 3 in the previous list) by doing the following.

1. Under the Window tab in Eclipse, select Show View (see Figure 1.6). At the bottom of that menu, choose Other.

Figure 1.6
Eclipse Show View menu.
Source: *The Eclipse Foundation.*

2. Choose Devices on that menu and click the OK button. You should see a new panel and tab where you would normally see the console or LogCat at the bottom of the Eclipse screen. Figure 1.7 shows that my Toshiba tablet is connected. When I run an application from Eclipse, it is displayed on my tablet rather than on an emulator.

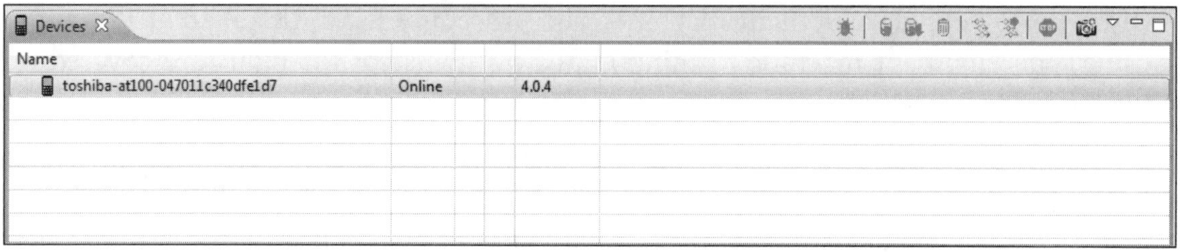

Figure 1.7
Eclipse Devices panel.
Source: *The Eclipse Foundation.*

Step 4 in the preceding list is done to the individual application's manifest file. The Android Developers web page, http://developer.android.com/guide/developing/device. html, states that inside the `<application>` tags you should enter the following line.

```
android:debuggable="true"
```

The page further states that this is unnecessary when using Eclipse, but I'm adding it here in case you might use a different IDE. The default value for `android:debuggable` is `"false"`. Remember to remove this line from the manifest before you deploy the application, or at least set it to `"false"`.

As long as we are configuring our development environment here, it is a good time to configure your digital signature. If you are already developing Android apps for distribution either internally or on the app market, you certainly have already done this. If not, this is a good time to prepare a `keystore`.

You will use a program called `keytool` to create your signature file. `keytool` is actually part of the Java SDK, not Android's. It is found in the `/bin` subdirectory of the `JRE` directory. You can find it with the search utility of your development computer's operating system if you are not sure how to find and navigate the Java SDK's directory structure. You can find a comprehensive description of what the `keytool` utility actually does and how to get the most from it at the following web page: http://docs. oracle.com/javase/1.5.0/docs/tooldocs/solaris/keytool.html.

The following command and switches give you enough information on the screen to prepare a suitable key to sign your applications with.

```
keytool -genkey -v -keystore ?????.keystore -alias ????? -keyalg RSA -validity 5000
```

Note

The pattern of five question marks in the command line indicates values you can choose on your own. For convenience sake, I use the same value in both sets of question marks. The value for the -alias field is case sensitive, so be careful to make a note of which letters, if any, you capitalize.

The -genkey switch simply creates a key. -v means *verbose*, and it allows the user to see the key in human-readable form. The -keystore switch allows you to determine the location for storing the key; it defaults to the user's home directory. (See the previous note about naming the keystore file. Use .keystore as the extension.) The -alias switch helps secure your key. You will use this alias when you use the key later to sign an app. The -keyalg switch specifies the encryption algorithm used for the key. RSA are the three last initials for the algorithm's developers: Rivest, Shamir, and Aldeman. The -validity switch specifies the number of days the key is good for. Subsequent versions of the same application must be signed with the same signature key, or the Android operating system on the target device will not allow the update.

Once you enter the keytool command at a terminal prompt, you will be asked several questions whose answers will be used to develop the key. Finally, you will be asked if the information is correct, and a key file will be generated and stored in your home directory with the name you prescribed and the .keystore extension.

SUMMARY OF KEY CONCEPTS

- The Java SDK Standard Edition (J2SE), the Eclipse integrated development environment (IDE), and the Android software development toolkit (SDK) are all freely available for download on the Internet. There are plenty of configuration guides similar to the content of this chapter available on the Internet as well.

- New revisions and releases of these three key components of the Android development environment appear constantly, as do new versions of the Android operating system for the Android devices. When you do your initial configuration of your development environment, be sure to select the latest stable versions of all components.

- Using an actual Android device wired to the development platform is preferable to using an emulator. As stated in the chapter, this will likely require the installation of an additional driver for each device you attempt to connect. Even after you install a driver successfully, Eclipse will not recognize some devices. In this case, you may simply have to resort to using an emulator.

■ Publishing your application, whether through a public marketplace such as the Google PlayStore or through internal distribution, requires the application to be signed. Likewise, upgrades to an application already deployed need to be signed with the same key, or the upgrade will not work. Once you create your keystore file, make a note of where it is on your development system, because its path and filename are required for actually signing the application. You can copy the keystore file and put it in another location for safekeeping.

SUGGESTED PROJECTS

■ Study Android's guide for preparing applications for publication, documenting the version, and signing the application with a digital signature, found at the following URLs, respectively.

http://developer.android.com/tools/publishing/preparing.html

http://developer.android.com/tools/publishing/versioning.html

http://developer.android.com/tools/publishing/app-signing.html

The last URL explains how to use the key described at the end of the chapter.

■ Create an application, which can be as simple as the basic configuration created when you start a new project or as complex as you care to make it. Follow the steps in the guides just listed to produce a signed .apk file. Because Android applications do not need to be obtained through an official marketplace, their creator can deploy them through virtually any means. Test your application by attaching the signed .apk file to yourself, and then open the email on your Android device. The device will detect the attachment and prompt you to install it. Choose Install, and then enjoy your newly created application.

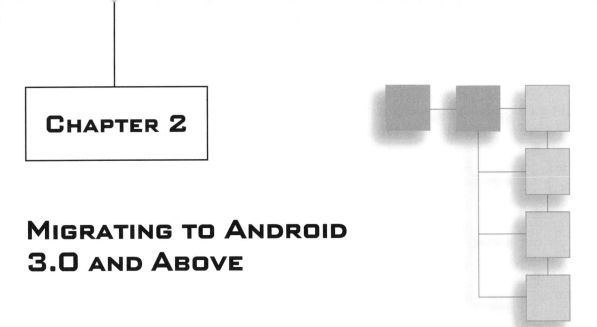

CHAPTER 2

MIGRATING TO ANDROID 3.0 AND ABOVE

A QUICK ECLIPSE REFRESHER

What's new for Android development actually starts with the Android software development toolkit (SDK) and Eclipse. There are changes to the project setup that allow the developer to have a little more control over package naming, project naming, and launch icon control in the newer versions of the SDK. An important difference is the default naming of the main activity class and the XML file that describes the screen layout. Before we get into these changes and where you will encounter them, let's do a quick review of how to get an Android development project going in Eclipse.

Let's assume at this point that you have correctly configured Eclipse with Java and the Android SDK. It's time to write the first application. If you have used Eclipse before, you know how to start a project. If not, here's what you need to know about projects. Eclipse creates a directory, or folder, called Workspace to store your programming projects. When Eclipse is installed, the installer is prompted for the desired location for this directory. After installation, Eclipse allows for the creation of a new Workspace directory and allows you to change the Workspace directory each time you open Eclipse.

Traditionally, any time you started a new project, Eclipse would ask for a project name and create a subdirectory (subfolder) in the Workspace directory for the project, using the chosen project name for the subdirectory name. However, in the new Eclipse add-on for Android, the developer is prompted for three entries: the application name, which will appear on the device with the launch icon once the application is deployed (and in the emulator during development); the project name, which will be used by Eclipse; and the package name. The package name is a little more complicated and refers to the Java structure referred to as a package. Simply put, a *package* is a related set of classes. Your project could contain many classes, related to each other by a single purpose: to provide the functionality of your Android app. All the package names in the Android system must be unique. To be sure that whatever you are adding will not coincidentally match anything else, a reverse-domain-style naming system is used. The Java convention for naming packages is sort of a web domain name backwards, such as com.sheusi.SomeProject. You should note that reverse-domain naming is the convention here. You need not own a domain name; you can just make one up. (You can learn more about package naming at http://download.oracle.com/javase/tutorial/java/package/namingpkgs.html.)

During project setup, the developer is also prompted to pick both the build SDK and the minimum required SDK. Previously, the minimum required SDK had to be set in the manifest file after the project was set up and in development. See Figure 2.1 for the new project setup panel.

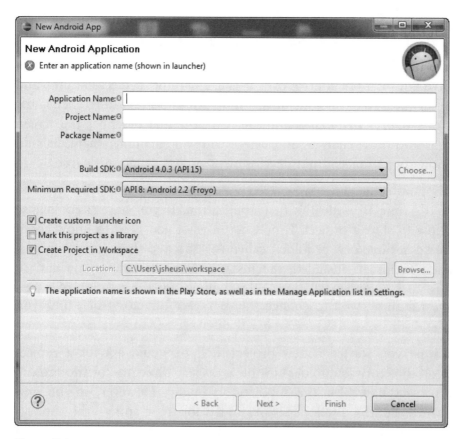

Figure 2.1
Eclipse New Android Application panel.
Source: The Eclipse Foundation.

The lower the application programming interface (API) you choose, the more inclusive you will be of devices that will run your application. On the other hand, the lower the number you choose, the fewer features of devices and advances in the Android platform your application will be able to take advantage of. Table 2.1 shows the complete list of versions and corresponding APIs at the time of this writing.

Once you click the Next button at the bottom of the panel, you can select the launch image from a handful of built-in clip art images by clicking the Clipart button; or you can choose your own by choosing the Image button. The launch image is what the user will select on his device to start your application. You also have the option of using text instead of an icon or changing the shape and color of the launch icon. See Figure 2.2. Previously, the stock Android icon was used automatically, and the

Table 2.1   Android Versions, API Levels, and Code Names

Platform Version	API Level	VERSION_CODE
Android 4.1	16	JELLY BEAN
Android 4.0	14	ICE CREAM SANDWICH
Android 3.2	13	HONEYCOMB_MR2
Android 3.1.x	12	HONEYCOMB_MR1
Android 3.0.x	11	HONEYCOMB
Android 2.3.4	10	GINGERBREAD_MR1
Android 2.3.3		
Android 2.3.2		
Android 2.3.1	9	GINGERBREAD
Android 2.3		
Android 2.2.x	8	FROYO
Android 2.1.x	7	ECLAIR_MR1
Android 2.0.1	6	ECLAIR_0_1
Android 2.0	5	ECLAIR
Android 1.6	4	DONUT
Android 1.5	3	CUPCAKE
Android 1.1	2	BASE_1_
Android 1.0	1	BASE

Source: http://developer.android.com/guide/appendix/api-levels.html

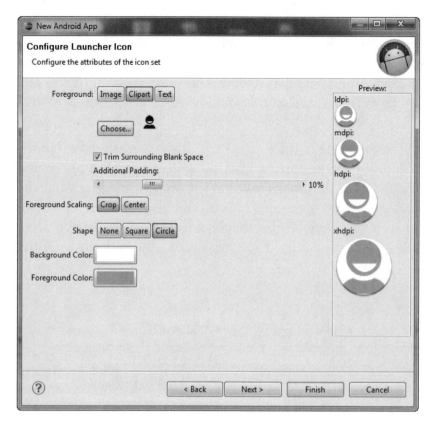

Figure 2.2
Eclipse Configure Launcher Icon panel.
Source: The Eclipse Foundation.

developer had to supply the launch icons by adding them to the appropriate sub-folders in the resource folder and setting the icon name in the manifest file.

The main activity class name no longer defaults to the project name but is called MainActivity. Likewise, the main screen's layout XML file, which previously defaulted to main.xml, now defaults to activity_main.xml. However, as you click through your setup screens, you will arrive at the screen shown in Figure 2.3, which lets you change these filenames if you wish.

After you click the Finish button, Eclipse creates an empty project framework for you. Eclipse is a powerful, versatile development environment that can be complicated and intimidating. It is easy to click the wrong place with the mouse and change the appearance of the whole editor. If nothing else, it takes practice. Figure 2.4 is an illustration of the entire Eclipse screen with the essential areas labeled. If any of these accidently "disappear" on you, you can probably restore them by choosing Window on the menu bar, choosing Show View, and finally choosing the panel you want to

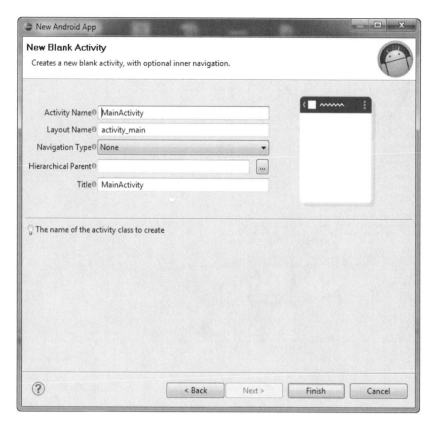

Figure 2.3
Eclipse IDE screen.
Source: The Eclipse Foundation.

restore. If you accidentally minimize the editor screen, look for an icon on the right side of the screen displaying a pencil on a piece of paper. Click this to restore the editor.

The right side of the screen is the editor space. If you are familiar with Eclipse, you will recognize this. On the left side is the Package Explorer window. You will find a list for all the projects in your workspace, as described earlier. If you click on your newly created project, you see a breakdown of the components of the project Eclipse created. It's a combination of directories, subdirectories, and files. As mentioned before, their correct organization is essential to a successful project build, so you should leave them organized as they are, although you will be adding files as the project goes on. The breakdown should look like Figure 2.5.

The first listing is a subdirectory called src. This subdirectory or subfolder contains all the source code for the class(es) you intend to create for your application. You should recognize the package name that you used in the dialog box in the first level

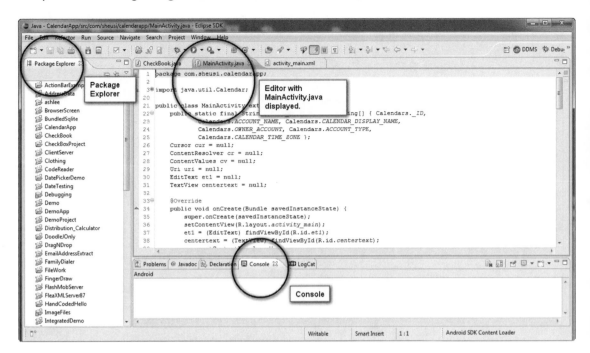

Figure 2.4
Eclipse IDE screen.
Source: The Eclipse Foundation.

below the src icon, and the activity name you chose with the JAVA extension added. This is the primary class of the application.

Next is the directory named gen. The primary file here is called R.java, and it is created based on your configuration of the main.xml and strings.xml at a minimum. You can read this file; it looks like any other Java class, but as Eclipse warns, you do not modify it. The SDK will automatically regenerate it at compile time as you modify other components of the project.

The next component is a collection of API files based on the version you chose in the dialog box in the beginning. It will be numbered based on your choice; it happens to be Android 2.2 in the illustration, but the number can be different for different projects. You likely will not need to deal with this section of the project.

Following that is a directory called res, which is short for resources. It contains folders whose names begin with drawable; these contain graphics files such as the launch icons for the application. You will find more on that topic in Chapter 9, "Deployment and Versioning." The layout and values subdirectories under res contain XML files. The layout directory contains XML files that configure the screens of

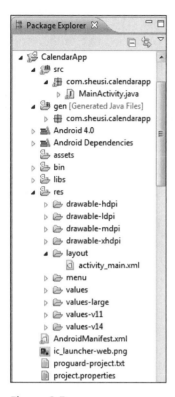

Figure 2.5
Eclipse Package Explorer.
Source: The Eclipse Foundation.

the application. The `values` folder contains values for text strings and a couple of other data types you might use in your application. If you make assignments here in the XML file, they will be available throughout the coded application. These XML files together allow you to design the whole user interface without having to write a single line of Java code.

Finally, we come to the `AndroidManifest.xml` file. You can view this file as the "instruction book" that the target device uses to run the application. It contains things like permissions to use features on the device such as the GPS system, references to the files that should be included when the application is bundled up for deployment (hence the inclusion of the word *manifest* in the filename), version and revision numbers, API information, and so on. This file is important to the application, and you should take care to construct it correctly.

One of the biggest benefits to using an integrated development environment (IDE) such as Eclipse over using a simple editor to write source code is the extensive error detection and debugging facilities included in the IDE. This feature is not new with the newer APIs, but it is worth mentioning. The common errors that occur in application development fall into one of three common categories: syntax, logic, and run-time. The second type, the logic error, is essentially impossible for the IDE to detect and diagnose because these errors are flaws in the approach to solving the problem that the application is meant to do. Some causes are incorrect formulas, complex decision structures that are designed incorrectly, and misapplication of essential values. For example, consider the following method to convert Fahrenheit to Celsius.

```
public double FtoC(double f){
return   5.0 / 9.0 * f - 32;
}
```

Syntactically, this method is okay, and the application it is part of will work quite nicely. However, the value produced when the method is called will not be what the programmer expects because of the missing parentheses. The method that follows is correct.

```
public double FtoC(double f){
return   5.0 / 9.0 * (f - 32);
}
```

The IDE cannot second-guess your intentions; therefore, it cannot help you with this kind of error. The others are different. Take syntax errors, for example. These errors can include missing or incorrectly matching curly braces in code, missing semicolons at the end of a line, incorrect uppercase or lowercase letters, and so on. In other words, they're what we could call "spelling and grammar." These errors could also be use of classes without including the correct import statements, mistakes in variable scope, and other language-based errors. Here, the IDE will generally highlight mistakes right on the editor screen and not let you run the application on the screen or in the editor. In fact, these are the most obvious and easiest errors to fix. Figure 2.6 is a screenshot with an Eclipse error indicator to the left of the code lines.

The error, indicated by a red circle, indicates a missing semicolon at the end of the line, a *punctuation* error, so to speak. If you spot one of these and you don't

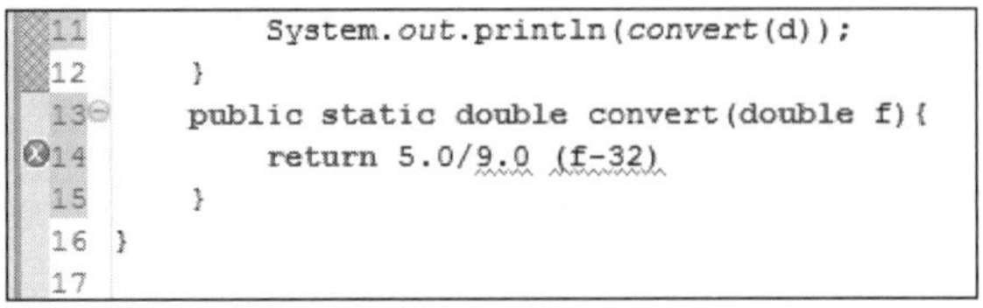

Figure 2.6
Error markers in the Eclipse editor.
Source: The Eclipse Foundation.

immediately know what the problem is, hold the mouse pointer over the red circle (or square, in the case of certain errors) a moment, and an explanation of the error appears.

The last type of error, the run-time error, can be the most frustrating. That is because this error occurs when the application is running, and there is no indication at compile time that anything is wrong. A run-time error turns up in the emulator when the application is running and generally looks like Figure 2.7.

Figure 2.7
A run-time error indication in the emulator.
Source: The Eclipse Foundation.

What's more, due to the nature of run-time errors, they don't occur every time the application runs. Unlike syntax errors, when run-time errors occur, the emulator gives no explanation. Frustrating, indeed! This is where the Debug perspective in Eclipse is the biggest help.

The error in Figure 2.7 is the result of the following application code.

```
package com.sheusi.Debugging;

import android.app.Activity;
import android.os.Bundle;

public class DebuggingActivity extends Activity {
    /** Called when the activity is first created. */
    @Override
```

```java
public void onCreate(Bundle savedInstanceState) {
    super.onCreate(savedInstanceState);
    setContentView(R.layout.main);
    int bogus[]=new int[5];

    for(int ct=0;ct<=5;++ct){
    bogus[ct]=ct;
    }

    }
}
```

Close examination reveals that we are outrunning the array of integers, which causes an unchecked Java exception: ArrayIndexOutOfBounds Exception. Java programmers are familiar with exception handling. To look at the Debug perspective in Eclipse, choose View Perspective under the Window menu, and choose Debug. You will see a screen similar to Figure 2.8.

Figure 2.8
Eclipse Debug perspective.
Source: The Eclipse Foundation.

In the lower-right corner is a panel with a tab marked LogCat. This is the first place to check for the source of the error. Any text in red is what you should examine. Look at the close-up in Figure 2.9.

Notice the line Caused by: java.lang.ArrayIndexOutOfBoundsException. Here is our problem. Now we know what to look for in our code to correct the problem. Let's go back and fix the problem with a try-catch block. In the catch portion, we will print some diagnostics. Notice that we cannot use the typical printStackTrace( ) on

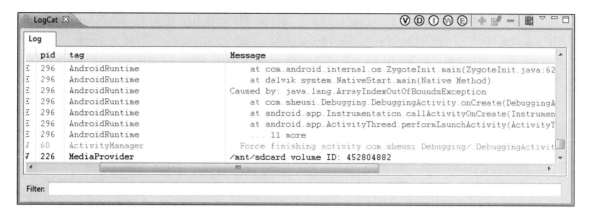

Figure 2.9
Eclipse LogCat panel.

a mobile application to help us. Instead, we can use the logger. Notice the changes in the following code.

```java
package com.sheusi.Debugging;

import android.app.Activity;
import android.os.Bundle;
import android.util.Log;
public class DebuggingActivity extends Activity {
    /** Called when the activity is first created. */
    @Override
    public void onCreate(Bundle savedInstanceState) {
        super.onCreate(savedInstanceState);
        setContentView(R.layout.main);
        int bogus[]=new int[5];
        try{
        for(int ct=0;ct<=5;++ct){
        bogus[ct]=ct;
        }
        }catch(ArrayIndexOutOfBoundsException aioe){
        String err;
        if(aioe.getMessage()==null)
            err="Outran Array";
        else
            err=aioe.getMessage();
        Log.i("Error Here",err);
        }
    }
}
```

You see that we added a `try-catch` block, a `Log` statement, and an additional `import` statement to include the android `Log` class on our namespace. The `try-catch` block allows the application to run, but if we take another look at the debug screen, we find the `LogCat` section shown in Figure 2.10.

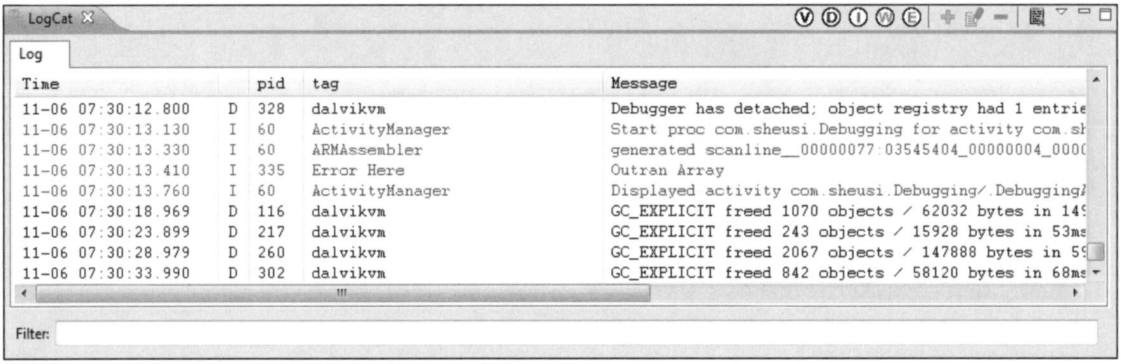

Figure 2.10
Eclipse LogCat panel showing user Log messages.
Source: The Eclipse Foundation.

Under `tag`, we see `Error Here`, which was the tag specified as the first argument in the `Log.i ( )` method call and the message we specified. If the exception had a message to print, it would have appeared in place of `Outran Array`. We can use the `Log` class methods in place of the traditional `printStackTrace( )`. The `I` to the left of the `pid` column indicates that this is an INFO, or informational message. This is specified by the use of the `.i( )` method in the `Log` class. Other common choices are `D` for DEBUG, `E` for ERROR, and `W` for WARNING.

Now that we are acquainted (or reacquainted as the case may be) with Eclipse and the new Android plug-ins, let us look at some of the new features in the Android user interface and how to take advantage of them.

Android 3.0, or Honeycomb, was the first Android release designed for tablet use. There are several subtle improvements to the operating system, some of which are not even visible to the user. Other improvements, in contrast, are highly visible and appealing to both the user and the developer; two of these are the Action Bar and Fragments. The Action Bar is an improved alternative to the Options menu on older devices, which was activated by the hardware menu button. *Fragments* are constructs that allow the developer to build *subscreens*, for lack of a better term, which modularize the screen and provide reusable portions of the user interface. We will examine the Action Bar first.

The Action Bar

The Action Bar is similar to the menu bar on a desktop application, but it's not identical. One might say the Action Bar is better because a selection on the Action Bar can bring up a drop-down list as a typical menu bar would, or it can bring up a built-in service or another activity. Because many devices that support Android 3.0 now and in the future will not have the hardware menu button, developers at Android recommend that applications developers begin to migrate away from the traditional options menu model to the Action Bar. For instance, my own Toshiba Thrive tablet does not have hardware buttons.

You can easily upgrade current applications designed for older devices. Applications designed for new devices are backward compatible for the most part. You will read about some examples of how to accomplish this in code.

To maintain compatibility for legacy applications, you may want to run on multiple platforms; devices running 3.0 and up that have no hardware buttons display a screen image of the old hardware buttons, such as the Back button and the Home button, as well as an added button image that displays a column of thumbnail-sized screens representing the recently run applications when selected. See Figure 2.11.

These buttons can become "ghosted" at times to allow a more pleasant user experience, such as while a video is running the full screen. For example, if a user is watching a movie using Netflix, all the button images turn into translucent dots. If the user

Figure 2.11
Android 3.0 on emulator showing button images at the lower left.
Source: The Eclipse Foundation.

taps the screen, the button images are restored to their normal state, and other Netflix-specific controls appear.

To maintain compatibility with legacy applications that use an options menu, a fourth button image, called an *Overflow button*, is added to the previously mentioned three. This image consists of three stacked lines or short dashes. Touching this image button on a running legacy application brings up the menu choices that were written into the application to allow for a consistent user. If the application is upgraded to 3.0 or higher, this action Overflow button is moved to the right side of the Action Bar, which is displayed by default and provides the same functionality.

To run an experiment to demonstrate the changes in the Options menu system and to look at how the Action Bar works, we will start with a simple menu application taken from my first book, *Android Application Development for Java Programmers*. There are actually two types of menus: the Options menu and the Context menu. The Options menu, which is what we are addressing in this exercise, has choices similar to a typical pull-down menu in a computer application. The Context menu is similar to those activated by right-clicking on a computer application. Our menu will offer three choices: two dummy choices and a third that will be coded to close the application.

The following two XML files are `main.xml`, which provides the primary screen display, and `mymenu.xml`, which defines the menu choices.

```xml
<?xml version="1.0" encoding="utf-8"?>
<LinearLayout xmlns:android="http://schemas.android.com/apk/res/android"
    android:orientation="vertical"
    android:layout_width="fill_parent"
    android:layout_height="fill_parent"
    >
<TextView
    android:layout_width="fill_parent"
    android:layout_height="wrap_content"
    android:text="@string/hello"
    />
</LinearLayout>
```

The `mymenu.xml` file begins here.

```xml
<?xml version="1.0" encoding="utf-8"?>
<menu xmlns:android="http://schemas.android.com/apk/res/android">
    <item android:id="@+id/dummy"
        android:icon="@drawable/icon"
        android:title="Do Something"/>
    <item android:id="@+id/anotherdummy"
        android:icon="@drawable/icon"
```

```
            android:title="Do Something Else"/>
    <item android:id="@+id/close"
        android:icon="@drawable/icon"
        android:title="Close"/>
</menu>
```

Finally, what follows are the manifest file and the actual activity code.

```
<?xml version="1.0" encoding="utf-8"?>
<manifest xmlns:android="http://schemas.android.com/apk/res/android"
    package="com.sheusi.MenuStuff"
    android:versionCode="1"
    android:versionName="1.0">
    <uses-sdk android:minSdkVersion="8"
        android:targetSdkVersion="8"/>

    <application android:icon="@drawable/icon"
        android:label="@string/app_name">
        <activity android:name=".MenuWerx"
                android:label="@string/app_name">
            <intent-filter>
                <action android:name="android.intent.action.MAIN" />
                <category android:name="android.intent.category.LAUNCHER" />
            </intent-filter>
        </activity>

    </application>
</manifest>
```

Finally, this is the Java code for the main activity.

```java
package com.sheusi.MenuStuff;
import android.app.Activity;
import android.os.Bundle;
import android.view.Menu;
import android.view.MenuInflater;
import android.view.MenuItem;

public class MenuWerx extends Activity {
    /** Called when the activity is first created. */

     @Override
    public boolean onCreateOptionsMenu(Menu menu){
        MenuInflater inflater=getMenuInflater();
        inflater.inflate(R.menu.mymenu,menu);

        return super.onCreateOptionsMenu(menu);

    }
    @Override
```

```
public boolean onOptionsItemSelected(MenuItem mi){
    if(mi.getItemId()==R.id.dummy){
        //do nothing
        return true;
    }
    if(mi.getItemId()==R.id.anotherdummy){
        //again, do nothing
        return true;
    }
    if(mi.getItemId()==R.id.close){
        this.finish();
        return true;
    }
    return true;
}
@Override
public void onCreate(Bundle savedInstanceState) {
    super.onCreate(savedInstanceState);
    setContentView(R.layout.main);

}
}
```

Notice that in the manifest both the target and the minimum SDK versions are 8, which specifies Android 2.2 as the target environment. By reading the code, you will notice that the only menu button that actually does anything is the Close button. You may also notice by reading the `mymenu.xml` file that the image on the menu choices is the stock Android icon. Of course, the applications programmer can specify any other image he chooses. Figure 2.12 is an image of the application running on an emulator configured with Android 2.2.

Running the same application with no code, XML, or manifest alterations on an Android 3.0 device will look like Figure 2.13. The image displayed shows the menu image button (the fourth image on the bottom left of the screen, a grid-shaped object) and the open menu across the bottom of the screen.

Next, we will change the target SDK version in the manifest file to 11, which corresponds to Android 3.0. We will leave the minimum SDK at 8 to preserve backward compatibility. Figure 2.14 shows the Action Bar near the top of the screen. By default, the image bar shows the launch icon and the application name (upper left). At the upper-right corner, you will notice the Overflow button I pointed out earlier. Clicking the Overflow button reveals a drop-down with my three menu choices.

If we don't change anything but the manifest, we bring our application's user interface up to the Android 3.x level. But a few steps can make it even more attractive.

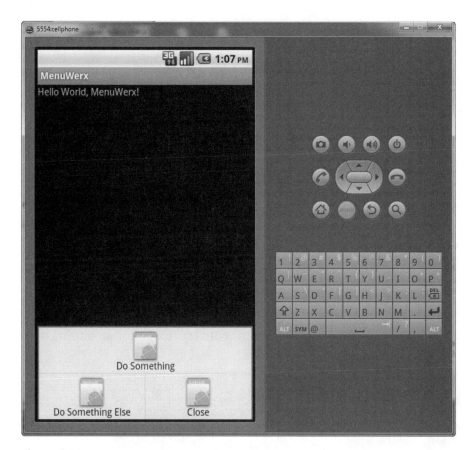

Figure 2.12
Menu demo application on Android 2.2 emulator.
Source: The Eclipse Foundation.

First, to make some code changes that bring the application more in line with the improvements in 3.0 and higher, we need to change the build target in Eclipse. You can do this by right-clicking the project name in the Package Explorer and choosing Properties at the bottom of the list. Choose Android in the new list, and you will see the panel illustrated in Figure 2.15. Click the check box for Android 3.0, and click the Enter button at the bottom.

Next, we will take the menu choices out of the action Overflow button and place them directly on the Action Bar. As nice as the Action Bar is, it is only so long, and only so many items will fit. Whatever is left, as you can imagine, will go into the overflow, so prioritize your order to make the important ones appear on the Action Bar. Revise your menu.xml file to look like the following file listing, adding

```
android:showAsAction="ifRoom|withText"
```

to each menu item.

```
<?xml version="1.0" encoding="utf-8"?>
<menu xmlns:android="http://schemas.android.com/apk/res/android">
<item android:id="@+id/dummy"
    android:showAsAction="ifRoom|withText"
    android:icon="@drawable/icon"
    android:title="Do Something"/>
<item android:id="@+id/anotherdummy"
    android:showAsAction="ifRoom|withText"
    android:icon="@drawable/icon"
    android:title="Do Something Else"/>
<item android:id="@+id/close"
    android:showAsAction="ifRoom|withText"
    android:icon="@drawable/icon"
    android:title="Close"/>
</menu>
```

If you do not change the build target, Eclipse does not recognize the directive,
android:showAsAction, and you get an error when you try to run the application.

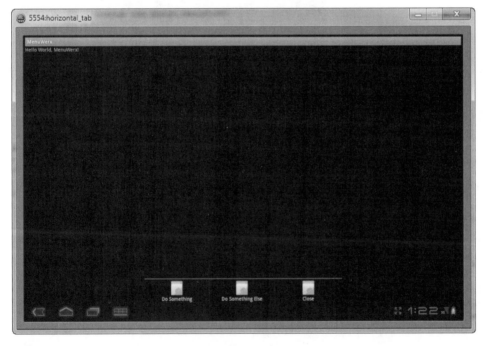

Figure 2.13
Menu demo application on Android 3.0 emulator with a build target of 8.
Source: The Eclipse Foundation.

Figure 2.14
Menu demo application of Android 3.2 emulator with a build target of 11.
Source: The Eclipse Foundation.

Run the application again and notice the change on the Action Bar shown in Figure 2.16.

If you don't want to use the Action Bar, you can add the following line to the `<application>` element of your manifest.

```
android:theme="@android:style/Theme.Holo.NoActionBar"
```

Of course, if you eliminate the Action Bar, you must do something else with your menu.

To help provide an Android-consistent application, the Android User Experience (UX) group has made dozens of icons for Action Bar directives available for download at http://developer.android.com/design/downloads/index.html.

You can find a comprehensive guide to the Action Bar at http://developer.android.com/design/patterns/actionbar.html.

The guide presents tips on the Action Bar design, a chart to determine the number of action items, depending on the screen width in DP (density-independent pixels), and so on.

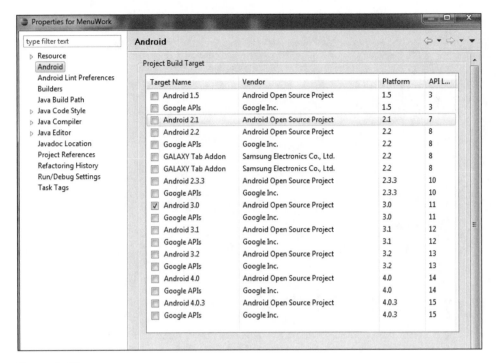

Figure 2.15
Build Target selection from project properties.
Source: The Eclipse Foundation.

FRAGMENTS

Fragments allow you to take the large tablet surface and divide it into several more easily handled sections. You can reuse the sections from screen to screen (activity to activity) and preserve and recall them while maintaining state. Fragments have their own life cycle, similar to the activity that hosts them, but the hosting activity affects them. For example, when an activity is paused, its fragments are paused; when the activity is destroyed, its fragments are as well. See the fragment life cycle diagram in Figure 2.17.

Anatomically, fragments consist of a class that extends the Fragment class or a subclass of the Fragment class, and their layout is drawn from an XML file similar to that of the hosting activity. Fragment "space" can be built into the hosting activity's XML file just as controls such as buttons and text fields are, or they can be added dynamically, similar to the way a developer might add a control dynamically. In fact, a fragment can exist without a user interface and just manage some background activity.

Figure 2.16
Android 3.2 emulator showing application with revised Action Bar.
Source: The Eclipse Foundation.

An application can manage its fragments to suit the device it is running on. For example, two fragments might be displayed side by side on a tablet in a given application, but the same application running on a handset might display one at a time, one triggering the display of the other.

Like activities, several methods are associated with the stages in the life cycle of a fragment, but not all have to be used. The essential methods for the fragment are onCreate( ), onCreateView( ), and onPause( ).

The first method, onCreate( ), is called when the fragment is created. In your application, you would initialize essential components that you intend to maintain as the fragment is paused or stopped and resumed. The second, onCreateView( ), is called when the fragment is to be drawn on the screen. Here, the fragments use the corresponding XML file to dictate the layout, and the method returns a View object to represent the fragment to the activity. If the fragment has no user interface, a "null" can be returned. The onPause( ) method is called as the user leaves the fragment. The developer should write code to save any data that is essential to the application, such as posting to a data table, saving files, or closing streams, because there is no guarantee that the user will return to the fragment during the life of the activity.

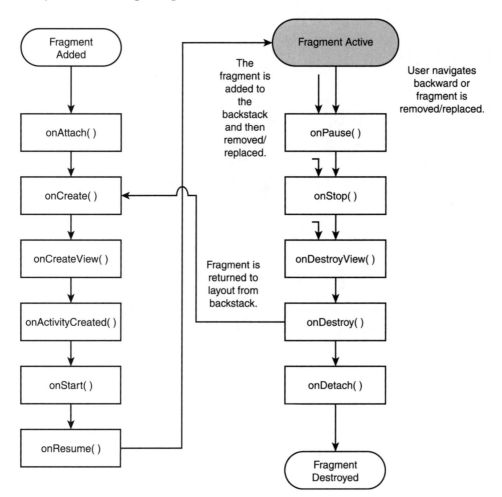

Figure 2.17
Fragment life cycle.
Source: © 2013 Cengage Learning®, All Rights Reserved.

As mentioned earlier, there are two ways to add fragments with user interfaces to activities: by providing a placeholder in the activity's XML file, or by adding the fragment at run-time. Following is an example of an XML file for the main activity in an application, which provides a place for the fragment to be added to the screen. Look for the fragment tags near the center of the XML file.

```
<?xml version="1.0" encoding="utf-8"?>
<LinearLayout xmlns:android="http://schemas.android.com/apk/res/android"
    android:id="@+id/mainlayout"
    android:layout_width="fill_parent"
    android:layout_height="fill_parent"
    android:orientation="vertical" >
```

```
<TextView
    android:layout_width="wrap_content"
    android:layout_height="wrap_content"
    android:text="An activity with a fragment." />
<fragment
    android:id="@+id/frag_space"
    android:layout_width="wrap_content"
    android:layout_height="wrap_content"
    class="com.sheusi.SimpleFragments.BlankFragment" >
</fragment>
<Button
    android:id="@+id/f1button"
    android:layout_width="wrap_content"
    android:layout_height="wrap_content"
    android:text="Toggle fragments in defined space." >
</Button>
```

```
</LinearLayout>
```

Pay particular attention to the fragment element in the sample file. First, notice that the space is given an "id" attribute that identifies it in the activity's code. Also notice the unusual "class" attribute, which identifies the fragment's class. The more conventional attribute, "android:name", can be used in place of the "class" attribute. It might be more appropriate to say the fragment's *initial* class, because fragments can be swapped in and out of a given space. There will be more on this later in the chapter. Finally, notice that there is an "id" value in the LinearLayout element. This is essential when adding fragments dynamically, because a ViewGroup object is needed to host a fragment, and the LinearLayout identified will be the ViewGroup object used by the activity.

Manipulating fragments in an activity while the application is running requires the use of an instance of the FragmentTransaction class. An instance is returned from the beginTransaction( ) method of an instance of a TransactionManager class. The getFragmentManager( ) method of the Activity class returns the latter. Instances of the fragments are produced by declaring a Fragment variable and assigning it by calling the constructor of the desired fragment's class. For example,

```
MyFragment mf=new MyFragment( );
```

When you create a fragment instance, its onAttach(), onCreate(), onCreateView(), and onActivityCreated() methods run in that order, as indicated in the life cycle chart illustrated earlier.

Actual manipulation of the fragments begins with the `beginTransaction( )` call described earlier and ends with a call to the `commit( )` method of the `FragmentTransaction` object produced by the `beginTransaction( )` call.

Shown next is the source code for a simple activity that has a button to toggle between two fragments whose space is defined in the `main.xml` file, like the one illustrated earlier. Each fragment is designed to distinguish one from the other, although they are essentially the same functionally, each having a button to clear an included text field.

```
package com.sheusi.SimpleFragments;

import android.app.Activity;
import android.os.Bundle;
import android.app.FragmentManager;
import android.app.Fragment;
import android.app.FragmentTransaction;
// for OS versions below 3.0, use the following packages for compatibility
//import android.support.v4.app.FragmentActivity;
//import android.support.v4.app.Fragment;
import android.view.View;
import android.widget.*;
// for versions less than 3.0, extend android.support.v4.app.FragmentActivity
public class SimpleFragmentsActivity extends Activity {
    /** Called when the activity is first created. */
    EditText et1 = null;
    Fragment f = null;
    Fragment f2 = null; // second fragment
    LinearLayout ll = null;
    FragmentManager fm = null;
    Button frag1Button = null;
    EditText fragEditText = null;

    @Override
    public void onCreate(Bundle savedInstanceState) {
        super.onCreate(savedInstanceState);
        setContentView(R.layout.main);
        ll = (LinearLayout) findViewById(R.layout.main);
        f = new SimpleFragmentClass();
        f2 = new SimpleFragTwo();
        fm = this.getFragmentManager();
        FragmentTransaction ft = fm.beginTransaction();
        ft.replace(R.id.frag_space, f);
        ft.commit();
        frag1Button = (Button) findViewById(R.id.f1button);
```

```
frag1Button.setOnClickListener(new View.OnClickListener() {
    public void onClick(View v) {
        FragmentTransaction ft = fm.beginTransaction();
        if (f.isResumed()) {
            ft.replace(R.id.frag_space, f2);
            ft.commit();
        } else {
            ft.replace(R.id.frag_space, f);
            ft.commit();
        }// end if-else
    }
});
    }
}
```

In the next section of code listings are three different fragment classes. The first is a dummy fragment class. When you swap fragments in a defined space, the results may not be desirable. My experience is that the second fragment appears along with the first when the swap button is used initially, rather than replacing the first as desired. Postings on popular reference sites report similar experiences and suggest different workarounds. My suggestion is to create a fragment class with a corresponding XML file that has no controls and that will be the one referenced by the `main.xml` file. You saw this in the `main.xml` file illustrated earlier, specifically this line.

```
class="com.sheusi.SimpleFragments.BlankFragment"
```

Here is the dummy fragment class's source code.

```
package com.sheusi.SimpleFragments;

import android.app.Fragment;
import android.view.LayoutInflater;
import android.view.ViewGroup;
import android.view.View;
import android.os.Bundle;

public class BlankFragment extends Fragment {
    @Override
    public void onActivityCreated(Bundle savedInstanceState) {
        super.onActivityCreated(savedInstanceState);
    }
    @Override
    public View onCreateView(LayoutInflater li, ViewGroup vg,
            Bundle savedInstanceState) {
        View fragView = li.inflate(R.layout.fragment_dummy, vg, false);
        return fragView;
    }
```

```
    @Override
    public void onViewCreated(View view, Bundle savedInstanceState) {
        // required switch to API 13, from 11
        super.onViewCreated(view, savedInstanceState);

    }

    @Override
    public void onCreate(Bundle saved) {
        super.onCreate(saved);
    }

    @Override
    public void onPause() {
        super.onPause();
        // called when user leaves this fragment
        // save anything that should be saved here, e.g., open files, records, etc.,
        // because the fragment may never be accessed again
    }
    @Override
    public void onResume() {
        super.onResume();
    }
}
```

I have included overrides of essential methods, but because the class has no functionality, they are virtually blank. Following are the remaining two fragment classes that the main activity class uses.

```
package com.sheusi.SimpleFragments;

import android.widget.*;
import android.app.Fragment;
import android.view.LayoutInflater;
import android.view.ViewGroup;
import android.view.View;
import android.os.Bundle;

public class SimpleFragmentClass extends Fragment {
    String id = null;
    EditText et1 = null;
    Button b1 = null;

    @Override
    public void onActivityCreated(Bundle savedInstanceState) {
        super.onActivityCreated(savedInstanceState);
        et1 = (EditText) getView().findViewById(R.id.et1);
        et1.setText("The Original Fragment");
        b1 = (Button) getView().findViewById(R.id.b1);
```

```java
        b1.setOnClickListener(new View.OnClickListener() {
            public void onClick(View v) {
                et1.setText("");
            }
        });
    }

    @Override
    public View onCreateView(LayoutInflater li, ViewGroup vg,
            Bundle savedInstanceState) {
        // notice this code, how it is assigned here, not in on-create,
        // and that we create an instance of the View class and return it
        View fragView = li.inflate(R.layout.simplefraglayout, vg, false);
        return fragView;
    }

    @Override
    public void onCreate(Bundle saved) {
        super.onCreate(saved);

    }

    @Override
    public void onPause() {
        super.onPause();
        // called when user leaves this fragment
        // save anything that should be saved here, e.g., open files, records, etc.,
        // because the fragment may never be accessed again

    }

}
package com.sheusi.SimpleFragments;

import android.widget.*;
import android.app.Fragment;
import android.view.LayoutInflater;
import android.view.ViewGroup;
import android.view.View;
import android.os.Bundle;

public class SimpleFragTwo extends Fragment {
    String id = null;
    EditText et1 = null;
    Button b1 = null;

    @Override
    public void onActivityCreated(Bundle savedInstanceState) {
        super.onActivityCreated(savedInstanceState);
```

```
            et1 = (EditText) getView().findViewById(R.id.etfrag2);
            et1.setText("The Second Fragment");
            b1 = (Button) getView().findViewById(R.id.bfrag2);
            b1.setOnClickListener(new View.OnClickListener() {
                public void onClick(View v) {
                    et1.setText("");
                }
            });
        }

        @Override
        public View onCreateView(LayoutInflater li, ViewGroup vg,
                Bundle savedInstanceState) {
            // notice this code, how it is assigned here, not in on-create,
            // and that we create an instance of View and return it
            View fragView = li.inflate(R.layout.simplefragtwo, vg, false);

            return fragView;
        }

        @Override
        public void onViewCreated(View view, Bundle savedInstanceState) {
            // required switch to API 13, from 11
            super.onViewCreated(view, savedInstanceState);

        }

        @Override
        public void onCreate(Bundle saved) {
            super.onCreate(saved);

        }

        @Override
        public void onPause() {
            super.onPause();
            // called when user leaves this fragment
            // save anything necessary here, e.g., open files, records, etc.
            // because the fragment may never be accessed again

        }

        @Override
        public void onResume() {
            super.onResume();

        }
    }
```

The corresponding XML files for the classes appear here. First is `simplefragment layout.xml`.

```xml
<?xml version="1.0" encoding="utf-8"?>
<LinearLayout xmlns:android="http://schemas.android.com/apk/res/android"
    android:id="@+id/myfrag"
    android:layout_width="match_parent"
    android:layout_height="wrap_content"
    android:orientation="horizontal"
    android:tag="fragment_one" >

    <TextView
        android:layout_width="wrap_content"
        android:layout_height="wrap_content"
        android:text="This is a fragment"
        android:textSize="20dp" />

    <EditText
        android:id="@+id/et1"
        android:layout_width="wrap_content"
        android:layout_height="wrap_content"
        android:minWidth="350dp"
        android:textSize="20dp" />

    <Button
        android:id="@+id/b1"
        android:layout_width="wrap_content"
        android:layout_height="wrap_content"
        android:text="Click to Clear Text" />

</LinearLayout>
```

The XML file for `simplfragtwo` begins here.

```xml
<?xml version="1.0" encoding="utf-8"?>
<LinearLayout xmlns:android="http://schemas.android.com/apk/res/android"
    android:id="@+id/myfrag2"
    android:layout_width="match_parent"
    android:layout_height="wrap_content"
    android:orientation="horizontal"
    android:tag="fragment_two" >

    <TextView
        android:layout_width="wrap_content"
        android:layout_height="wrap_content"
        android:text="This is the second fragment"
        android:textSize="20dp" />
```

```
<EditText
    android:id="@+id/etfrag2"
    android:layout_width="wrap_content"
    android:layout_height="wrap_content"
    android:minWidth="350dp"
    android:textSize="20dp" />

<Button
    android:id="@+id/bfrag2"
    android:layout_width="wrap_content"
    android:layout_height="wrap_content"
    android:text="Click to Clear Text" />
```

```
</LinearLayout>
```

There is nothing especially unusual about these XML files, except that they have an android:id attribute to identify the fragments in the activity.

When the main activity runs, it immediately replaces the dummy fragment with the first useful fragment. From there on, the button built into the activity toggles between the useful activities. The isResumed( ) method tests which fragment is active at any given time, and in turn determines which one to replace the active one with.

The screen for the running application might look like Figure 2.18.

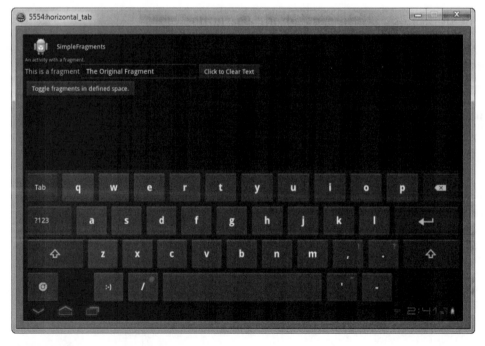

Figure 2.18
Emulator running application with fragments.
Source: The Eclipse Foundation.

The second method to switch among fragments involves adding and removing fragments dynamically, much as a developer might add or remove buttons and other controls. This method might be considered more appropriate if your intention is to manipulate fragments from a running application, because it avoids the problems inherent in defining the fragment space in the main.xml as we did earlier. On the other hand, this method may take a little more planning on the developer's part regarding screen layout in the main.xml file.

In the second example, we will add fragments dynamically. You will note some changes in the main activity file. Also, just to change things up, I introduce a new fragment that has two EditText controls and a button that takes the content of the first, converts it to uppercase, and prints it in the second. The user can type the text to be converted in the first text field. Following is the revised XML file for the main activity, main.xml. Notice that the fragment tags are removed. Also notice the ID in the LinearLayout element; it is used in the activity code as a reference to the ViewGroup to which the fragments must be added.

```xml
<?xml version="1.0" encoding="utf-8"?>
<LinearLayout xmlns:android="http://schemas.android.com/apk/res/android"
    android:id="@+id/mainlayout"
    android:layout_width="fill_parent"
    android:layout_height="fill_parent"
    android:orientation="vertical"

    >

    <TextView
        android:layout_width="wrap_content"
        android:layout_height="wrap_content"
        android:text="An activity with a fragment." />

    <Button
        android:id="@+id/f2button"
        android:layout_width="wrap_content"
        android:layout_height="wrap_content"
        android:text="Toggle fragments added dynamically" >
    </Button>

</LinearLayout>
```

The following is the revised activity source code.

```java
package com.sheusi.SimpleFragments;

import android.app.Activity;
import android.os.Bundle;
```

```java
import android.app.FragmentManager;
import android.app.Fragment;
import android.app.FragmentTransaction;

//import android.support.v4.app.FragmentActivity;
//import android.support.v4.app.Fragment;
import android.view.View;
import android.widget.*;

// for versions less than 3.0, extend android.support.v4.app.FragmentActivity
public class SimpleFragmentsActivity extends Activity {
    /** Called when the activity is first created. */
    EditText et1 = null;
    Fragment f2 = null; // second fragment
    Fragment dynafrag = null;
    LinearLayout ll = null;
    FragmentManager fm = null;
    Button frag2Button = null;

    @Override
    public void onCreate(Bundle savedInstanceState) {
        super.onCreate(savedInstanceState);
        setContentView(R.layout.main);
        ll = (LinearLayout) findViewById(R.layout.main);
        f2 = new SimpleFragTwo();
        dynafrag = new DynaFrag();
        fm = this.getFragmentManager();
        FragmentTransaction dft = fm.beginTransaction();
        dft.add(R.id.mainlayout, dynafrag);
        dft.commit();
        frag2Button = (Button) findViewById(R.id.f2button);

        frag2Button.setOnClickListener(new View.OnClickListener() {
            public void onClick(View v) {

                FragmentTransaction dft = fm.beginTransaction();
                if (dynafrag.isResumed()) {

                    dft.remove(dynafrag);
                    dft.add(R.id.mainlayout, f2);
                    dft.commit();

                } else {
                    dft.remove(f2);
                    dft.add(R.id.mainlayout, dynafrag);
                    dft.commit();
```

```
            }// ends if-else
        }
    });
}
```

The Java code for the SimpleFragTwo and its corresponding XML file don't need to change. Following is the Java code and the XML file for the new fragment called dynafrag.

```java
package com.sheusi.SimpleFragments;

import android.widget.*;
import android.app.Fragment;
import android.view.LayoutInflater;
import android.view.ViewGroup;
import android.view.View;
import android.os.Bundle;
public class DynaFrag extends Fragment {
    String id = null;
    EditText et1 = null;
    EditText et2 = null;
    Button b1 = null;

    @Override
    public void onActivityCreated(Bundle savedInstanceState) {
        super.onActivityCreated(savedInstanceState);

        et1 = (EditText) getView().findViewById(R.id.dynafrag_et);
        et2 = (EditText) getView().findViewById(R.id.dynafrag_et2);
        b1 = (Button) getView().findViewById(R.id.dynafrag_b1);
        b1.setOnClickListener(new View.OnClickListener() {
            public void onClick(View v) {
                et2.setText(et1.getText().toString().toUpperCase());
            }
        });
    }

    @Override
    public View onCreateView(LayoutInflater li, ViewGroup vg,
            Bundle savedInstanceState) {
        // notice this code, how it is assigned here, not in on-create,
        // and that we create an instance of View and return it
        View df = li.inflate(R.layout.dynamic_frag, vg, false);

        return df;
    }
```

```java
    @Override
    public void onViewCreated(View view, Bundle savedInstanceState) {
        // required switch to API 13, from 11
        super.onViewCreated(view, savedInstanceState);

    }

    @Override
    public void onCreate(Bundle saved) {
        super.onCreate(saved);

    }

    @Override
    public void onPause() {
        super.onPause();
        // called when user leaves this fragment
        // save anything that should be saved here, e.g., open files, records, etc.,
        // because the fragment may never be accessed again

    }

    @Override
    public void onResume() {
        super.onResume();

    }
}
```

Here is the XML file for the dynamic fragment.

```xml
<?xml version="1.0" encoding="utf-8"?>
<LinearLayout xmlns:android="http://schemas.android.com/apk/res/android"
    android:id="@+id/dynafrag"
    android:layout_width="match_parent"
    android:layout_height="wrap_content"
    android:background="#000000"
    android:orientation="vertical"
    android:tag="dynamic_frag" >

    <TextView
        android:layout_width="wrap_content"
        android:layout_height="wrap_content"
        android:text="This is a dynamically added fragment." />

    <EditText

        android:id="@+id/dynafrag_et"
        android:layout_width="wrap_content"
        android:layout_height="wrap_content"
        android:minWidth="300dp" />
```

```
<Button
    android:id="@+id/dynafrag_b1"
    android:layout_width="wrap_content"
    android:layout_height="wrap_content"
    android:text="Click to Copy Text from First EditText field" />

<EditText
    android:id="@+id/dynafrag_et2"
    android:layout_width="wrap_content"
    android:layout_height="wrap_content"
    android:minWidth="300dp" />
```

```
</LinearLayout>
```

When running, the revised application will look similar to Figure 2.19. Note, however, that illustrations are static images and do not indicate the functionality of an application. In the illustration, the second button, labeled Toggle Fragments Added Dynamically, causes fragments appearing below the button to alternate.

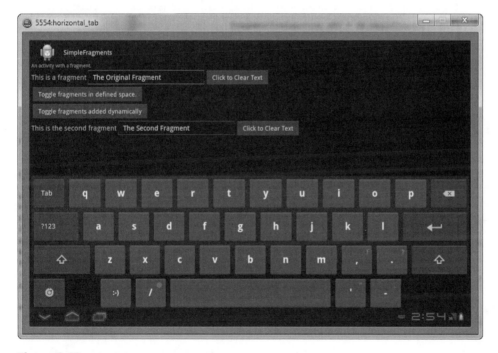

Figure 2.19
Emulator running application with dynamically added fragments.
Source: The Eclipse Foundation.

Fragments can communicate back and forth with their hosting activity. For example, for the hosting activity to gain a reference to a fragment, we declare a variable of the fragment's type and assign it using the `getFragmentManager( )` method. Look at the following example.

```
SomeFragmentClass  fragref = (SomeFragmentClass)getFragmentManager( ).findViewById
(R.id.frag_id);
```

`frag_id` is the ID used in the fragment's XML file. The fragment's methods can be called by the activity using the fragment's reference variable. Likewise, the fragment can access the activity's components by using its `getActivity( )` method. For example,

```
EditText parent_edittext = getActivity( ).findViewById(R.id.edittext_id);
```

`edittext_id` is the ID in the main activity's XML file element corresponding to the targeted `EditText` object.

The final noticeable user interface covered here is the new application programmer's interface or API for drag and drop. Drag and drop implementation in the application can be as plain and simple or as sophisticated and embellished as the programmer wants it to be. You can use the feature with anything from plain text in a `TextView` to an image from an `ImageView`; you can even use it with an `Intent`. As simple or complex as the programmer wants to be with his configuration of the drag and drop implementation, there are a few essential pieces. The first is some event that indicates to the system that a drag and drop operation should be started. Typically, this is a long click involving the user touching and holding his finger on the target control. To detect this gesture, we simply need to add an `OnLongClickListener` interface. To allow objects to receive a drop, we implement the `OnDragListener` interface. The second item we need to facilitate is a shadow, which is an image representing the object being dragged. This is done with a `View.DragShadowBuilder` object and can be as simple as taking the text from the source text field or as elaborate as a custom-designed image. Third and finally, we use a `ClipData` object to hold the data we want to transport.

The workhorse for the drag and drop operation is `OnDragListener`, which has several actions to which the programmer can write a response. The essentials are `ACTION_DRAG_STARTED`, `ACTION_DRAG_ENDED`, and `ACTION_DROP`.

To illustrate, let's review the code for the `DynaFrag` class listed earlier. Recall that it contained two text fields (`EditTexts`) and a button that converted the text in the top text field to uppercase and copied it to the bottom text field. We will revise that class so the user can drag the contents of the top text field to the bottom one. The implementation will be extremely simplified but functional. Because the top text field will be the source of the data, we will attach the OnLongClickListener to it. (In any other implementation, it is likely that the programmer would want several or all text fields to be potential sources from which to drag data, so it is easiest to implement the OnLongClickListener interface at the parent class level; then you can associate the individual text fields with the parent class's onLongClick( ) method. The same holds true with the OnDragListener, because there may be more than one likely drop target. This is how it is done in the example.)

The shadow will simply be the text held by the source text field. Because there is one and only one source in the example, the text field is identified by its variable name. The revised fragment, DragDropFragment.java, is listed here.

```java
package com.sheusi.SimpleFragments;

import android.widget.*;
import android.app.Fragment;
import android.view.DragEvent;
import android.view.LayoutInflater;
import android.view.ViewGroup;
import android.view.View;
import android.os.Bundle;
import android.view.View.OnDragListener;
import android.view.View.OnLongClickListener;
import android.content.ClipData;
import android.content.ClipDescription;
import android.graphics.Color;

public class DragDropFrag extends Fragment implements OnDragListener,
        OnLongClickListener {
    String id = null;
    EditText et1 = null;
    EditText et2 = null;
    Button b1 = null;

    @Override
    public void onActivityCreated(Bundle savedInstanceState) {
        super.onActivityCreated(savedInstanceState);
        et1 = (EditText) getView().findViewById(R.id.dynafrag_et);
        et2 = (EditText) getView().findViewById(R.id.dynafrag_et2);
        et1.setOnLongClickListener(this);
        et2.setOnDragListener(this);
        b1 = (Button) getView().findViewById(R.id.dynafrag_b1);
        b1.setOnClickListener(new View.OnClickListener() {
            public void onClick(View v) {
                et2.setText(et1.getText().toString().toUpperCase());
            }
```

```
        });
    }

    @Override
    public View onCreateView(LayoutInflater li, ViewGroup vg,
             Bundle savedInstanceState) {
        // notice this code, how it is assigned here, not in on-create,
        // and that we create an instance of View and return it
        View df = li.inflate(R.layout.dynamic_frag, vg, false);

        return df;
    }

    @Override
    public void onViewCreated(View view, Bundle savedInstanceState) {
        // required switch to API 13, from 11
        super.onViewCreated(view, savedInstanceState);

    }

    @Override
    public void onCreate(Bundle saved) {
        super.onCreate(saved);

    }

    @Override
    public void onPause() {
        super.onPause();
        // called when user leaves this fragment
        // save anything that should be saved here, e.g., open files, records, etc.,
        // because the fragment may never be accessed again

    }

    @Override
    public void onResume() {
        super.onResume();

    }

    public boolean onLongClick(View v) {
        View.DragShadowBuilder vdsb = new View.DragShadowBuilder(et1);
        String cliptag = "myClipTag";
        v.setTag(cliptag);
        ClipData.Item cdi = new ClipData.Item(((TextView) v).getText()
                 .toString());
        String[] mimeTypes = { ClipDescription.MIMETYPE_TEXT_PLAIN };
        ClipData cd = new ClipData((CharSequence) v.getTag(), mimeTypes, cdi);
        v.startDrag(cd, vdsb, null, 0);
        return false;
```

```
    }
    public boolean onDrag(View v, DragEvent de) {
        if (de.getAction() == DragEvent.ACTION_DRAG_STARTED) {
            v.setBackgroundColor(Color.BLUE);
        }
        if (de.getAction() == DragEvent.ACTION_DROP) {
            ClipData.Item cdi = de.getClipData().getItemAt(0);
            v.setBackgroundColor(Color.BLACK);
        }
        if (de.getAction() == DragEvent.ACTION_DRAG_ENDED) {
            return de.getResult();
        }
        return false;
    }
}
```

As you read the code, pay attention to the new `import` statements at the top to include the necessary classes. The essential piece of the `onDrag( )` method that we must include to implement the `OnDragListener` interface is the code for `DragEvent.ACTION_DROP`. This is where the value is placed in the target text field. The code for `DragEvent.ACTION_DRAG_STARTED` turns all eligible targets blue for the application user's benefit; likewise, `DragEvent.ACTION_DRAG_ENDED` turns the background black again. Any eligible target that was attached to this listener, if there were multiple ones, would turn blue. You can find a comprehensive and reasonably easy-to-understand reference to Android drag and drop at http://developer.android.com/guide/topics/ui /drag-drop.html.

Simplified examples are shown here in the chapter so you can get an idea of how they are coded, how they look, and what their potential may be in a useful, custom application.

SUMMARY OF KEY CONCEPTS

- While the basic functionality of Eclipse and the APIs for Java and Android is consistent, subtle changes are being made to these all the time. It could be as simple as a menu change, and in the language packages there can be new classes, new methods, and new functionality to keep up with the evolving operating systems, hardware, and user interfaces. It is important to continually check for upgrades. Sometimes, as in the case of Java, the developer is notified that updates are available; other times, as in the case of Eclipse, there may be a menu choice that checks for updates. It pays to belong to user groups in social networks on the Internet and read the postings. Another good idea is to check with the websites managed by the software providers themselves.

■ Some of the changes in the Android operating system from version to version are subtle, whereas others are dramatic. The tablet device and Android 3.0 have brought new opportunities for useful application development. The introduction of Android 4.0 continues to bring improvement. This chapter focuses on only a few of them. You should research the changes in the versions and the corresponding Android APIs to discover other features that might be to your advantage in producing useful applications.

■ The Action Bar eliminates the need for the hardware menu button and provides more functionality than the old-style menus. Android allows for use of the Action Bar while maintaining compatibility with older devices that have the hardware menu button.

■ Fragments allow the developer to modularize groups of controls and their functionality into reusable pieces. Screens can be assembled by using combinations of fragments, and fragments can be brought from screen to screen, added and removed dynamically, and ported from application to application. Although they're not the solution to every problem, they provide a reusable and predictable structure for application building.

REVIEW QUESTIONS

You can find the answers to these review questions in the appendix at the end of the book.

1. In the Eclipse application manager, user-written Java classes are stored in the _____ directory within the project.

2. Three classifications of common errors are _____, _____, and _____.

3. The onscreen structure that replaces the menu system is the _____.

4. Choices that cannot fit on the Action Bar are revealed by touching the _____ button.

5. The target and minimum versions for the SDK are specified in the application's _____ file.

6. To configure their layout at design time, fragments will have their own _____ file.

7. All fragments extend the _____ class.

8. Three essential methods of the `Fragment` class are _____, _____, and _____.

9. To perform a drag-and-drop sequence, the two necessary listeners are the _____ and the _____.

10. The image indicating the transferred item on its drag path is referred to as the _____.

SUGGESTED PROJECTS

- Take any of the applications you have written so far and add an Action Bar. At a minimum, include an entry to close the application. The body of the method can use the `finish( )` method to close the activity.

- *7 Little Words* is a game released by Blue Ox Technologies, Ltd., that is available on the Google Play Store. The goal is to assemble seven words by selecting syllables. Using this theme, take a large word and put each of its syllables into a separate `TextView`, preferably out of order. Allow the player to drag and drop the syllables, adding them to an equal number of empty `EditText` objects in order. A slightly more challenging variation is to add the syllables to one large `EditText` field.

- Design a simple fragment, and display it on the screen among other widgets. Try using an `ImageView` or a `WebView` among the others. Modify the main XML file to change the location of the fragment and observe the results. If you color the background of the fragment's outermost `ViewGroup` element, its bounds will be more visible.

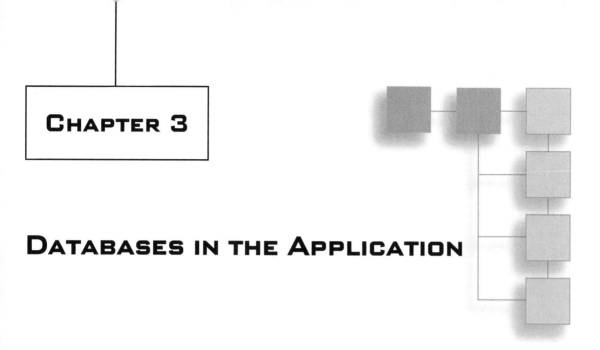

CHAPTER 3

DATABASES IN THE APPLICATION

BUNDLING A DATABASE

Chances are that any business application has some kind of database. It may be as simple as a single table used as a look-up such as a member list, contact list, or parts list, or it can be as complex as a multitable relational database that is at the heart of the application. Android uses the SQLite database management system as its onboard database. Because of the obvious hardware constraints in a mobile device, SQLite is limited and not as versatile and sophisticated as, say, Microsoft Access or even MySQL, and it is certainly no Oracle. Some missing features found in other databases are views, triggers, and stored procedures; furthermore, only left joins are supported. On the other hand, SQLite is reasonably easy to implement in an application and can exchange data with other databases through downloadable drivers.

SQLite is part of the Android application development kit; therefore, no extra download is necessary for the developer, and no additional libraries or external JARs have to be included when the application is being developed. Construction and maintenance of the SQLite database can be done as the application is used, just as a person adds, edits, and deletes people from her contact list on her smart phone. An alternative is the database being predefined in the application and being updated through downloads to the device. Finally, the database can be bundled with the application when it is delivered to the end user. It is often recommended that you bundle an initial data set with an app, even if you can download a newer one on first run. This allows tables without cellular connections to run the app even if it is disconnected from the Internet the first time the application is loaded.

If the goal of the database is to provide look-up information to the end user, and the end user is not expected to have to modify data on his own, the amount of data is not conveniently added at run-time, or connectivity may not be available at run-time, an ideal solution may be to bundle data with the application. To run through an example of this process, we will build an application that includes the zip codes for the United States for look-up purposes. Obviously, there would be no need or logic to the end user having the ability to add, edit, or delete zip codes, but the developer might want to include the ability for the user to specify a subset of zip codes, such as all zip codes for a given state. There are more than 42,000 zip codes in the table, so this is not a data table we would want to load by hand. Also, it is information that the developer wouldn't want to leave at the mercy of available connectivity on the road. (Remember, the advantage of mobile devices is their mobility!) So by its nature, the zip code table is a good example to use.

You can find a usable, downloadable zip code table at www.unitedstateszipcodes.org /zip-code-database/.

The first step is to convert the zip code table to an SQLite table. The data table at this site comes in CSV format and can be read by either Microsoft Excel or Microsoft Access. (It's assumed you have access to one or both of these applications.) If you are using Access, you can import it as comma-delimited text. If you are using Excel, simply right-click the download and choose Open with Excel. Once you have the data table in Excel or Access, you have to get it into SQLite. This requires two things: the creation of an SQLite database, and a "bridge" from Access or Excel to SQLite. For the balance of this discussion, I will use Access as the data source. You need an application to create an SQLite database on the development machine; for this, you can download an application called SQL Database Browser from http://sourceforge. net/projects/sqlitebrowser/files/latest/download.

When you unzip the download, you will find one executable file. Just double-click it to start the SQLite browser. With this, you will create a database to hold the zip code table. I named my database `AndroidDatabase`. Do this by choosing New Database under the File menu. See Figure 3.1.

For any database that you want to bundle with an Android application, you need to create a table called `android_metadata` with a single field called `locale`. You can do that using the Create Table icon on SQLite Database Browser's toolbar, which is a table symbol with a yellow star on it. After you create the table, choose the Execute SQL tab and enter the following code to enter a single record.

```
insert into "android_metadata" values('en_US')
```

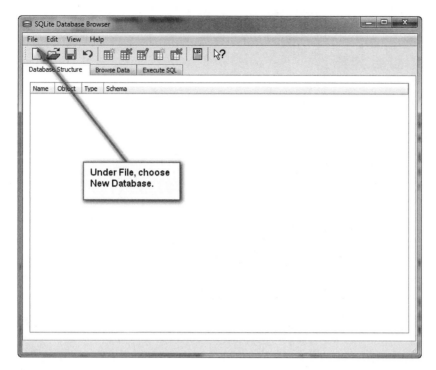

Figure 3.1
New database using SQLite Browser.
Source: SourceForge.net.

Thus far, we have created one table in our database, which contains one record. The next step is to export the zip code table to this SQLite database. To do this, we need to download an SQLite driver. I downloaded this from www.ch-werner.de/sqliteodbc.

This site was available at the time of this writing, but if it's not when you're reading this, you can search for another source. The download contains a file called `sqliteodbc.exe`. Just execute that file to install the driver. After you have installed the driver, you need to register your newly created SQLite as a data source. If you are using Windows, find Data Sources (ODBC) in the Control Panel. It should either have its own icon or be listed in Administrative Tools. In Windows 7, you may need to click the arrow point to the right of the Control Panel in the search bar and choose All Control Panel Items. (See Figure 3.2.) When you find it and click it, you bring up the ODBC Data Source Administrator dialog box. (See Figure 3.3.) With the User DSN tab active, click the Add button on the right, choose the appropriate newly installed SQLite driver (probably SQLite 3 ODBC Driver), and then click the OK button. When you do this, another dialog box pops up for you to choose your SQLite database wherever you saved it on your machine. When this is complete, you should be good to go. You can find a comprehensive guide to this process at http://web.synametrices.com/SQLite.htm.

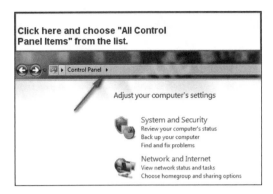

Figure 3.2
Follow this diagram to find Administrative Tools in Windows 7.
Source: Microsoft® Corporation.

After we create the Open Database Connectivity (ODBC) data source, we need to get back to Microsoft Access. At this point, we should have an Access database with the imported zip code table. We now need to export that table to SQLite using our new ODBC connection. Be sure your zip code data table is selected (or any table you wish to export, for that matter), and if you are using Access 2007 or above, use the External Data tab and find More in the Export Ribbon. (See Figure 3.4.)

In the More section, you should find ODBC Database as one of the choices. Choose that, and you will see a confirmation pop up to be sure you picked the correct table to export. Continue on, and in the Select Data Source dialog box, choose the Machine

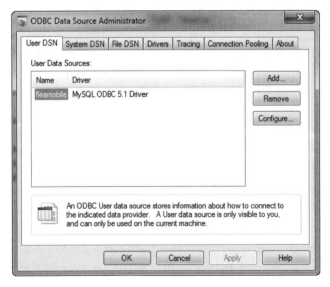

Figure 3.3
ODBC Data Source Administrator dialog box in Windows 7.
Source: Microsoft® Corporation.

Figure 3.4
Export Ribbon in Microsoft Access 2010.
Source: Microsoft® Corporation.

Data Source tab and find your SQLite database in the list. Choose it and click OK to complete the transfer.

There is one step left to making a SQLite database suitable for bundling with an Android application: giving the primary key field _id. You can do this with the SQLite Database Browser program that we used earlier or any other method you may be aware of. In SQLite Database Browser, use the Table Edit function. Figure 3.5 shows the structure of my usable Android database.

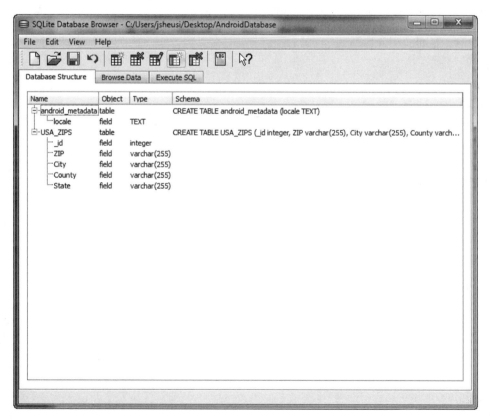

Figure 3.5
SQLite Database Browser showing structures of tables for the Android application.
Source: SourceForge.net.

You only need to add this database to the Assets folder in your Android application. Unfortunately, an Android application cannot use a database from the location it occupies in the bundled application. You must copy it to the location in the application's directory tree specified by the following path: /data/data/*the_application _package_name*/databases/. What's more, we probably don't want to do this every time the application is run, which would simply waste load time for the application. Checking for the database in the proper location as well as copying it from Assets if necessary is done with methods in a class called SQLiteOpenHelper, which is in the android.database.sqlite package. The programmer extends this class to suit the application, adding the appropriate paths, database, and table names; extra methods as necessary; and overridden methods. Following is the code for the extended class used in our demonstration. We will include this as a class to our application in Eclipse.

```
class myDBHelper extends SQLiteOpenHelper {
    private String dbpath = "/data/data/com.sheusi.BundledSqlite/databases/";
    private String dbname = "AndroidDatabase";
    private SQLiteDatabase myData = null;
    private Context myContext = null;

    public myDBHelper(Context c) {
        super(c, "AndroidDatabase", null, 1);
        myContext = c;
    }

    public void createDataBase() {
        boolean dbExists = checkForDataBase();

        if (dbExists == true) {
            // no need to do anything
        } else {
            this.getReadableDatabase();
            xferDataBase();
        }

    }

    private boolean checkForDataBase() {

        SQLiteDatabase test = null;
        try {
            String myPath = dbpath + dbname;
            test = SQLiteDatabase.openDatabase(myPath, null,
                    SQLiteDatabase.OPEN_READONLY);
        } catch (SQLiteException e) {

        }
        if (test != null)
```

```java
                test.close();

        if (test != null)
            return true;
        else
            return false;
    }

    private void xferDataBase() {
        try {
            InputStream myInput = myContext.getAssets().open(dbname);
            String outFile = dbpath + dbname;
            OutputStream myOutput = new FileOutputStream(outFile);
            byte[] buffer = new byte[1024];
            int length;
            while ((length = myInput.read(buffer)) > 0)
                myOutput.write(buffer, 0, length);
            myOutput.flush();
            myOutput.close();
            myInput.close();
        } catch (IOException ioe) {
        }
    }

    public SQLiteDatabase openDataBase() {
        try {
            String myPath = dbpath + dbname;
            myData = SQLiteDatabase.openDatabase(myPath, null,
                    SQLiteDatabase.OPEN_READONLY);
        } catch (SQLException sqle) {
        }
        return myData;
    }

    @Override
    public synchronized void close() {
        if (myData != null) {
            myData.close();
            super.close();
        }
    }

    @Override
    public void onCreate(SQLiteDatabase sqldb) {

    }

    @Override
```

```
    public void onUpgrade(SQLiteDatabase sqldb, int oldVersion, int newVersion) {

    }

}// ends class
```

You should be careful to enter the name of the path and database correctly. Also be careful to use the path separators (/) in the correct locations. Notice that the .getAssets( ) method of the Context class abstracts the location of the Assets folder in the Package Manager of Eclipse at design time.

The rest of the application's source code is quite simple. It uses an instance of the database helper class to open the database, transferring first if necessary. Then it runs a simple query to draw records for a single state, Rhode Island. After that, it populates an EditText field with the zip codes and their corresponding cities and state. (Listing the state is technically superfluous because the query specifies the state, but it's just a demonstration.) This demonstration merely shows how we can take advantage of a bundled database; admittedly, the user interface leaves plenty of room for improvement. Following is the source code for the main Activity class, followed by the main.xml file.

```
package com.sheusi.BundledSqlite;

import android.app.Activity;
import android.os.Bundle;
import android.widget.*;
import android.database.*;
import android.database.sqlite.*;
import android.content.*;
import java.io.*;

public class BundledSqliteActivity extends Activity {
    /** Called when the activity is created. */
    EditText et = null;
    Context myContext = null;
    SQLiteDatabase ad = null;
    myDBHelper mdbh = null;

    @Override
    public void onCreate(Bundle savedInstanceState) {
        super.onCreate(savedInstanceState);
        setContentView(R.layout.main);
        et = (EditText) findViewById(R.id.et);
        myContext = this.getApplicationContext();
        mdbh = new myDBHelper(myContext);
        mdbh.createDataBase();
```

```
    ad = mdbh.openDataBase();
    Cursor c = ad.rawQuery("select * from USA_ZIPS where state=?",
            new String[] { "RI" });
    c.moveToFirst();
    while (!c.isAfterLast()) {

        et.append(c.getString(1) + ":" + c.getString(2) + ":"
                + c.getString(4) + "\n");
        c.moveToNext();
    }
    c.close();
    }

}
```

The XML file for the main activity's form appears below.

```
<?xml version="1.0" encoding="utf-8"?>
<LinearLayout xmlns:android="http://schemas.android.com/apk/res/android"
    android:layout_width="fill_parent"
    android:layout_height="fill_parent"
    android:orientation="vertical" >

    <TextView
        android:layout_width="match_parent"
        android:layout_height="wrap_content"
        android:text="@string/hello" />

    <EditText
        android:id="@+id/et"
        android:layout_width="match_parent"
        android:layout_height="wrap_content"
        android:scrollbars="vertical" />

</LinearLayout>
```

In reality, it is likely that even though it is desirable for a database to be bundled with an application, the data contained might need to be updated from time to time. In a small business environment, it is feasible that the tablets that are to be taken on the road are accessible to the in-house IT specialist on a daily basis, or at least at some periodic interval. An application can be modified to draw a database from an external device that can be updated on a timely basis as often as necessary. With that in mind, an application similar to the example presented can draw data from a flash drive instead of the Assets folder in the bundle.

I chose the Toshiba Thrive tablet for myself because it has a standard USB port, to which I can add a flash drive or a USB hub. To test this concept, I downloaded an area code data table from http://databases.about.com/od/access/a/areacodes.htm, in native Microsoft Access format. I added the required primary key with the field name, _id (I removed the primary key designation from the area code field in Access), and exported it to my AndroidDatabase file as I did earlier with the zip codes. I then made the following modifications to the database helper class. The commented lines (//) reflect the original code, and the new code follows directly below it. Here are the changes to the xferDataBase( ) method in the helper class.

```
//InputStream myInput = myContext.getAssets().open(dbname);
File f =new File("/mnt/usb0/part0/AndroidDatabase");
FileInputStream myInput=new FileInputStream(f);
```

Then I made this change to the checkForDataBase( ) method.

```
//       if (test != null)
//            return true;
//       else
//            return false;
return false;
```

First, I had to change the source of the data file. I determined the correct path for the USB drive using the DDMS perspective in Eclipse. To get to the DDMS perspective, choose the Window menu on Eclipse, and then choose Open Perspective. If DDMS is not an immediate choice, choose Other and you will find it. The path for the Thrive is /mnt/usb0/part0/. See Figure 3.6.

Second, I ignored the test for whether or not the database was ever copied into the usable location (/data/data/pkgname/databases/) because I wanted to be sure my USB database was copied every time for testing purposes. In production, the copy routine might be a separate process that requires a button activation and an authorization to transfer new data. The change in the code returns false every time to be sure new data is transferred.

Finally, in the Activity class, the query has to change to poll the area code table instead of the zip code table, and the fields to be listed in the EditText field have to change. There is no filter in the area code query, as you can see; all the area codes and their regions are listed in the EditText field. There is no need to change anything else in the application.

```
//Cursor c = ad.rawQuery("select * from USA_ZIPS where state=?",
//            new String[] { "RI" });
    Cursor c=ad.rawQuery("select * from Area_Codes order by Region",new String[]{});
    c.moveToFirst();
```

```
while (!c.isAfterLast()) {

      //et.append(c.getString(1) + ":" + c.getString(2) + ":"
      //        + c.getString(4) + "\n");
      et.append(c.getString(1).substring(0,3)+":"+c.getString(2)+ "\n");
      c.moveToNext();
}
```

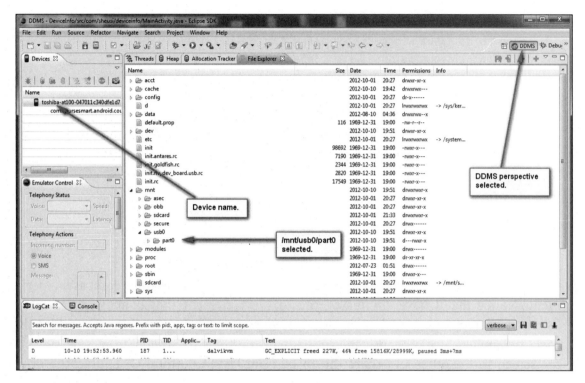

Figure 3.6
DDMS perspective in Eclipse.
Source: The Eclipse Foundation.

DISPLAYING THE TABLE WITH A LISTVIEW

Let's take a time out from working with the data itself and look at a more attractive display of the table on the screen. The ideal widget to use for this purpose is the ListView, which is a descendant of the AdapterView class, which in turn is a descendant of the ViewGroup class. One or more ListView widgets can be added to a ViewGroup, such as a LinearLayout, RelativeLayout, or whatever is desirable. Typically, this would be the primary "container" in the main.xml file. The way the contents of the ListView will actually appear is defined in a separate XML file; the ListView is essentially a placeholder in the XML file, in which it appears as an element. With that in mind, look at the `main.xml` file listed here.

```xml
<?xml version="1.0" encoding="utf-8"?>
<LinearLayout xmlns:android="http://schemas.android.com/apk/res/android"
    android:layout_width="fill_parent"
    android:layout_height="fill_parent"
    android:orientation="vertical" >

    <TextView
        android:layout_width="match_parent"
        android:layout_height="wrap_content"
        android:text="@string/hello" />

    <ListView
        android:id="@+id/headerlist"
        android:layout_width="match_parent"
        android:layout_height="wrap_content" />

    <ListView
        android:id="@+id/recordlist"
        android:layout_width="match_parent"
        android:layout_height="wrap_content" />

</LinearLayout>
```

This is the XML file we will use to replace the one in our original database experiment. Notice that I have eliminated the `EditText` element that contained our table listings and replaced it with two `ListView` elements. They are given IDs and only basic parameters, which cause the individual `ListViews` to stretch from one side of the screen to the other and share the space from top to bottom. Of course, the programmer can do whatever he wants with these parameters. I have included two `ListViews` because one will contain the field names from the table to be displayed, and the other will contain the actual records. This will provide a table display similar to what you would see in the Datasheet View in Microsoft Access. (You might recall in our simple `EditText` listing that the field names themselves were never displayed.) Because we are talking about XML files, let's get them all out of the way here. The following are the XML definitions for the field name portion of the display (`header.xml`) and the display for the actual records (`records.xml`).

```xml
<?xml version="1.0" encoding="utf-8"?>
<LinearLayout xmlns:android="http://schemas.android.com/apk/res/android"
    android:id="@+id/fieldlayout"
    android:layout_width="match_parent"
    android:layout_height="wrap_content"
    android:background="#000099"
```

```
    android:orientation="horizontal"
    android:paddingBottom="6dp"
    android:paddingTop="4dp" >

    <TextView
        android:id="@+id/fieldname1"
        android:layout_width="80dp"
        android:layout_height="wrap_content"
        android:layout_weight="1"
            android:textColor="#ffffff"
        android:textSize="20dp"/>

    <TextView
        android:id="@+id/fieldname2"
        android:layout_width="80dp"
        android:layout_height="wrap_content"
        android:layout_weight="1"
            android:textColor="#ffffff"
        android:textSize="20dp"/>

    <TextView
        android:id="@+id/fieldname3"
        android:layout_width="80dp"
        android:layout_height="wrap_content"
        android:layout_weight="1"
            android:textColor="#ffffff"
        android:textSize="20dp"/>

</LinearLayout>
```

This is the beginning of the header.xml file.

```
<?xml version="1.0" encoding="utf-8"?>
<LinearLayout xmlns:android="http://schemas.android.com/apk/res/android"
    android:id="@+id/recordlayout"
    android:layout_width="match_parent"
    android:layout_height="wrap_content"
    android:background="#990000"
    android:orientation="horizontal"
    android:paddingBottom="6dp"
    android:paddingTop="4dp" >

    <TextView
        android:id="@+id/field1"
        android:layout_width="80dp"
        android:layout_height="wrap_content"
        android:layout_weight="1"
            android:textColor="#ffffff"
```

```
                android:textSize="20dp"/>
        <TextView
            android:id="@+id/field2"
            android:layout_width="80dp"
            android:layout_height="wrap_content"
            android:layout_weight="1"
                android:textColor="#ffffff"
            android:textSize="20dp"/>
        <TextView
            android:id="@+id/field3"
            android:layout_width="80dp"
            android:layout_height="wrap_content"
            android:layout_weight="1"
                android:textColor="#ffffff"
            android:textSize="20dp"/>

</LinearLayout>
```

The difference between the two displays is subtle in this example. The only differences between the two are the element IDs and the background colors. Notice, though, that both the LinearLayouts have a horizontal orientation. This is not typical for Linear Layouts when they are the base for a main.xml file but is essential here, so be careful to set them to horizontal orientation.

The code for implementing a multicolumn ListView, which we must do in our case, is far from intuitive, so we will take it in steps. First, you should note that we set some of the code back to the use of the zip code table and reset the code to check for the existence of the database before we copy it from the Assets directory. The first set of modifications only provides for printing the field names on the screen. The process to print the records is similar, but to keep things simple, we will look at the field names and the actual records one at a time. Also, remember that we are eliminating the use of the EditText and replacing it with two ListViews. The first set of changes is the additional object declarations listed in the code snippit that follows. (The entire Activity code will be presented at the end of this discussion.)

```
//EditText et;
// declarations for dressed-up record list
ListView header = null;
String[] fieldnames = null;
SimpleAdapter headeradapter = null;
HashMap<String,String> headermap = null;
ArrayList<HashMap<String, String>> headerlist = null;
//
```

First, as I mentioned earlier, we have eliminated the use of the `EditText`. Then we have declared a `ListView`, an array of `String` objects to hold the field names, a `SimpleAdapter` to supply content to the `ListView` on the screen, a `HashMap` object to hold values taken from the data table as key-value pairs, and an `ArrayList` to hold multiple rows of data. The `HashMap` and `ArrayList` classes are found in the `java.util` package, so be sure to add them to your `include` statements.

```
header = (ListView) findViewById(R.id.headerlist);
```

The preceding line is found near the top of the `onCreate( )` method, where we typically assign variable names to items found in the XML files.

```
Cursor c = ad.rawQuery("select * from USA_ZIPS where state=?",
                new String[] { "RI" });
        // Cursor c=ad.rawQuery("select * from Area_Codes order by Region",new
        // String[]{});
        fieldnames = c.getColumnNames();
        headermap = new HashMap<String, String>();
        headermap.put("fn1", fieldnames[1]);
        headermap.put("fn2", fieldnames[2]);
        headermap.put("fn3", fieldnames[4]);
        headerlist = new ArrayList<HashMap<String, String>>();
        headerlist.add(headermap);
        headeradapter = new SimpleAdapter(this, headerlist, R.layout.header,
                new String[] { "fn1", "fn2", "fn3" }, new int[] {
                        R.id.fieldname1, R.id.fieldname2, R.id.fieldname3 });
        header.setAdapter(headeradapter);
```

A lot is happening in this section of code. First, using the `Cursor` object, we can extract the field names as an array of `Strings`. We are only interested in the City, State, and Zip Code fields in this example, which have index values of 1, 2, and 4. Remember that the array is zero based. Next, we add the field names and their keys `fn1`, `fn2`, and `fn3` to the `ArrayList` we declared, which holds two `Strings`. The key names `fn1`, `fn2`, and `fn3` are arbitrary and are not dependent on any other code at this point. Next, the `ArrayList` is added to the `HashMap`, which is composed of `ArrayLists`.

Finally, the `SimpleAdapter` is constructed with five parameters: the application's context, the `HashMap`, the XML file that provides the layout, the key values that contain the actual data through their paired items, and finally the IDs for the elements in the XML file. It may seem strange that the IDs for the elements are arrays of integers rather than `Strings`, but remember that in the `R.java` file, each of the elements in the various directories is assigned hex values. Look at the `R.java` file, and you will see this.

This code will produce the view of the field names you see in Figure 3.7.

Figure 3.7
Structured presentation of field names on emulator.
Source: The Eclipse Foundation.

The following is some additional code to add the actual records to our screen. First, here are some additional declarations.

```
//-------------- Declaration of objects for displaying the records
ListView records=null;
SimpleAdapter recordadapter=null;
HashMap<String,String> recordmap = null;
ArrayList<HashMap<String, String>> recordlist = null;
```

Here's an additional assignment in the onCreate( ) method.

```
records= (ListView) findViewById(R.id.recordlist);
```

Finally, the code takes records from the Cursor object, adds them to the list view, and displays them. The commented code in this section is left over from the original EditText version of our record display application.

```
recordlist=new ArrayList<HashMap<String,String>>();
    while (!c.isAfterLast()) {
        recordmap=new HashMap<String, String>();
     recordmap.put("r1",c.getString(1));
```

```
        recordmap.put("r2",c.getString(2));
        recordmap.put("r3",c.getString(4));
        recordlist.add(recordmap);
            // et.append(c.getString(1) + ":" + c.getString(2) + ":"
            // + c.getString(4) + "\n");
            // et.append(c.getString(1).substring(0,3)+":"+c.getString(2)+
            // "\n");
            c.moveToNext();
    }// ends while
    c.close();
    recordadapter=new SimpleAdapter(this,recordlist,R.layout.records,
            new String[]{"r1","r2","r3"}, new int[] {R.id.field1,
R.id.field2,R.id.field3});
    records.setAdapter(recordadapter);
```

Make a note that the recordmap variable is reassigned inside the loop that cycles through all the records; otherwise, you may just repeat the same record many times.

Here is the cleaned-up code in its entirety.

```
package com.sheusi.BundledSqlite;

import android.app.Activity;
import android.os.Bundle;
import android.widget.*;
import android.database.*;
import android.database.sqlite.*;
import android.content.*;
import java.io.*;
import android.util.Log;
import java.util.*;

public class BundledSqliteActivity extends Activity {
    /** Called when the activity is first created. */

    Context myContext = null;
    SQLiteDatabase ad = null;
    myDBHelper mdbh = null;
    ListView header = null;
    String[] fieldnames = null;
    SimpleAdapter headeradapter = null;
    HashMap<String, String> headermap = null;
    ArrayList<HashMap<String, String>> headerlist = null;
    ListView records = null;
    SimpleAdapter recordadapter = null;
    HashMap<String, String> recordmap = null;
    ArrayList<HashMap<String, String>> recordlist = null;
```

```java
@Override
public void onCreate(Bundle savedInstanceState) {
    super.onCreate(savedInstanceState);
    setContentView(R.layout.main);
    header = (ListView) findViewById(R.id.headerlist);
    records = (ListView) findViewById(R.id.recordlist);
    myContext = this.getApplicationContext();
    mdbh = new myDBHelper(myContext);
    mdbh.createDataBase();
    ad = mdbh.openDataBase();
    Cursor c = ad.rawQuery("select * from USA_ZIPS where state=?",
            new String[] { "RI" });
    fieldnames = c.getColumnNames();
    headermap = new HashMap<String, String>();
    headermap.put("fn1", fieldnames[1]);
    headermap.put("fn2", fieldnames[2]);
    headermap.put("fn3", fieldnames[4]);
    headerlist = new ArrayList<HashMap<String, String>>();
    headerlist.add(headermap);
    headeradapter = new SimpleAdapter(this, headerlist, R.layout.header,
            new String[] { "fn1", "fn2", "fn3" }, new int[] {
                    R.id.fieldname1, R.id.fieldname2, R.id.fieldname3 });
    header.setAdapter(headeradapter);
    c.moveToFirst();
    recordlist = new ArrayList<HashMap<String, String>>();
    while (!c.isAfterLast()) {
        recordmap = new HashMap<String, String>();
        recordmap.put("r1", c.getString(1));
        recordmap.put("r2", c.getString(2));
        recordmap.put("r3", c.getString(4));
        recordlist.add(recordmap);
        c.moveToNext();
    }// ends while
    c.close();
    recordadapter = new SimpleAdapter(this, recordlist, R.layout.records,
            new String[] { "r1", "r2", "r3" }, new int[] { R.id.field1,
                    R.id.field2, R.id.field3 });
    records.setAdapter(recordadapter);
}

}

class myDBHelper extends SQLiteOpenHelper {
    private String dbpath = "/data/data/com.sheusi.BundledSqlite/databases/";
```

```java
private String dbname = "AndroidDatabase";
private SQLiteDatabase myData = null;
private Context myContext = null;

public myDBHelper(Context c) {
    super(c, "AndroidDatabase", null, 1);
    myContext = c;
}

public void createDataBase() {
    boolean dbExists = checkForDataBase();

    if (dbExists == true) {
        // no need to do anything
    } else {
        this.getReadableDatabase();
        xferDataBase();
    }

}

private boolean checkForDataBase() {

    SQLiteDatabase test = null;
    try {
        String myPath = dbpath + dbname;
        test = SQLiteDatabase.openDatabase(myPath, null,
                SQLiteDatabase.OPEN_READONLY);
    } catch (SQLiteException e) {

    }
    if (test != null)
        test.close();

    if (test != null)
        return true;
    else
        return false;

}

private void xferDataBase() {
    try {
        InputStream myInput = myContext.getAssets().open(dbname);
        String outFile = dbpath + dbname;
        OutputStream myOutput = new FileOutputStream(outFile);
        byte[] buffer = new byte[1024];
        int length;
```

```
            while ((length = myInput.read(buffer)) > 0)
                myOutput.write(buffer, 0, length);
            myOutput.flush();
            myOutput.close();
            myInput.close();
            Log.i("info", "data transferred");
        } catch (IOException ioe) {
            Log.i("info", "data didn't transfer");
        }
    }

    public SQLiteDatabase openDataBase() {
        try {
            String myPath = dbpath + dbname;
            myData = SQLiteDatabase.openDatabase(myPath, null,
                    SQLiteDatabase.OPEN_READONLY);
        } catch (SQLException sqle) {
        }
        return myData;
    }

    @Override
    public synchronized void close() {
        if (myData != null) {
            myData.close();
            super.close();
        }
    }

    @Override
    public void onCreate(SQLiteDatabase sqldb) {

    }

    @Override
    public void onUpgrade(SQLiteDatabase sqldb, int oldVersion, int newVersion) {

    }
}// ends class
```

The final running application should look like Figure 3.8. The application as written will fill the whole screen, which is probably not the way you would want it in production, but it serves as a demonstration. One nice feature when you split the field names from the actual records in two different ListViews, aside from the fact that the background, font color, and style can be different, is that when the list of records is scrolled, the field names stay locked.

Figure 3.8
Structured listing of zip codes with their cities and states on emulator.

Source: The Eclipse Foundation.

BUILDING A TABLE AT RUN-TIME

Often the database doesn't have to be preloaded in the application; it can be created and built incrementally as the application is used. For example, a business might deploy tablets for employees to use in the field to take applications, collect survey data, conduct event registrations, and so on. Data, once collected, can be transmitted to a central collection point if necessary or downloaded once the worker returns to the main office. The framework of the database, or the table names and their field descriptions and characteristics (metadata), is contained in the application's coding, but the data is collected at run-time.

Those familiar with database operations are familiar with the acronym CRUD, which stands for create, read, update, and delete—four main operations done on a data table. The SQLite's classes have methods for these specific operations, with a built-in parameter list for each. For example, the `SQLiteDatabase` class has one `query( )` method that returns a `Cursor` object and requires seven specific arguments. The definition of the method is as follows:

```
query( String table-name, String[ ] column-names, String selection-description, String[]
selection-arguments, String group-by, String having…, String order-by).
```

This query essentially performs a read operation on a table. It doesn't add or change existing records; it simply reads them. The Cursor object that is returned is similar to the ResultSet object returned by a query in Java Standard Edition's Statement.query( ) method. Implementation of that code sample might look like this:

```
Cursor c=query( "members", null, "subject=?",new String[]
{"android"},null,null,"pagecount");
```

This is equivalent to the SQL statement *select * from members where subject='android' order by pagecount.*

When a database application is designed for a server or an individual's desktop or laptop, typically the database portion is done on a database management system (for example, Microsoft Access, MySQL, and Oracle), and the front end is done separately. The front end application, or the user interface, is built to assume that the database portion exists and is functioning. Indeed, this is the beauty of modern relational database management system (RDBMS) middleware; the data operations are independent of and abstracted from the front-end application. On the other hand, in a mobile application, unless data is provided by a content provider, the database operation is integrated into the application. SQLite does not offer ODBC connectivity or JDBC as J2SE does. So the programmer has a chicken-and-egg dilemma. If she designs the application to construct data tables each time the application is started, existing data is always overwritten and lost. If she doesn't include the construction of the data tables, they may never exist. Obviously, the solution is to check for the tables' existence before creating them. We did a similar thing with our bundled tables using the database helper object in the previous exercise, but the Android Context class contains the method openOrCreateDatabase( ), which returns an instance of the SQLiteDatabase class and has a built-in check for the database's existence.

To round out the CRUD queries, the Update query syntax is as follows:

```
update(table-name,ContentValues cv,String selection-description,String[]
selection-arguments);
```

The symbols are as follows: table-name is the name of the table to update, cv is an instance of the ContentValues class, selection-description is the specifier for which record(s) to update, and selection-arguments is the specification for the selection description. The method returns an integer that indicates how many records were updated.

The Insert query syntax is as follows:

```
insert(table-name,null column hack,ContentValues cv);
```

The symbols are as follows: `table-name` is the name of the table to update, the `null column hack` allows the insertion of a record with no values (normally we would give that a value of `null`), and `cv` is an instance of the `ContentValues` class that holds the field values to insert. The `insert` method returns a long value indicating the number of the record that was inserted or a minus one (−1) if the `insert` operation failed.

Finally, the `Delete` query syntax is as follows:

```
delete(table-name,String selection-description,selection-arguments);
```

Like the previous two examples, `table-name` represents the table to modify, `selection-description` indicates which field(s) to check for targeting the deletion, and `selection-arguments` indicates which values in those fields to delete for. This method also returns an integer indicating how many records were deleted.

The following exercise simulates the collection of membership data for a club. The database to create consists of a single table containing member information. The data table will use an auto-increment integer as a unique field, just as we used in the bundled table examples. However, we will use an email address as our unique member identifier. Our demographics will consist of first name, last name, street address, city, state, zip code, phone number, and email address. The screen will consist of `EditText` fields to fill in with the values for the records and buttons to search for members by email address, to add or update a record, to delete a given record, or to clear the form. The application has a single screen, and its layout XML file is as follows.

```xml
<?xml version="1.0" encoding="utf-8"?>
<LinearLayout xmlns:android="http://schemas.android.com/apk/res/android"
    android:layout_width="fill_parent"
    android:layout_height="fill_parent"
    android:orientation="vertical" >

    <TextView
        android:layout_width="fill_parent"
        android:layout_height="wrap_content"
        android:text="Android Developer's Association" />

    <TableLayout
        android:layout_width="fill_parent"
        android:layout_height="wrap_content" >

        <TableRow
            android:layout_width="wrap_content"
            android:layout_height="wrap_content" >
```

```xml
            <TextView
                android:layout_width="wrap_content"
                android:layout_height="wrap_content"
                android:layout_weight=".5"
                android:text="Email Address:" />

            <EditText
                android:id="@+id/et_email"
                android:layout_width="wrap_content"
                android:layout_height="wrap_content"
                android:layout_weight=".5"
                android:background="#808080"
                android:text="" />
        </TableRow>

        <TableRow
            android:layout_width="wrap_content"
            android:layout_height="wrap_content" >

            <Button
                android:id="@+id/retrievebutton"
                android:layout_width="wrap_content"
                android:layout_height="wrap_content"
                android:layout_weight=".5"
                android:text="Retrieve" />
        </TableRow>

        <TableRow
            android:layout_width="wrap_content"
            android:layout_height="wrap_content" >

            <TextView
                android:layout_width="wrap_content"
                android:layout_height="wrap_content"
                android:layout_weight=".5"
                android:text="First Name:" />

            <EditText
                android:id="@+id/et_fname"
                android:layout_width="wrap_content"
                android:layout_height="wrap_content"
                android:layout_weight=".5"
                android:background="#404040"
                android:text="" />
        </TableRow>

        <TableRow
            android:layout_width="wrap_content"
```

```
            android:layout_height="wrap_content" >

        <TextView
            android:layout_width="wrap_content"
            android:layout_height="wrap_content"
            android:layout_weight=".5"
            android:text="Last Name:" />

        <EditText
            android:id="@+id/et_lname"
            android:layout_width="wrap_content"
            android:layout_height="wrap_content"
            android:layout_weight=".5"
            android:background="#606060"
            android:text="" />
    </TableRow>

    <TableRow
        android:layout_width="wrap_content"
        android:layout_height="wrap_content" >

        <TextView
            android:layout_width="wrap_content"
            android:layout_height="wrap_content"
            android:layout_weight=".5"
            android:text="Address:" />

        <EditText
            android:id="@+id/et_address"
            android:layout_width="wrap_content"
            android:layout_height="wrap_content"
            android:layout_weight=".5"
            android:background="#404040"
            android:text="" />
    </TableRow>

    <TableRow
        android:layout_width="wrap_content"
        android:layout_height="wrap_content" >

        <TextView
            android:layout_width="wrap_content"
            android:layout_height="wrap_content"
            android:layout_weight=".5"
            android:text="City:" />

        <EditText
            android:id="@+id/et_city"
```

```
            android:layout_width="wrap_content"
            android:layout_height="wrap_content"
            android:layout_weight=".5"
            android:background="#606060"
            android:text="" />
    </TableRow>

    <TableRow
        android:layout_width="wrap_content"
        android:layout_height="wrap_content" >

        <TextView
            android:layout_width="wrap_content"
            android:layout_height="wrap_content"
            android:layout_weight=".5"
            android:text="State:" />

        <EditText
            android:id="@+id/et_state"
            android:layout_width="wrap_content"
            android:layout_height="wrap_content"
            android:layout_weight=".5"
            android:background="#404040"
            android:text="" />
    </TableRow>

    <TableRow
        android:layout_width="wrap_content"
        android:layout_height="wrap_content" >

        <TextView
            android:layout_width="wrap_content"
            android:layout_height="wrap_content"
            android:layout_weight=".5"
            android:text="Zip:" />

        <EditText
            android:id="@+id/et_zip"
            android:layout_width="wrap_content"
            android:layout_height="wrap_content"
            android:layout_weight=".5"
            android:background="#606060"
            android:text="" />
    </TableRow>

    <TableRow
        android:layout_width="wrap_content"
        android:layout_height="wrap_content" >
```

```xml
        <TextView
            android:layout_width="wrap_content"
            android:layout_height="wrap_content"
            android:layout_weight=".5"
            android:text="Phone:" />

        <EditText
            android:id="@+id/et_phone"
            android:layout_width="wrap_content"
            android:layout_height="wrap_content"
            android:layout_weight=".5"
            android:background="#404040"
            android:text="" />
    </TableRow>

    <TableRow
        android:layout_width="wrap_content"
        android:layout_height="wrap_content" >

        <Button
            android:id="@+id/savebutton"
            android:layout_width="wrap_content"
            android:layout_height="wrap_content"
            android:layout_weight=".5"
            android:text="Save" />

        <Button
            android:id="@+id/clearbutton"
            android:layout_width="wrap_content"
            android:layout_height="wrap_content"
            android:layout_weight=".5"
            android:text="Clear" />

        <Button
            android:id="@+id/deletebutton"
            android:layout_width="wrap_content"
            android:layout_height="wrap_content"
            android:layout_weight=".5"
            android:text="Delete from Table" />
    </TableRow>
</TableLayout>
</LinearLayout>
```

The code consists of a single activity and is as follows.

```java
package com.sheusi.Membership;

import android.app.Activity;
```

```
import android.os.Bundle;
import android.database.*;
import android.database.sqlite.*;
import android.view.*;
import android.widget.*;
import android.content.*;

public class MembershipActivity extends Activity {
    /** Called when the activity is first created. */
    SQLiteDatabase database = null;
    Button retrieve = null;
    Button save = null;
    Button delete = null;
    Button clear = null;
    EditText email = null;
    EditText fname = null;
    EditText lname = null;
    EditText address = null;
    EditText city = null;
    EditText state = null;
    EditText zip = null;
    EditText phone = null;
    Context myContext = null;

    @Override
    public void onCreate(Bundle savedInstanceState) {
        super.onCreate(savedInstanceState);
        setContentView(R.layout.main);
        myContext = this.getApplicationContext();

this.setRequestedOrientation(android.content.pm.ActivityInfo.SCREEN_ORIENTATION
_PORTRAIT);
        // build table if it doesn't exist already
        database = openOrCreateDatabase("membership.db",
                SQLiteDatabase.CREATE_IF_NECESSARY, null);
        database.setLockingEnabled(true);
        if (checkForTable() != true)
            database.execSQL("create table members(_id integer primary key
autoincrement, email text, fname text, lname text, address text, city text, state text,
zip text, phone text)");

        // end build
        retrieve = (Button) findViewById(R.id.retrievebutton);
        save = (Button) findViewById(R.id.savebutton);
        delete = (Button) findViewById(R.id.deletebutton);
        clear = (Button) findViewById(R.id.clearbutton);
```

```
email = (EditText) findViewById(R.id.et_email);
fname = (EditText) findViewById(R.id.et_fname);
lname = (EditText) findViewById(R.id.et_lname);
address = (EditText) findViewById(R.id.et_address);
city = (EditText) findViewById(R.id.et_city);
state = (EditText) findViewById(R.id.et_state);
zip = (EditText) findViewById(R.id.et_zip);
phone = (EditText) findViewById(R.id.et_phone);
email.setText(null);
fname.setText(null);
lname.setText(null);
address.setText(null);
city.setText(null);
state.setText(null);
zip.setText(null);
phone.setText(null);
retrieve.setOnClickListener(new View.OnClickListener() {
    public void onClick(View v) {
        // if record exists, retrieve it; if not, give toast message
        String key = email.getText().toString();
        Cursor c = database.query("members", null, "email=?",
                new String[] { key }, null, null, null, null);
        if (c.getCount() == 0)
            Toast.makeText(myContext, "no record exists",
                    Toast.LENGTH_SHORT).show();
        else {
            c.moveToFirst();
            fname.setText(c.getString(2));
            lname.setText(c.getString(3));
            address.setText(c.getString(4));
            city.setText(c.getString(5));
            state.setText(c.getString(6));
            zip.setText(c.getString(7));
            phone.setText(c.getString(8));
        }

    }
});
save.setOnClickListener(new View.OnClickListener() {
    public void onClick(View v) {
        // if record exists, update it; if not, insert it
        String key = email.getText().toString();
        Cursor c = database.query("members", null, "email=?",
                new String[] { key }, null, null, null, null);
        if (c.getCount() > 0) { // it exists, so update
```

```java
                    ContentValues cv = new ContentValues();
                    cv.put("fname", fname.getText().toString());
                    cv.put("lname", lname.getText().toString());
                    cv.put("address", address.getText().toString());
                    cv.put("city", city.getText().toString());
                    cv.put("state", state.getText().toString());
                    cv.put("zip", zip.getText().toString());
                    cv.put("phone", phone.getText().toString());

                    database.update("members", cv, "email=?",
                            new String[] { key });

                } else { // doesn't exist so insert
                    ContentValues cv = new ContentValues();
                    cv.put("email", key);
                    cv.put("fname", fname.getText().toString());
                    cv.put("lname", lname.getText().toString());
                    cv.put("address", address.getText().toString());
                    cv.put("city", city.getText().toString());
                    cv.put("state", state.getText().toString());
                    cv.put("zip", zip.getText().toString());
                    cv.put("phone", phone.getText().toString());
                    database.insert("members", null, cv);
                }

            }
        });
        delete.setOnClickListener(new View.OnClickListener() {
            public void onClick(View v) {
                String key = email.getText().toString();
                database.delete("members", "email=?", new String[] { key });
                email.setText(null);
                fname.setText(null);
                lname.setText(null);
                address.setText(null);
                city.setText(null);
                state.setText(null);
                zip.setText(null);
                phone.setText(null);
                Toast.makeText(myContext, "Record was deleted.",
                        Toast.LENGTH_SHORT).show();

            }
        });
        clear.setOnClickListener(new View.OnClickListener() {
            public void onClick(View v) {
```

```
                    email.setText(null);
                    fname.setText(null);
                    lname.setText(null);
                    address.setText(null);
                    city.setText(null);
                    state.setText(null);
                    zip.setText(null);
                    phone.setText(null);

                }
            });
    }

    public boolean checkForTable() {
        Cursor c = database.query("sqlite_master", null, "type=? and name=?",
                new String[] { "table", "members" }, null, null, null);
        if (c.getCount() > 0)
            return true;
        else
            return false;
    }

    @Override
    public void onStop() {
        super.onStop();
        email.setText(null);
        fname.setText(null);
        lname.setText(null);
        address.setText(null);
        city.setText(null);
        state.setText(null);
        zip.setText(null);
        phone.setText(null);
        database.close();
    }
}
```

When the application runs, it will look like Figure 3.9.

SQLite allows you to stick with standard SQL query syntax to some extent by using the rawQuery( ) method of the SQLiteDatabase class. The rawQuery( ) method generally takes two parameters: the query statement as a String object, and the selection-arguments as an array of strings. For example, to substitute a raw query for our Retrieve button in Figure 3.9, we might use this.

Figure 3.9
Membership application on the emulator.
Source: The Eclipse Foundation.

```
Cursor c=database.rawQuery("Select * from members where email=?",
new String[]{key});
```

instead of this.

```
Cursor c = database.query("members", null, "email=?",
new String[] { key }, null, null, null, null);
```

For more complicated queries, SQLite offers a class called SQLiteQueryBuilder. It builds the query in several steps and then executes its own query( ) method to return a cursor. Although it is not required for a query as simple as the one we executed earlier, it might be done like the following using an SQLiteQueryBuilder object. If you want to use it, remember to put the following import statement at the top of your class.

```
import android.database.sqlite.SQLiteQueryBuilder;
```

The implementation might look like the following:

```
SQLiteQueryBuilder sqlqb=new SQLiteQueryBuilder();
                         sqlqb.setTables("members");
                         Cursor c=sqlqb.query(database,null,"email=?",new
String[]{key},null,null,null);
```

The first `null` argument causes the query to return all the fields instead of fields you may choose to specify: the last three `nulls` group-by, having..., and sort order. As I said earlier, in this case, an `SQLiteQueryBuilder` is overkill for the query at hand, but you can substitute this code on your own and give it a try.

SUMMARY OF KEY CONCEPTS

SQLite is the database management system employed by Android devices. Information on SQLite can be found at www.sqlite.org. You should review this website, especially the documentation and support areas.

A successful data-based application depends on a clear understanding of database design, data types, relations, and SQL. Although the examples in this chapter involve a single table of simple design for illustrative purposes, in reality it is likely that the data maintained will be much more complicated. You would do well to look at outside resources covering relational database design and SQL. A place to start is at www.w3schools.com/sql/.

Open Database Connectivity (ODBC) is middleware used by an operating system for accessing database management systems (DBMS). You can find information on ODBC for Windows 7 at http://windows.microsoft.com/is-IS/windows7/Using-the-ODBC-Data-Source-Administrator. You should review this website for help configuring SQLite on the development machine if necessary.

The `SimpleAdapter`, `ArrayList`, and `HashMap` classes are essential to presenting data in a pleasing fashion to the user. Study these classes, and practice them by making modifications to the examples shown in this chapter.

REVIEW QUESTIONS

You can find the answers to these review questions in the appendix at the end of the book.

1. The database manager used in Android devices as well as other handhelds and tablets is _____.

2. Middleware that connects the Windows 7 operating system to database management software running on the computer is _____.

3. A field whose value is unique to every record in a data table is called the _____.

4. A database bundled with an application can be used by the application in its current location at run-time, true or false? _____

5. Instances of the `HashMap` class are used to maintain data in _____ - _____ pairs.

6. The Eclipse perspective that allows access to the directory tree as well as other components of a connected device or an emulator is the _____ perspective.

7. The Android class that holds query results is the _____class.

8. The last parameter in `SQLiteDatabase` class's `query( )` method controls the _____ of the returned data.

9. The `rawQuery( )` method of the `SQLiteDatabase` class allows the programmer to structure queries using _____ syntax.

10. The UI control or widget used to display a list is the _____.

Suggested Projects

■ Search the Internet for other lists you can download as a table in CSV, DBF, or some other standard format, and substitute it for the zip code table used in the first exercise. Edit the `Activity` class and the layout XML file as necessary and test the application.

■ Develop an application to keep an inventory of your computer books or equipment based on the last exercise in this chapter.

■ Research SQLite, and compare and contrast it to another open source database management product such as MySQL, PostgreSQL, or Derby.

■ Write examples of SQLite query statements that will create, read, update, and delete records from a given table.

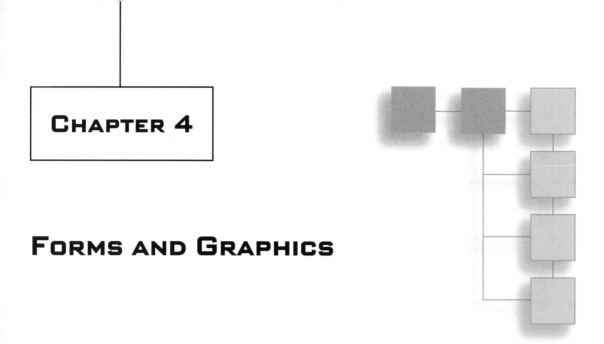

CHAPTER 4

FORMS AND GRAPHICS

FORMS WITH PICK-LISTS

The big advantage of the tablet over the handset is the amount of usable space on the screen. Even with the "soft" keyboard up there is a lot of visible, available space for your application. Of course, any screen, whether it is on a tablet or a PC, needs some planning if it is to provide an ideal user experience. Hopefully you have had some experience with ViewGroup classes such as the LinearLayout and RelativeLayout as well as the common controls such as the EditText, Button, and ListView classes. Indeed, if you have done the exercises presented in the previous chapters, you have seen how they work.

If you are using the latest Android toolkit and the latest add-in for Eclipse, you may have noticed that new projects default to the RelativeLayout instead of the LinearLayout. You also will have noticed that the single TextView, which holds the "Hello" message, no longer appears on the top of the screen, but in the middle. In the RelativeLayout, the screen objects are positioned in relation to another given object that is identified by its given android:id parameter, which is a nice way to plan the screen. If you noticed this, you undoubtedly noticed the improved graphic designer view when you edited the main XML file. Not so apparent, on the other hand, is that Android has deprecated the AbsoluteLayout ViewGroup class.

If you are planning a screen, it is helpful to know its dimensions in pixels. This is especially true if you know the device's specifications in advance, which would be the case if you are lucky enough to specify the device that will be deployed with your applications on it. You can get these dimensions from the documentation for the device if it is available, or you can do a little research on the Internet. Alternatively, you can get the dimensions from the device itself. Your application can get the dimensions from the device and make calculations based on them at run-time. This is helpful if your application must be adjusted for different devices or if you need to scale graphics at run-time.

Aside from screen dimensions, it is ideal to be able to determine at design time whether the screen will display in portrait or in landscape mode. It is best if you can lock the screen in one or the other mode so your thought-out design isn't spoiled by the user turning the device the wrong way. Although these two features are easy enough to use, they are not intuitive like many of the common programming techniques and requirements are. I find myself having to look them up each time.

With that in mind, let's look at the following experiment. The application's screen will contain two TextViews: one to display the width dimension and the other to display the height. It will also have two buttons: one for the user to select landscape orientation and the other to select portrait. These two buttons lock the application in the chosen orientation no matter how the device itself is held. If you are fortunate enough to be able to try the application on a real tablet device, you will notice that the dimensions displayed will change, depending on the screen orientation. Of course, there is probably no practical reason why you would want the application's user to be able to swap orientations at run-time; this is just an exercise to show the code that does so. Likewise, there is probably no reason to display the screen dimensions, but the application shows how to get the values so you can use them internally and for planning purposes. Following is the XML file for the main screen. You will notice that I am using the RelativeLayout, which is currently the default layout for new applications started in Eclipse. Also, I am basing the positions of my components on the single default TextView object, which normally holds the "Hello" message. Look at the code snippet here.

```
<TextView
        android:id="@+id/first"
        android:layout_width="wrap_content"
        android:layout_height="wrap_content"
        android:layout_centerHorizontal="true"
        android:layout_centerVertical="true"
        android:background="#aaaaaa"
        android:padding="@dimen/padding_medium"
        android:text=""
        android:width="400dp"
        tools:context=".MainActivity"
/>
```

Eclipse creates one `TextView` and puts it dead center on the screen using the `android:layout_centerHorizontal` and `android:layout_centerVertical` attributes. I have added to it an `android:id` attribute and an `android:background` attribute to give it a shade of gray for a color, and I have removed the predefined text. I have also set the `android:width` attribute to 400dp. The specification *dp* stands for device-independent pixel (*dip* could also be used), which is an abstract unit based on the density of a given screen. It is based on a 160-pixel screen and adjusts accordingly. If you use px as your unit, your dimension is based on the actual pixel density of the deployed device's screen. There is plenty of documentation on writing applications that are to run on devices with varying screen sizes and densities, and it can be confusing. However, I find that using the dp specification works fine in most cases. The entire XML file with another `TextView` and two buttons added looks like this.

```xml
<RelativeLayout xmlns:android="http://schemas.android.com/apk/res/android"
    xmlns:tools="http://schemas.android.com/tools"
    android:layout_width="match_parent"
    android:layout_height="match_parent" >

    <TextView
        android:id="@+id/first"
        android:layout_width="wrap_content"
        android:layout_height="wrap_content"
        android:layout_centerHorizontal="true"
        android:layout_centerVertical="true"
        android:background="#aaaaaa"
        android:padding="@dimen/padding_medium"
        android:text=""
        android:width="400dp"
        tools:context=".MainActivity" />

    <TextView
        android:id="@+id/second"
        android:layout_width="wrap_content"
        android:layout_height="wrap_content"
        android:layout_below="@+id/first"
        android:layout_centerHorizontal="true"
        android:background="#bbbbbb"
        android:padding="@dimen/padding_medium"
        android:text=""
        android:width="400dp"
        tools:context=".MainActivity" />

    <Button
        android:id="@+id/b1"
        android:layout_width="wrap_content"
```

```
        android:layout_height="wrap_content"
        android:layout_below="@+id/second"
        android:layout_centerHorizontal="true"
        android:padding="@dimen/padding_medium"
        android:text="Set Landscape"
        tools:context=".MainActivity" />

    <Button
        android:id="@+id/b2"
        android:layout_width="wrap_content"
        android:layout_height="wrap_content"
        android:layout_below="@+id/b1"
        android:layout_centerHorizontal="true"
        android:padding="@dimen/padding_medium"
        android:text="Set Portrait"
        tools:context=".MainActivity" />

</RelativeLayout>
```

The rest of the XML file's objects are positioned based on each other, with the second TextView based on the first and so on. All contain the android:centerHorizontal attribute to center them horizontally.

The code for the main activity file follows.

```
package com.sheusi.screentrix;

import android.os.Bundle;
import android.app.Activity;
import android.content.pm.ActivityInfo;
import android.view.Menu;
import android.view.*;
import android.widget.*;
import android.util.DisplayMetrics;

public class MainActivity extends Activity {
    TextView tv1 = null;
    TextView tv2 = null;
    Button b1 = null;
    Button b2 = null;

    @Override
    public void onCreate(Bundle savedInstanceState) {
        super.onCreate(savedInstanceState);
        setContentView(R.layout.activity_main);
        tv1 = (TextView) findViewById(R.id.first);
        tv2 = (TextView) findViewById(R.id.second);
        b1 = (Button) findViewById(R.id.b1);
```

```
        b2 = (Button) findViewById(R.id.b2);
        b1.setText("Set to Landscape");
        b2.setText("Set to Portrait");

        b1.setOnClickListener(new View.OnClickListener() {
            public void onClick(View v) {
                MainActivity.this
.setRequestedOrientation(ActivityInfo.SCREEN_ORIENTATION_LANDSCAPE);

            }
        });
        b2.setOnClickListener(new View.OnClickListener() {
            public void onClick(View v) {
                MainActivity.this
.setRequestedOrientation(ActivityInfo.SCREEN_ORIENTATION_PORTRAIT);

            }
        });
        DisplayMetrics metrics = new DisplayMetrics();
        this.getWindowManager().getDefaultDisplay().getMetrics(metrics);
        tv1.setText("Height in pixels: " + String.valueOf(metrics.heightPixels));
        tv2.setText("Width in pixels: " + String.valueOf(metrics.widthPixels));
    }

    @Override
    public boolean onCreateOptionsMenu(Menu menu) {
        getMenuInflater().inflate(R.menu.activity_main, menu);
        return true;
    }

}
```

The following four lines obtain and display the length and width of the screen in pixels.

```
DisplayMetrics metrics = new DisplayMetrics();
this.getWindowManager().getDefaultDisplay().getMetrics(metrics);
tv1.setText("Height in pixels: " + String.valueOf(metrics.heightPixels));
tv2.setText("Width in pixels: " + String.valueOf(metrics.widthPixels));
```

The following line changes and locks the screen to portrait mode.

```
MainActivity.this.setRequestedOrientation(ActivityInfo
.SCREEN_ORIENTATION_PORTRAIT);
```

One point to note about this line that prompted me to print it here is the use of the class name in front of this. Because the listener for the button is built as an in line class, the word this no longer refers to the main activity class as it does when we obtain the screen metrics in the earlier code. The explicit designation of the activity class name (`MainActivity`) takes care of this. That's also true for the button that locks the screen in horizontal mode. The screen of the emulator running this application should look like Figure 4.1, shown on this page and the next.

As convenient as it is to have an attachable standard PC keyboard or at least a reasonably large "soft" keyboard, it is nice to reduce the number of keystrokes on a form. If we can incorporate pick-lists into our application that allow the user to either drag and drop or choose by touching the desired record and cause the action to fill in some necessary fields on a form, we can make data entry easier for the user. We have already seen how to make a look-up table with a database in the background, and we have seen how to build a simple form that adds, edits, or deletes records from another table. The next example shows how to combine the two operations to make data entry more convenient. For the sake of clarity, this example will not use data tables in the background but will simply mock up an entry screen and a pick-list to demonstrate the desired effect. We will use an abbreviated list of cities, states, and zip codes in a list; we will also use some blanks to fill in with our choice from the list.

The form is similar to the one we used in our database exercise, but the data entered doesn't go anywhere; it's just there for demonstration. Following are the three XML

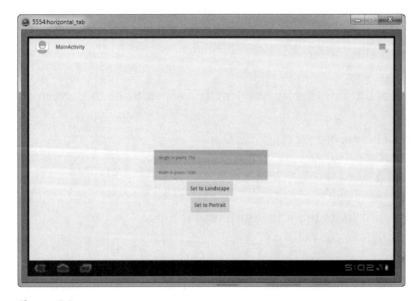

Figure 4.1
a) Emulator running dimension detection application in landscape mode.
Source: The Eclipse Foundation.

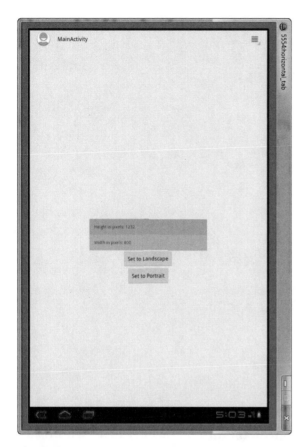

Figure 4.1
b) Emulator running dimension detection application in portrait mode.
Source: The Eclipse Foundation.

files we will use. The header.xml and records.xml files are essentially the same as those used earlier in Chapter 3, "Databases in the Application." They appear again here.

```xml
<?xml version="1.0" encoding="utf-8"?>
<LinearLayout xmlns:android="http://schemas.android.com/apk/res/android"
    android:id="@+id/fieldlayout"
    android:layout_width="match_parent"
    android:layout_height="wrap_content"
    android:background="#000099"
    android:orientation="horizontal"
    android:paddingBottom="6dp"
    android:paddingTop="4dp" >
```

```
<TextView
    android:id="@+id/fieldname1"
    android:layout_width="80dp"
    android:layout_height="wrap_content"
    android:layout_weight="1"
    android:textColor="#ffffff"
    android:textSize="20dp"/>

<TextView
    android:id="@+id/fieldname2"
    android:layout_width="80dp"
    android:layout_height="wrap_content"
    android:layout_weight="1"
    android:textColor="#ffffff"
    android:textSize="20dp"/>

<TextView
    android:id="@+id/fieldname3"
    android:layout_width="80dp"
    android:layout_height="wrap_content"
    android:layout_weight="1"
    android:textColor="#ffffff"
    android:textSize="20dp"/>

</LinearLayout>
```

The XML file for the actual record portion of the display begins here. The background color attribute in the LinearLayout element is different from that of the header. This is a matter of style and is up to the application designer. I think it's nice to show slight contrast between the field names and the actual records.

```
<?xml version="1.0" encoding="utf-8"?>
<LinearLayout xmlns:android="http://schemas.android.com/apk/res/android"
    android:id="@+id/recordlayout"
    android:layout_width="match_parent"
    android:layout_height="wrap_content"
    android:background="#990000"
    android:orientation="horizontal"
    android:paddingBottom="6dp"
    android:paddingTop="4dp" >

<TextView
    android:id="@+id/field1"
    android:layout_width="80dp"
    android:layout_height="wrap_content"
    android:layout_weight="1"
    android:textColor="#ffffff"
    android:textSize="20dp" />
```

```
<TextView
    android:id="@+id/field2"
    android:layout_width="80dp"
    android:layout_height="wrap_content"
    android:layout_weight="1"
    android:textColor="#ffffff"
    android:textSize="20dp" />

<TextView
    android:id="@+id/field3"
    android:layout_width="80dp"
    android:layout_height="wrap_content"
    android:layout_weight="1"
    android:textColor="#ffffff"
    android:textSize="20dp" />

</LinearLayout>
```

The XML file for the main screen is a little different from the one we used in Chapter 3. There is no Search button, just field names and blanks. There is also an abbreviated pick-list at the top to select a city, state, and zip code combination. Touching any of the rows displayed puts the corresponding values in the main form's blanks. Following is the main XML file.

```
<RelativeLayout xmlns:android="http://schemas.android.com/apk/res/android"
    xmlns:tools="http://schemas.android.com/tools"
    android:layout_width="match_parent"
    android:layout_height="match_parent" >

<ListView
    android:id="@+id/headerlist"
    android:layout_width="match_parent"
    android:layout_height="wrap_content" />

<ListView
    android:id="@+id/recordlist"
    android:layout_width="match_parent"
    android:layout_height="wrap_content"
    android:layout_below="@+id/headerlist" />

<TextView
    android:id="@+id/centertext"
    android:layout_width="wrap_content"
    android:layout_height="wrap_content"
    android:layout_below="@+id/recordlist"
    android:padding="@dimen/padding_medium"
    android:text="Touch a row above to fill in the blanks below."
    tools:context=".MainActivity" />
```

```xml
<TableLayout
    android:layout_width="fill_parent"
    android:layout_height="wrap_content"
    android:layout_below="@+id/centertext" >

    <TableRow
        android:layout_width="wrap_content"
        android:layout_height="wrap_content"
        android:padding="10dp" >

        <TextView
            android:layout_width="wrap_content"
            android:layout_height="wrap_content"
            android:maxWidth="150dp"
            android:minWidth="150dp"
            android:text="First Name:" />

        <EditText
            android:id="@+id/et_fname"
            android:layout_width="wrap_content"
            android:layout_height="wrap_content"
            android:minWidth="300dp"
            android:text=""
            android:textSize="20dp" />

    </TableRow>

    <TableRow
        android:layout_width="wrap_content"
        android:layout_height="wrap_content"
        android:padding="10dp" >

        <TextView
            android:layout_width="wrap_content"
            android:layout_height="wrap_content"
            android:maxWidth="150dp"
            android:minWidth="150dp"
            android:text="Last Name:" />

        <EditText
            android:id="@+id/et_lname"
            android:layout_width="wrap_content"
            android:layout_height="wrap_content"
            android:minWidth="300dp"
            android:text=""
            android:textSize="20dp" />

    </TableRow>
```

```
<TableRow
    android:layout_width="wrap_content"
    android:layout_height="wrap_content"
    android:padding="10dp" >

    <TextView
        android:layout_width="wrap_content"
        android:layout_height="wrap_content"
        android:maxWidth="150dp"
        android:minWidth="150dp"
        android:text="Address:" />

    <EditText
        android:id="@+id/et_address"
        android:layout_width="wrap_content"
        android:layout_height="wrap_content"
        android:minWidth="300dp"
        android:text=""
        android:textSize="20dp" />
</TableRow>

<TableRow
    android:layout_width="wrap_content"
    android:layout_height="wrap_content"
    android:padding="10dp" >

    <TextView
        android:layout_width="wrap_content"
        android:layout_height="wrap_content"
        android:maxWidth="150dp"
        android:minWidth="150dp"
        android:text="City:" />

    <EditText
        android:id="@+id/et_city"
        android:layout_width="wrap_content"
        android:layout_height="wrap_content"
        android:minWidth="300dp"
        android:text=""
        android:textSize="20dp" />
</TableRow>

<TableRow
    android:layout_width="wrap_content"
    android:layout_height="wrap_content"
    android:padding="10dp" >
```

```xml
        <TextView
            android:layout_width="wrap_content"
            android:layout_height="wrap_content"
            android:maxWidth="150dp"
            android:minWidth="150dp"
            android:text="State:" />

        <EditText
            android:id="@+id/et_state"
            android:layout_width="wrap_content"
            android:layout_height="wrap_content"
            android:minWidth="300dp"
            android:text=""
            android:textSize="20dp" />
    </TableRow>

    <TableRow
        android:layout_width="wrap_content"
        android:layout_height="wrap_content"
        android:padding="10dp" >

        <TextView
            android:layout_width="wrap_content"
            android:layout_height="wrap_content"
            android:maxWidth="150dp"
            android:minWidth="150dp"
            android:text="Zip:" />

        <EditText
            android:id="@+id/et_zip"
            android:layout_width="wrap_content"
            android:layout_height="wrap_content"
            android:minWidth="300dp"
            android:text=""
            android:textSize="20dp" />
    </TableRow>

    <TableRow
        android:layout_width="wrap_content"
        android:layout_height="wrap_content"
        android:padding="10dp" >

        <TextView
            android:layout_width="wrap_content"
            android:layout_height="wrap_content"
            android:maxWidth="150dp"
            android:minWidth="150dp"
            android:text="Phone:" />
```

```
        <EditText
            android:id="@+id/et_phone"
            android:layout_width="wrap_content"
            android:layout_height="wrap_content"
            android:minWidth="300dp"
            android:text=""
            android:textSize="20dp" />
    </TableRow>
</TableLayout>
</RelativeLayout>
```

The source code for the activity is simple considering the job it does. Remember that we are just using a handful of cities and zips that are hard-coded into the arrays; the same goes for the header row. Because we are not using a data table, there are no field names to read; therefore, we will just hard-code some field names. The onItemClickListener( ) assigned to the records ArrayList object does the bulk of the work. You will notice that the listener assigned is actually an inner class subclassed from the OnItemClickListener interface in the android.widget.AdapterView package.

Another thing you might notice is that I added a line of code to freeze the screen in portrait mode. This allows ample room for the whole form and the pick-list above it. It reduces the size of the keyboard, but because the amount of necessary typing is reduced, this is a fair trade-off. If your application will have a fixed number of values in a pick-list and they are likely to remain constant, there are other ways to handle them besides a data table. You could hard-code them as we do in this exercise, or you could bundle them as a text file or in XML or JSON format as we will see in Chapter 7, "Using External Data."

Here is the Java code for the main activity.

```
package com.sheusi.integrateddemo;

import java.util.ArrayList;
import java.util.HashMap;
import android.os.Bundle;
import android.app.Activity;
import android.content.Context;
import android.content.pm.ActivityInfo;
import android.view.Menu;
import android.view.View;
import android.widget.EditText;
import android.widget.AdapterView;
import android.widget.ListView;
import android.widget.SimpleAdapter;
```

```java
public class MainActivity extends Activity {
    Activity myActivity = null;
    Context myContext = null;
    ListView header = null;
    String[] fieldnames = null;
    SimpleAdapter headeradapter = null;
    HashMap<String, String> headermap = null;
    ArrayList<HashMap<String, String>> headerlist = null;
    ListView records = null;
    SimpleAdapter recordadapter = null;
    HashMap<String, String> recordmap = null;
    ArrayList<HashMap<String, String>> recordlist = null;
    EditText fname = null;
    EditText lname = null;
    EditText addr = null;
    EditText city = null;
    EditText state = null;
    EditText zip = null;

    @Override
    public void onCreate(Bundle savedInstanceState) {
        super.onCreate(savedInstanceState);
        setContentView(R.layout.activity_main);
        this.setRequestedOrientation(ActivityInfo.SCREEN_ORIENTATION_PORTRAIT);
        header = (ListView) findViewById(R.id.headerlist);
        records = (ListView) findViewById(R.id.recordlist);
        myContext = this.getApplicationContext();
        myActivity = this;
        fname = (EditText) findViewById(R.id.et_fname);
        lname = (EditText) findViewById(R.id.et_lname);
        addr = (EditText) findViewById(R.id.et_address);
        city = (EditText) findViewById(R.id.et_city);
        state = (EditText) findViewById(R.id.et_state);
        zip = (EditText) findViewById(R.id.et_zip);
        headermap = new HashMap<String, String>();
        headermap.put("fn1", "City");
        headermap.put("fn2", "State");
        headermap.put("fn3", "Zip Code");
        headerlist = new ArrayList<HashMap<String, String>>();
        headerlist.add(headermap);
        headeradapter = new SimpleAdapter(this, headerlist, R.layout.header,
                new String[] { "fn1", "fn2", "fn3" }, new int[] {
                        R.id.fieldname1, R.id.fieldname2, R.id.fieldname3 });
```

```
        header.setAdapter(headeradapter);
        recordlist = new ArrayList<HashMap<String, String>>();

        recordmap = new HashMap<String, String>();
        recordmap.put("r1", "Bristol");
        recordmap.put("r2", "RI");
        recordmap.put("r3", "02809");
        recordlist.add(recordmap);
        recordmap = new HashMap<String, String>();
        recordmap.put("r1", "New Brunswick");
        recordmap.put("r2", "NJ");
        recordmap.put("r3", "08989");
        recordlist.add(recordmap);
        recordmap = new HashMap<String, String>();
        recordmap.put("r1", "Andover");
        recordmap.put("r2", "MA");
        recordmap.put("r3", "05544");
        recordlist.add(recordmap);
        recordmap = new HashMap<String, String>();
        recordmap.put("r1", "Georgetown");
        recordmap.put("r2", "MD");
        recordmap.put("r3", "21930");
        recordlist.add(recordmap);

        recordadapter = new SimpleAdapter(this, recordlist, R.layout.records,
                new String[] { "r1", "r2", "r3" }, new int[] { R.id.field1,
                        R.id.field2, R.id.field3 });
        records.setAdapter(recordadapter);

        records.setOnItemClickListener(new MyOnItemClickListener());
    }
    class MyOnItemClickListener implements AdapterView.OnItemClickListener {
        public void onItemClick(AdapterView<?> parent, View view, int pos,
                long id) {
            city.setText(recordlist.get(pos).get("r1"));
            state.setText(recordlist.get(pos).get("r2"));
            zip.setText(recordlist.get(pos).get("r3"));

        }

        public void onNothingSelected(AdapterView<?> parent) {
        }

    }

    @Override
    public boolean onCreateOptionsMenu(Menu menu) {
        getMenuInflater().inflate(R.menu.activity_main, menu);
```

```
        return true;
    }

}
```

The running application should look like Figure 4.2.

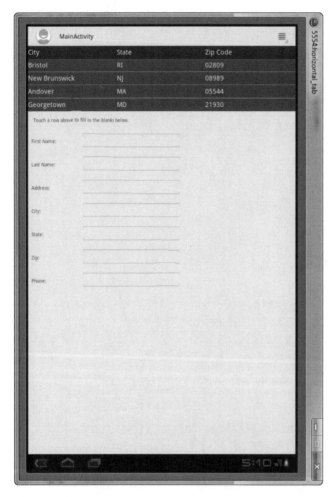

Figure 4.2
Emulator running pick-list and form combination application.
Source: The Eclipse Foundation.

SUBCLASSING CONTROLS

The time will come when you will need to make certain controls such as buttons or text fields behave in a fashion that is different from their default behaviors. For example, a text field may need to detect a particular keystroke, a button will need to perform a specific task, and so on. Anyone with any object-oriented programming

(OOP) experience knows that you can just attach a listener of one type or another to accomplish the specific task or modify the XML or source code for a cosmetic change on a control or widget. However, if you want to use a control with a custom feature or features over and over again, maybe across different applications, it can be tedious to rewrite the special code each time. In these cases, it is convenient to create subclasses of the common widgets to suit your needs. You can write such subclasses as inner classes (which sort of defeats the purpose of modularity), or you can write them as separate Java class files in a given project and then include it if necessary in other projects.

There are two ways to include a widget or a widget's subclass in an application. You can do it in the Java code by creating an object of the appropriate `ViewGroup` class (`LinearLayout`, for example) and linking it to the `ViewGroup` you used in your XML file, and then use the object's `add( )` method to add your control; or you can simply add the control or its subclass to the XML file at design time. (Notice that I tend to use the terms *control* and *widget* interchangeably.) The latter technique is what we will use here.

The first example of subclassed widgets is a simple one, involving the appearance of two text fields. It probably has no practical value other than to illustrate the point. This time we will look at the Java file first.

```
package com.sheusi.Screens;

import android.app.Activity;
import android.os.Bundle;
import android.widget.*;
import android.content.Context;
import android.util.AttributeSet;
import android.graphics.Color;

public class Screens extends Activity {
    /** Called when the activity is first created. */

    @Override
    public void onCreate(Bundle savedInstanceState) {
        super.onCreate(savedInstanceState);
        setContentView(R.layout.main);
    }

    public static class BigText extends TextView {
        public BigText(Context c) {
            super(c);
            this.setBackgroundColor(Color.WHITE);
            this.setTextSize((float) 30.0);
            this.setText("This is my big text");
        }
    }
```

```java
    public BigText(Context c, AttributeSet attrs) {
        super(c, attrs);
        this.setBackgroundColor(Color.WHITE);
        this.setTextSize((float) 30.0);
        this.setText("This is my big text");
    }

    public BigText(Context c, AttributeSet attrs, int baseStyle) {
        super(c, attrs, baseStyle);
        this.setBackgroundColor(Color.WHITE);
        this.setTextSize((float) 30.0);
        this.setText("This is my big text");
    }
  }
}
```

An Android application source code cannot get much simpler than this. No doubt you can spot the cosmetic treatments on the TextView that the subclass provides. What is important to note here is that there are three constructors. If you look at the Android documentation on the Internet at http://developer.android.com/ reference/android/widget/TextView.html, you will see that the TextView class does indeed have three constructors. All three are not required in every situation, but including them makes a subclass more versatile. The important thing is the "super( )" calls to the parent class constructor; if these are missing, you get a run-time error indicating that the subclass object could not be inflated. This can be frustrating to a new applications programmer because this run-time error is not particularly intuitive. (It pays to be familiar with Eclipse's LogCat and Debug perspectives as well.)

Here is an example of another subclass of the TextView widget, this time as its own class file.

```java
package com.sheusi.Screens;

import android.content.Context;
import android.graphics.Color;
import android.util.AttributeSet;
import android.widget.TextView;

public class RedText extends TextView {
    public RedText(Context c) {
        super(c);
        this.setBackgroundColor(Color.RED);
        this.setTextSize((float) 30.0);
        this.setText("This is my big RED text");
    }
```

```
public RedText(Context c, AttributeSet attrs) {
    super(c, attrs);
    this.setBackgroundColor(Color.RED);
    this.setTextSize((float) 30.0);
    this.setText("This is my big RED text");
}
public RedText(Context c, AttributeSet attrs, int baseStyle) {
    super(c, attrs, baseStyle);
    this.setBackgroundColor(Color.RED);
    this.setTextSize((float) 30.0);
    this.setText("This is my big RED text");
}
}
```

The two subclasses are essentially the same, except the latter has a red background added, and the text is slightly different. The important difference in the two is how they are represented in the main XML file, listed here.

```
<?xml version="1.0" encoding="utf-8"?>
<LinearLayout xmlns:android="http://schemas.android.com/apk/res/android"
    android:orientation="vertical"
    android:layout_width="fill_parent"
    android:layout_height="fill_parent"
    >
<view
    class="com.sheusi.Screens.Screens$BigText"
    android:layout_width="wrap_content"
    android:layout_height="wrap_content"
    />
<view
    class="com.sheusi.Screens.RedText"
    android:layout_width="wrap_content"
    android:layout_height="wrap_content"
    android:id="@+id/red"
    />
</LinearLayout>
```

Notice that both use the generic view element descriptor. Next, notice the class attribute. The first has a value of com.sheusi.Screens.Screens$BigText, which indicates that BigText is an inner class component of the outer class, Screens. It is common Java syntax. Just be careful to get it correct. In this case, the package name is com.sheusi.Screens. The second, being a class in its own right, is simply designated as com.sheusi.Screens.RedText.

Neither of these EditText subclasses has an object variable reference in the main Java file, so both will just appear on the screen. The running application should look like Figure 4.3.

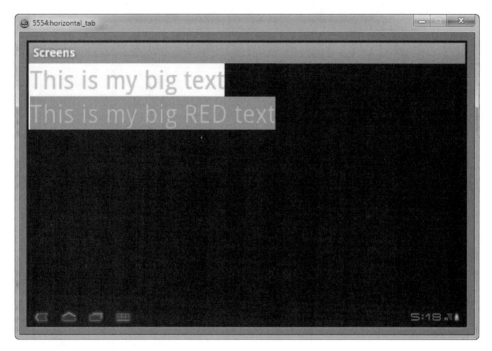

Figure 4.3
Application in emulator displaying two subclasses of the TextView class.
Source: The Eclipse Foundation.

The next example is probably a little more useful. This time we will subclass an EditText widget and add code to validate the data entry. For the sake of demonstration, let's assume that we have a numeric field for which monetary values must be entered in increments of .25. The easiest thing we can do is specify the keypad used for this field; we will use a numeric keypad to discourage entry of alpha characters. Next, we can look for a decimal point. If none is found, we can assume that a whole number was entered, such as 15. In that case, we will add .00 and make it 15.00. Then we will multiply by 100 to convert to whole cents. Finally, we can use the modulus operator and check for a zero remainder. If we get zero, the value entered is valid. If we don't get zero, we will pop up a notice that the number entered was an invalid entry and return the cursor to that field. It's not perfect, but it's good enough for demonstration purposes.

We will detect when the user leaves the field using an OnFocusChangeListener. To make this customized EditText field reusable over several applications, we will write it into its own class and bundle the listener with it. Following is our extended EditText class code.

```java
package com.sheusi.subclasses;

import android.content.Context;
import android.util.AttributeSet;
import android.view.View;
import android.widget.EditText;
import android.widget.Toast;
import android.content.res.Configuration;
class SpecialEditText extends EditText implements View.OnFocusChangeListener {
    Context myContext;

    public SpecialEditText(Context c) {
        super(c);
        myContext = c;
        this.setInputType(Configuration.KEYBOARD_12KEY);
        this.setOnFocusChangeListener(this);
    }

    public SpecialEditText(Context c, AttributeSet attrs) {
        super(c, attrs);
        myContext = c;
        this.setInputType(Configuration.KEYBOARD_12KEY);
        this.setOnFocusChangeListener(this);
    }

    public SpecialEditText(Context c, AttributeSet attrs, int baseStyle) {
        super(c, attrs, baseStyle);
        myContext = c;
        this.setInputType(Configuration.KEYBOARD_12KEY);
        this.setOnFocusChangeListener(this);
    }

    public void onFocusChange(View v, boolean hasfocus) {

        if (hasfocus) {
            // do nothing; focus just came in
        } else {

            // do validation check, because user just left the field
            String value = this.getText().toString();
            if (!value.contains(".")) {
                value = value + ".00";
                this.setText(value);
```

```
        }
        int numvalue = Integer.parseInt(value) * 100;
        if (numvalue % 25 != 0) {
            Toast.makeText(myContext, "Invalid entry", Toast.LENGTH_SHORT)
                    .show();

            this.requestFocus(); // should work, but doesn't. Unresolved
                                 // Android bug.
            // use line below to return to field with invalid entry.
            v.post(new Runnable() {
                public void run() {
                    requestFocus();
                }
            });
        }
    }
}
```

Again, I defined all three constructors. Even though the class implements the listener, we must still assign the onboard listener to the class. This is done in each constructor. The validation code should be easy to follow. The code that returns the cursor to the field in case of an invalid entry is far from intuitive and is annotated in the listing. Currently, the requestFocus( ) method does not work correctly; it actually creates another cursor in the requesting field, placing two on the screen at once, but the cursor in the requesting field is not active. A little research on the Internet turned up the solution used in the code.

Here is the XML file for the main screen, which calls for the customized class.

```
<RelativeLayout xmlns:android="http://schemas.android.com/apk/res/android"
    xmlns:tools="http://schemas.android.com/tools"
    android:layout_width="match_parent"
    android:layout_height="match_parent" >

    <TextView
        android:id="@+id/textView1"
        android:layout_width="wrap_content"
        android:layout_height="wrap_content"
        android:layout_centerHorizontal="true"
        android:layout_centerVertical="true"
        android:padding="@dimen/padding_medium"
        android:text="@string/hello_world"
        tools:context=".MainActivity" />

    <view
```

```
        android:id="@+id/et1"
        android:layout_width="wrap_content"
        android:layout_height="wrap_content"
        android:layout_below="@+id/textView1"
        android:layout_centerHorizontal="true"
        android:layout_marginTop="44dp"
        class="com.sheusi.subclasses.SpecialEditText"
        android:ems="10" />
    <EditText
        android:id="@+id/et2"
        android:layout_width="wrap_content"
        android:layout_height="wrap_content"
        android:layout_below="@+id/et1"
        android:layout_centerHorizontal="true"
        android:layout_marginTop="44dp"
        android:ems="10" />

    <EditText
        android:id="@+id/et3"
        android:layout_width="wrap_content"
        android:layout_height="wrap_content"
        android:layout_below="@+id/et2"
        android:layout_centerHorizontal="true"
        android:layout_marginTop="44dp"
        android:ems="10" />
```

</RelativeLayout>

The additional EditText entries just give the cursor somewhere to go as we test the application. Notice again that we use the generic view (lowercase *v*) for our element tag and a reference to the package and class in the class attribute.

Finally, here is the main activity's Java file. Because all the real work is done in the SpecialEditText class file, the activity is fairly simple.

```
package com.sheusi.subclasses;

import android.os.Bundle;
import android.app.Activity;
import android.view.Menu;
import android.content.Context;

public class MainActivity extends Activity {
    SpecialEditText et1 = null;
    Context myContext = null;

    @Override
    public void onCreate(Bundle savedInstanceState) {
        super.onCreate(savedInstanceState);
```

```
        setContentView(R.layout.activity_main);
        myContext = this.getApplicationContext();
        et1 = (SpecialEditText) findViewById(R.id.et1);
    }

    @Override
    public boolean onCreateOptionsMenu(Menu menu) {
        getMenuInflater().inflate(R.menu.activity_main, menu);
        return true;
    }

}
```

The running application is illustrated in Figure 4.4.

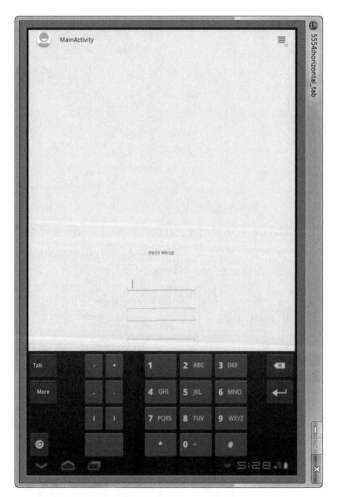

Figure 4.4
Application in emulator displaying a customized EditText class.
Source: The Eclipse Foundation.

EXTENDING THE TEXTVIEW WITH GRAPHICS

As uses expand for handheld devices in business, many applications are designed to accept and save signatures, by use of either a stylus or just a fingertip. You may have noticed that more and more small retail stores are using handheld devices such as mobile phones as roving cash registers. With a credit card swipe device attached to the handheld device, a salesperson on the floor can accept a credit card purchase on the spot without having to return to a sales counter. This is more convenient for the salesperson and the customer. Of course, such purchases (at least over $25) require a signature. An application to accept pledges or memberships or to prepare ID cards that is to be used in the field may also be a suitable use for an application that contains a signature component, not to mention proof of a delivery to be used by a delivery service.

You can create a signature field and many more graphic enhancements to an application by extending the TextView class, just as we extended in the earlier examples. Part of the application involves detecting a touch and placing a dot at a series of x,y coordinates as the user moves a stylus or finger on the screen; the rest involves converting the contents of the TextView to a bitmap file. Once a self-contained subclass of the TextView class is created, you can reuse it in any number of business applications.

Following is the source code of a class that can be used to collect signatures. In reality, it could be used as a doodle pad as well, if that was your intent, but because we are targeting business applications, we will stick with the signature intent. The logic behind the class is to collect a series of x,y coordinates that reflect the touch locations. As the user moves her finger or stylus on the screen, the change in location causes the application to save the new location in the series. The act of lifting the finger or stylus prompts the end of one series of dots, and the retouch starts another; this preserves the breaks in the motion, such as when the user moves from first name to last name or from letter to letter. The touch positions are saved as an ArrayList of the contained class called spot; each instance of this contains the x and y coordinates as well as an index value that indicates which letter or continuous series of touches the spot belongs to. The dots are connected by lines drawn and redrawn by the TextView's onDraw(Canvas) method.

```
package com.sheusi.Screens;

import java.util.ArrayList;
import android.graphics.Paint;
import android.content.Context;
import android.util.AttributeSet;
import android.widget.TextView;
import android.view.View.*;
```

```
import android.view.*;
import android.graphics.*;

class SignatureView extends TextView implements OnTouchListener {

    float oldx;
    float oldy;
    int myletter;
    int oldletter;
    ArrayList<spot> sig = new ArrayList<spot>();
    Paint paint = new Paint();

    public SignatureView(Context context) {
        super(context);
        this.setBackgroundColor(Color.WHITE);
        this.setHeight(120);
        this.setWidth(300);
        setFocusable(true);
        setFocusableInTouchMode(true);
        this.setOnTouchListener(this);
        paint.setColor(Color.BLACK);
        paint.setStyle(Paint.Style.STROKE);
        myletter = 1;// start with first letter
        sig.add(new spot(-1, -1, myletter));// starter seed, to prevent connect
                                            // at both ends

    }

    public SignatureView(Context context, AttributeSet attrs) {
        super(context, attrs);
        this.setBackgroundColor(Color.WHITE);
        this.setHeight(120);
        this.setWidth(300);
        setFocusable(true);
        setFocusableInTouchMode(true);
        this.setOnTouchListener(this);
        paint.setColor(Color.BLACK);
        paint.setStyle(Paint.Style.STROKE);
        myletter = 1;// start with first letter
        sig.add(new spot(-1, -1, myletter));// starter seed, to prevent connect
                                            // at both ends

    }

    public SignatureView(Context context, AttributeSet attrs, int baseStyle) {
        super(context, attrs, baseStyle);
        this.setBackgroundColor(Color.WHITE);
        this.setHeight(120);
```

```java
        this.setWidth(300);
        setFocusable(true);
        setFocusableInTouchMode(true);
        this.setOnTouchListener(this);
        paint.setColor(Color.BLACK);
        paint.setStyle(Paint.Style.STROKE);
        myletter = 1;// start with first letter
        sig.add(new spot(-1, -1, myletter));// starter seed, to prevent connect
                                            // at both ends
    }

    public ArrayList getSig() {
        return sig;
    }

    public void onDraw(Canvas c) {
        for (int ct = 1; ct <= myletter; ++ct) {
            for (spot s : sig) {
                if (oldx == 0) {
                    oldx = s.x;
                    oldy = s.y;
                }
                if (oldx >= 0 & oldy >= 0 & s.x >= 0 & s.y >= 0
                        & s.letter == ct & oldletter == ct) {
                    c.drawLine(oldx, oldy, s.x, s.y, paint);
                }
                oldx = s.x;
                oldy = s.y;
                oldletter = s.letter;
            }
        }
    }

    public boolean onTouch(View v, MotionEvent me) {
        if (me.getAction() == MotionEvent.ACTION_DOWN) {
        } else if (me.getAction() == MotionEvent.ACTION_MOVE) {
            sig.add(new spot((int) me.getX(), (int) me.getY(), myletter));
        } else if (me.getAction() == MotionEvent.ACTION_UP) {
            myletter++;
        }
        oldx = 0;
        oldy = 0;
        invalidate();
        return true;
    }
```

```
    public Bitmap export() {
        int width = this.getWidth();
        int height = this.getHeight();
        Bitmap viewBitmap = Bitmap.createBitmap(width, height,
                Bitmap.Config.ARGB_8888);
        Canvas canvas = new Canvas(viewBitmap);
        this.setCursorVisible(false);
        layout(0, 0, width, height);
        draw(canvas);
        this.setCursorVisible(true);
        return viewBitmap;
    }
}

class spot {
    int x;
    int y;
    int letter;

    public spot(int x, int y, int l) {
        this.x = x;
        this.y = y;
        this.letter = l;
    }
}
```

Certain "fabricated" dots are given −1, −1 coordinates to prevent some unwanted lines from being drawn. You might also notice that the class contains a method that can be used to export the drawing or signature as a bitmap image. The dimensions of the TextView itself are hard coded, so the size would be consistent whether the screen is in portrait or landscape mode. You could then save the image with the following code, which might be included in the main activity or some activity of the application. Again, all three constructors for the subclass are included.

```
public void saveImageToJPG(Bitmap sigimage) {
        try {
            String chosenfilename = "???.jpg";
            OutputStream fOut = this.getApplicationContext().openFileOutput(
                    chosenfilename, MODE_WORLD_READABLE);
            sigimage.compress(Bitmap.CompressFormat.JPEG, 50, fOut);
            fOut.flush();
            fOut.close();
        } catch (Exception e) {
            // catch all exceptions
        }
    }
```

In the preceding code, the compress( ) method belongs to the Bitmap class and specifies the encoding algorithm, usually either JPEG or PNG, the quality reflected as a value from zero to one hundred (zero being the smallest size but poorest quality), and the filename to write to. Note that the variable name, sigimage in the preceding example, would have to be declared in the main activity and assigned to an instance of the SignatureView class that was identified by an ID assigned in the main.xml file, using a line of code like the following.

```
sigimage=(SignatureView)findViewById(R.id.sigimage);
```

The following code could be added to the activity to ensure that the signature field comes up empty each time the application is restarted.

```
public void onStop( ){
super.onStop( );
this.finish( );
}
```

The XML entry for the SignatureView extension of the TextView class is done the same as earlier examples. The SignatureView class has been included in the application we looked at earlier, which displayed two customized TextViews. The revised main XML file is as follows.

```
<?xml version="1.0" encoding="utf-8"?>
<LinearLayout xmlns:android="http://schemas.android.com/apk/res/android"
    android:layout_width="fill_parent"
    android:layout_height="fill_parent"
    android:orientation="vertical" >

    <view
        android:layout_width="wrap_content"
        android:layout_height="wrap_content"
        class="com.sheusi.Screens.SignatureView" />

    <view
        android:layout_width="wrap_content"
        android:layout_height="wrap_content"
        class="com.sheusi.Screens.Screens$BigText" />

    <view
        android:id="@+id/red"
        android:layout_width="wrap_content"
        android:layout_height="wrap_content"
        class="com.sheusi.Screens.RedText" />

</LinearLayout>
```

Unless you want to add the code that saves the signature to a file and add a button to activate it, you can leave the `Screens.java` code alone. Just add the `SignatureView` class file to the package and use the preceding XML file listing. Your running application should look like Figure 4.5.

The last graphic application we will look at in this chapter is one that collects user input for a Pareto Chart and then displays the chart as a subclass of the `TextView` widget. If you are not familiar with the Pareto Chart, there is plenty of information on the Internet about what it is and how to construct one using Microsoft Excel. In a nutshell, a Pareto Chart is a graphic display of the causes of a given problem whose frequencies are represented by a vertical bar chart, with their cumulative percentages superimposed as a line chart. It's like the 80-20 rule it is based on, which says that if you concentrate on the handful of causes that compose 80 percent of the total, you can make the greatest impact on quality for the least investment of time and resources. The application collects a table of cause-and-frequency combinations in an `EditText` field, reorders them by frequency, computes individual and accumulating frequencies, and then constructs and displays the chart. This time the `TextView` object doesn't need a listener, but it requires a lot of manual coding to construct the graph.

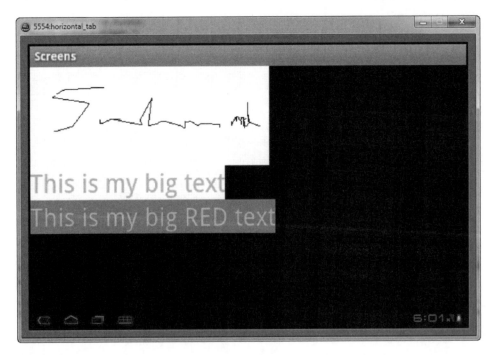

Figure 4.5
Application in emulator displaying SignatureView class.
Source: The Eclipse Foundation.

I have simplified the drawing calculations by predefining the size of the chart with dimensions that can be broken into nice round numbers. For example, with a width of 500 pixels, using a horizontal factor of 50 pixels divides the x axis into 10 equal parts. Using the first and tenth as borders, this leaves the second through the eighth parts to display up to eight bars for up to eight factors. The instructions given to the user onscreen limit input to eight factors. I also required frequencies, calculations, and plotting to be entered as integers.

Contrary to the way we handled subclasses earlier in the chapter, I chose to add the `graph` subclass to the `LinearLayout` on the right side of the screen dynamically in the Java code. (As you will see, there are two `LinearLayouts` embedded in the `Linear-Layout` that manages the whole screen: one on the left, and another on the right.) This gives me control over when the `graph` subclass appears and allows me to regenerate it more easily.

Once you study the code, you can make modifications as you wish, but for demonstration it is best to make the code as simple as possible. Use hard-coded numbers instead of calculated numbers where possible.

The application uses an internal class for the chart, which is the opposite of the method used for the `SignatureView` class in the previous example. It is also frozen to landscape view to control the user interface. Each factor used for the chart is stored as an instance of a class created specifically for that purpose, also written as an internal class. There is a minimal amount of error-checking for the data entry, but an example is provided for the user onscreen.

The most complicated work, in my opinion, is the calculating that goes into the graph itself. The hardest thing to get used to is that the 0,0 position on the graph is in the upper-left corner of the field, not the lower-left corner that intuition would dictate. This causes the vertical position of any given point (v) to be calculated as (height-in-pixels)–(v) instead of simply (v). It takes practice to get used to this.

First, let's get the main XML file out of the way.

```
<LinearLayout xmlns:android="http://schemas.android.com/apk/res/android"
    xmlns:tools="http://schemas.android.com/tools"
    android:id="@+layout/base"
    android:layout_width="match_parent"
    android:layout_height="match_parent"
    android:orientation="horizontal" >

    <LinearLayout
        android:id="@+layout/leftside"
        android:layout_width="wrap_content"
        android:layout_height="match_parent"
```

```
        android:layout_weight=".5"
        android:orientation="vertical" >

    <TextView
        android:id="@+id/tv1"
        android:layout_width="wrap_content"
        android:layout_height="wrap_content"
        android:text="Enter up to 8 factors and frequencies, separated by hyphens.
\nex.
Unresponsive-45 \n followed by carriage returns."
        android:textSize="24dp" />

    <TextView
        android:id="@+id/tv1"
        android:layout_width="wrap_content"
        android:layout_height="wrap_content"
        android:text="\nEnter frequencies as integers. All calculations will be
done in integers."
        android:textSize="24dp" />

    <TextView
        android:id="@+id/tv1"
        android:layout_width="wrap_content"
        android:layout_height="wrap_content"
        android:text="For more than 8, combine remaining factors with the eighth."
        android:textSize="24dp" />

    <EditText
        android:id="@+id/et1"
        android:layout_width="500dp"
        android:layout_height="wrap_content"
        android:background="#bbbbbb"
        android:maxLines="9"
        android:textSize="26dp" />

    <TableLayout
        android:layout_width="500dp"
        android:layout_height="wrap_content" >

        <TableRow>

            <Button
                android:id="@+id/b1"
                android:layout_width="500dp"
                android:layout_height="wrap_content"
                android:layout_weight=".5"
                android:text="Click to produce chart." />
```

```
            <Button
                android:id="@+id/b2"
                android:layout_width="500dp"
                android:layout_height="wrap_content"
                android:layout_weight=".5"
                android:text="Click to clear data." />
        </TableRow>
    </TableLayout>
</LinearLayout>

<LinearLayout
    android:id="@+layout/rightside"
    android:layout_width="wrap_content"
    android:layout_height="match_parent"
    android:layout_weight=".5"
    android:orientation="vertical" >

</LinearLayout>

</LinearLayout>
```

Because the Pareto Chart is added dynamically in the Java code, there is no need to include an element for it in the XML file. However, the right-side LinearLayout element requires an ID attribute, so we can link to it in the main activity's code. Also notice that the outer LinerLayout is set to horizontal orientation, causing the screen to be divided left to right. Following is the Java code for the main activity, which includes all the classes internally needed for the application.

```
package com.sheusi.paretochart;

import android.os.Bundle;
import android.app.Activity;
import android.content.Context;
import android.graphics.Canvas;
import android.graphics.Color;
import android.graphics.Paint;
import android.view.Menu;
import android.widget.*;
import android.view.*;
import android.util.DisplayMetrics;
import java.util.ArrayList;
import java.util.Collections;
import android.content.pm.ActivityInfo;

public class MainActivity extends Activity implements View.OnClickListener {
    LinearLayout ll = null;
    EditText et = null;
```

```
Button b1 = null;
Button b2 = null;
Context myContext = null;
MyPlot mp = null;

@Override
public void onCreate(Bundle savedInstanceState) {
    super.onCreate(savedInstanceState);
    setContentView(R.layout.activity_main);
    this.setRequestedOrientation(ActivityInfo.SCREEN_ORIENTATION_LANDSCAPE);
    myContext = this.getApplicationContext();
    ll = (LinearLayout) findViewById(R.layout.rightside);
    et = (EditText) findViewById(R.id.et1);
    b1 = (Button) findViewById(R.id.b1);
    b2 = (Button) findViewById(R.id.b2);
    b1.setOnClickListener(this);
    b2.setOnClickListener(this);
}

@Override
public void onClick(View v) {
    if (v == b2)
        et.setText("");
    else {
        int freqtotal = 0;
        int m_cumpercentage = 0;
        ArrayList<Factor> pareto = new ArrayList<Factor>();
        String[] lines;
        String[] pieces;
        String s = et.getText().toString();
        if (!s.contains("-")) {
            et.setText("Bad data formatting, use \nFactor-Frequency.\nUse
            button below to clear data.");
             return;
        }
        lines = s.split("\n");
        for (int ct = 0; ct < lines.length; ++ct) {
            if (lines[ct].contains("-")) {
                pieces = lines[ct].split("-");
                pareto.add(new Factor(pieces[0], Integer
                        .parseInt(pieces[1])));
```

```
            }
        }
        Collections.sort(pareto);
        Object[] farray = pareto.toArray();
        for (int x = 0; x < farray.length; ++x)
            freqtotal += ((Factor) farray[x]).getFrequency();
        System.out.println("freqtotal: " + String.valueOf(freqtotal));
        for (int x = 0; x < farray.length; ++x) {
            ((Factor) farray[x]).percentage = (((Factor) farray[x])
                    .getFrequency() * 100 / freqtotal);
            // problem in formula above

            m_cumpercentage += (((Factor) farray[x]).getFrequency() * 100 /
            freqtotal);
            ((Factor) farray[x]).cumpercentage = m_cumpercentage;
        }
        if (mp != null) {
            ll.removeView(mp);
            mp = null;
        }
        mp = new MyPlot(this.getApplicationContext(), farray);
        ll.addView(mp);
    }// ends if
}

@Override
public boolean onCreateOptionsMenu(Menu menu) {
    getMenuInflater().inflate(R.menu.activity_main, menu);
    return true;
}

// bring up a clean screen each time app is restarted
@Override
public void onStop() {
    super.onStop();
    et.setText("");
    if (mp != null) {
        ll.removeView(mp);
        mp = null;
    }

}
}
```

```
class Factor implements Comparable {
    String category;
    public int frequency;
    public int percentage;
    public int cumpercentage;

    public Factor(String n, int a) {
        category = n;
        frequency = a;
    }

    public int getFrequency() {
        return frequency;
    }

    @Override
    public int compareTo(Object o1) {
        if (this.frequency == ((Factor) o1).frequency)
            return 0;
        else if ((this.frequency) > ((Factor) o1).frequency)
            return -1;
        else
            return 1;
    }
}

class MyPlot extends TextView {
    Paint paint = new Paint();
    DisplayMetrics dm = new DisplayMetrics();
    private Object[] plots;
    private int hirawvalue;
    private int vfactor;
    private int count;
    private int column;

    public MyPlot(Context context, Object[] farray) {
        super(context);
        this.setBackgroundColor(Color.YELLOW);
        this.setHeight(500);
        this.setWidth(500);
        plots = farray;

    }

    @Override
    public void onDraw(Canvas c) {

        paint.setStrokeWidth(2);
        // draw right scale
```

```
count = 0;
int jump = 0;
while (count < 100) {
    c.drawText(String.valueOf(count) + "%", 450, 500 - jump * 50, paint);
    count = count + 10;
    ++jump;
}
c.drawText("100%", 450, 9, paint);
// draw left scale
hirawvalue = ((Factor) plots[0]).getFrequency();
vfactor = 500 / hirawvalue;
count = 0;
int interval = 0;
while (count <= hirawvalue) {
    c.drawText("-", 3, 500 - count * vfactor, paint);
    if (interval % 5 == 0)
        c.drawText(String.valueOf(interval), 6, 500 - count * vfactor,
                paint);
    ++interval;
    ++count;
}
// draw raw frequency bars and labels
paint.setStrokeWidth(20);
paint.setColor(Color.BLUE);
column = 1;
for (count = 0; count < plots.length; ++count) {
    c.drawLine(column * 50, 500, column * 50, 500
            - ((Factor) plots[count]).getFrequency() * vfactor, paint);
    c.drawText(((factor) plots[count]).category, column * 50, 500
            - ((Factor) plots[count]).getFrequency() * vfactor, paint);
    ++column;
}
// draw cumulative percentage dots
paint.setColor(Color.RED);
paint.setStrokeWidth(2);
column = 1;
for (count = 0; count < plots.length; ++count) {
    c.drawCircle((column * 50),
            (500 - ((Factor) plots[count]).cumpercentage * 5),
            (float) 2.0, paint);
    ++column;
}
// connect the dots
paint.setStrokeWidth(2);
```

```
        column = 1;
        for (count = 0; count < plots.length - 1; ++count) {
            c.drawLine(column * 50,
                    500 - ((Factor) plots[count]).cumpercentage * 5,
                    (column + 1) * 50,
                    500 - ((Factor) plots[count + 1]).cumpercentage * 5, paint);
            ++column;
        }
    }
}
```

Notice that the `Factor` implements the `Comparable` interface to allow us to customize how the factors will be sorted. Although the scale on the right side of the graph is based on 100, the scale on the left is based on the highest frequency value taken from user data. This value is represented by the variable `hirawvalue` (highest raw value). Figure 4.6 shows how the application should look when data is entered and the chart is generated.

The example might represent the results of a poll of spectators at an outdoor event asking why they thought the event was poorly attended.

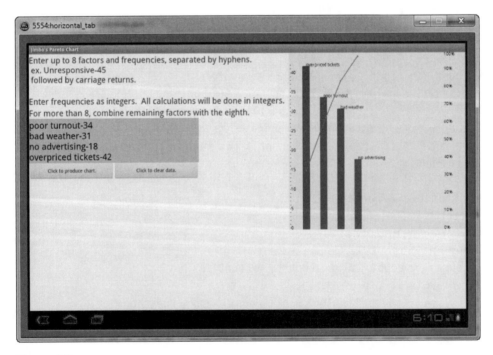

Figure 4.6
Application in emulator displaying Pareto Chart.
Source: The Eclipse Foundation.

SUMMARY OF KEY CONCEPTS

- The large screen size of a tablet device allows the developer to create a rich and dense user interface while allowing room for the onscreen keyboard. Although this book concentrates on choosing and locking either portrait or landscape orientation, the application developer can design a screen that adapts to either orientation at run-time.

- The developer can configure screen controls or widgets on the screen in the XML file at design time or add and remove them from the screen at run-time. Using fragments discussed in Chapter 2, "Migrating to Android 3.0 and Above," the developer can swap large blocks of screen controls in and out of the application.

- The application developer can subclass widgets such as the `EditText` to include error checking and validation and then reuse these in a single application or across many applications. Likewise, a developer can subclass the `TextView` widget to display a graphical representation of data. Using bars, lines, or dots in virtually any number and color can provide a pleasant and informative user experience.

- The `SimpleAdapter`, `ArrayList`, and `HashMap` classes are essential to presenting data in a pleasing fashion to the user. Study these classes and practice them by modifying the examples shown in the chapter.

REVIEW QUESTIONS

You can find the answers to these review questions in the appendix at the end of the book.

1. Layout managers such as the `RelativeLayout` and the `LinearLayout` belong to a group of controls called _____.

2. The proper terms used for the horizontal and vertical orientation of the screen are _____ and _____ modes.

3. The layout that positions widgets based on their relation to other widgets on the screen is the _____.

4. The abbreviations dp and dip are short for _____.

5. One `LinearLayout` can be embedded in another on the screen, true or false? _____.

6. Write a single line of code that would lock the screen in portrait mode.

   _____

7. A method in all subclasses that refers to its parent class and is often used in a constructor is the _____.

8. What is the purpose of the modulus operator?

   _____.

9. Which listener class would a developer use to detect when a user leaves a particular widget on the screen, moving from one EditText to the next in a form, for example? _____.

10. The graph point 0,0 is located in which corner of its container?

    _____.

Suggested Projects

- Research, compare, and contrast the graphic formats JPEG, BMP, and PMG. What are their purposes, advantages, and disadvantages?

- Collect the average monthly temperatures for a given year and graph them, using the Pareto Chart exercise as a guide.

- Write a subclass for the EditText class that accepts a floating-point value and properly rounds it to the appropriate integer value when the user leaves the field. Write another that converts a text entry to all uppercase when the user leaves the field.

- Research the android:inputType="textPassword" attribute for text fields. Then write a simple demonstration for matching an account name from one EditText field to the password entered in another and indicate a match or no match as the user leaves the last field.

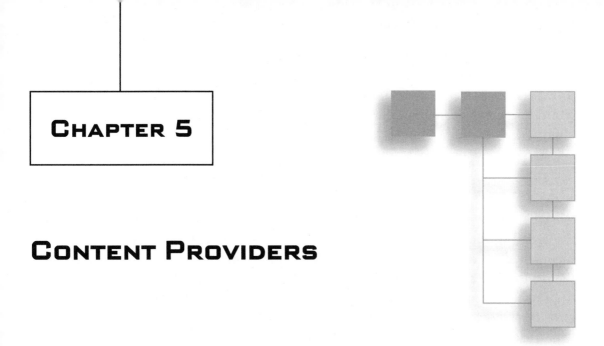

CHAPTER 5

CONTENT PROVIDERS

INTRODUCTION

Many of the operations of an Android handheld or tablet device that are typically used in their own right, such as a calendar, contact list, or photo gallery, are made available to applications through a system of content providers. Separate persons, places, things, and events that have essentially the same pieces of data associated with them lend themselves well to storage in data tables. In fact, this is true about content providers on the device. They are addressed as databases with data tables and respond to queries essentially the same as SQLite tables. Content providers are addressed as uniform resource identifiers (URIs) in the following format.

```
"content:// package.and.class.name / tablename"
```

For example, the first content provider we will look at will be calendars. A calendar's entries are held in a table called events, and when a user posts, reads, or modifies an event, it is addressed as follows.

```
"content://com.android.calendar/events"
```

To some extent, content providers prevent the applications programmer from having to reinvent the wheel each time an application needs to access the device's built-in applications. They also ensure that the user is accessing consistent, predictable sets of data from one specialized application to the next. Often the device will provide a user interface for the data tables that can be reached through a content provider, such as the ones the user of a device would use to enter a contact, enter an appointment, or retrieve an image from a gallery. Because content providers abstract access to the data maintained on the system, application designers are not bound to the device's user interfaces for this information. This is the feature that makes content providers particularly useful and interesting. The Android operating system even lets the applications programmer develop his own content provider and the data tables behind it.

CALENDARS AND EVENT POSTINGS

We will start by looking at the calendar as a content provider. Calendars are typically associated with and synchronized with a mail server associated with an email account maintained on the phone or tablet. Android allows multiple calendars to be used on the device and allows any one, a combination, or all their entries to be displayed at the same time on the built-in calendar application. For example, on my devices I have my Google Gmail account configured as well as my university email account, which uses Microsoft Exchange. Of course, neither email server resides on the device, but the accounts and their associated calendars are synced on the devices. Either of the calendars can be accessed at least two ways. First, the calendars can be accessed through the built-in "intent" available from Android that brings up the built-in user interface. Second, the calendars can be accessed through a posting operation similar to that used to add records to any SQLite database. To get our feet wet, so to speak, with content providers, and specifically the calendar content provider, we will write a little application that inventories the device's currently configured calendars. This is useful because later on we will need specific information from the calendar(s) to post events through an application.

We will start with a project called `CalendarApp`. This, as usual, will create one `TextView` in the main XML file that would normally hold the `"Hello"` greeting. We will add a multiline `EditText` field to the interface to hold information about the configured calendar(s). As is true many times throughout the book, the elegance of the user interface for many of the experiments is sacrificed for simplicity's sake, and this one is no exception. Sometimes in an effort to make an attractive, ready-for-prime-time user interface, the point of the exercise is lost. In this exercise especially, simplicity rules the day.

Note

I should point out that I am using an actual Android tablet to test my applications instead of an emulator, so the calendar data revealed is actually on the device. If you use an emulator, click the calendar app that is on the emulator and configure a calendar as instructed. Some of the classes used in this chapter require API 14, so configure an emulator for Android 4.0 if you are using one.

Here is the simple main XML file we will use to start.

```xml
<RelativeLayout xmlns:android="http://schemas.android.com/apk/res/android"
    xmlns:tools="http://schemas.android.com/tools"
    android:layout_width="match_parent"
    android:layout_height="match_parent" >

<TextView
        android:id="@+id/centertext"
        android:layout_width="wrap_content"
        android:layout_height="wrap_content"
        android:layout_centerHorizontal="true"
        android:layout_centerVertical="true"
        android:padding="@dimen/padding_medium"
        android:text=""
        tools:context=".MainActivity" />
<EditText
        android:id="@+id/et1"
        android:layout_width="wrap_content"
        android:layout_height="wrap_content"
        android:layout_centerHorizontal="true"
        android:layout_below="@+id/centertext"
        android:layout_centerVertical="true"
        android:padding="@dimen/padding_medium"
        tools:context=".MainActivity" />

</RelativeLayout>
```

If you are using an older configuration of Eclipse and the Android software development toolkit (SDK), you will have a LinearLayout by default. That is fine; just add an EditText element as I did earlier. All you need in that case are the android:layout_ width, android:layout_height, and android:id attributes.

The brief code that follows is all it takes to read some essential fields from the calendars table. To get a full list of the fields that the device carries, consult the Android documentation by searching Google for CalendarContract.Calendars.

Note

CalendarContract.Calendars requires API 14, which is for Android 4.0. The emulator must be configured for Android 4.0, or the device you use to test the application must have Android 4.0 or higher installed.

Most of the code has to do with querying the calendars table. The string array called CAL_RECORD is the list of fields we want to retrieve from the table, referred to as the *projection*. If you work with data tables, you know that a projection is just a subset of fields in a given table or join. The `ContentResolver` object resolves the query and returns the values to the `Cursor` object variable. We then cycle or iterate through the `Cursor` object and display the values that were specified in the `CAL_RECORD` array. Simple enough. The only thing here that might be confusing is the value assigned to the `Uri` object variable `Calendars.CONTENT_URI`. Don't let it bother you. You will see why in a minute.

```
package com.sheusi.calendarapp;

import android.os.Bundle;
import android.provider.CalendarContract.Calendars;
import android.app.Activity;
import android.view.Menu;
import android.database.Cursor;
import android.content.ContentResolver;
import android.content.ContentValues;
import android.net.Uri;
import android.widget.*;

public class MainActivity extends Activity {
    public static final String[] CAL_RECORD = new String[] { Calendars._ID,
            Calendars.ACCOUNT_NAME, Calendars.CALENDAR_DISPLAY_NAME,
            Calendars.OWNER_ACCOUNT, Calendars.ACCOUNT_TYPE,
            Calendars.CALENDAR_TIME_ZONE };
    Cursor cur = null;
    ContentResolver cr = null;
    Uri uri = null;
    EditText et1 = null;
    TextView centertext = null;

    @Override
    public void onCreate(Bundle savedInstanceState) {
        super.onCreate(savedInstanceState);
        setContentView(R.layout.activity_main);
        et1 = (EditText) findViewById(R.id.et1);
        centertext = (TextView) findViewById(R.id.centertext);
        cr = getContentResolver();
        uri = Calendars.CONTENT_URI;
        cur = cr.query(uri, CAL_RECORD, null, null, null);
        centertext.setText(String.valueOf(cur.getCount())
                + " calendars on the device.");
        if (cur.getCount() > 0) {
            for (int x = 0; x < cur.getCount(); ++x) {
                cur.moveToPosition(x);
```

```
        et1.append("Acct Name= " + cur.getString(0)
                    + "\nCalendar Display Name= " + cur.getString(1)
                    + "\nOwner Acct= " + cur.getString(2)
                    + "\nAccount Type= " + cur.getString(3)
                    + "\nCalendar Time Zone= " + cur.getString(4) + "\n\n");
            }
        }
    }

    @Override
    public boolean onCreateOptionsMenu(Menu menu) {
        getMenuInflater().inflate(R.menu.activity_main, menu);
        return true;
    }
}
```

After you run this code, make the following change and run it again.

Change

```
centertext.setText(String.valueOf(cur.getCount())+ " calendars on the device.");
```

to

```
centertext.setText(Calendars.CONTENT_URI.toString());
```

In the first TextView field, instead of seeing the count of calendars being maintained, you will see the resolution of the table in the format discussed at the beginning of the section, namely this.

```
"content://com.android.calendar/calendars"
```

Finally, note that the three nulls in the query simply specify that I want all the calendar records in natural order. (Query parameters, their values to match, and the order are null.)

Now that we have essential data on the calendars being maintained and synced by the Android system, let's look at how to post some events. The easiest is just to fire a system intent to bring up the default user interface for calendar entries. We can at least get a head start by posting some field entries, rather than just bringing up a blank entry screen. In this demonstration, we will hard-code some field values, but they could just as easily be taken from entry fields on a custom application's screen or from any other data source.

The way the code is written for this exercise instantly triggers the calendar intent, so the opening screen specified in the main.xml file never appears. Therefore, it is unnecessary to modify the main.xml file we used earlier. Leave it as is. Modify the Java file as indicated next.

```java
package com.sheusi.calendarapp;

import java.util.Calendar;

import android.os.Bundle;
import android.provider.CalendarContract.Calendars;
import android.provider.CalendarContract;
import android.provider.CalendarContract.Events;
import android.app.Activity;
import android.view.Menu;
import android.content.ContentResolver;
import android.content.ContentValues;
import android.net.Uri;
import android.widget.*;
import android.content.Intent;

public class MainActivity extends Activity {
    ContentResolver cr = null;
    ContentValues cv = null;
    Uri uri = null;
    EditText et1 = null;
    TextView centertext = null;

    @Override
    public void onCreate(Bundle savedInstanceState) {
        super.onCreate(savedInstanceState);
        setContentView(R.layout.activity_main);
        et1 = (EditText) findViewById(R.id.et1);
        centertext = (TextView) findViewById(R.id.centertext);
        cr = getContentResolver();
        uri = Calendars.CONTENT_URI;

        // add an event to a calendar
        Calendar begintime = Calendar.getInstance();
        Calendar endtime = Calendar.getInstance();
        begintime.set(2012, 9, 14, 17, 30);
        endtime.set(2012, 9, 14, 18, 00);
        long startMillis = begintime.getTimeInMillis();
        long endMillis = endtime.getTimeInMillis();

        // Intent style event entry

        Intent intent = new Intent(Intent.ACTION_INSERT)
                .setType("vnd.android.cursor.item/event");
        intent.putExtra(CalendarContract.EXTRA_EVENT_BEGIN_TIME, startMillis);
        intent.putExtra(CalendarContract.EXTRA_EVENT_END_TIME, endMillis);
        intent.putExtra(CalendarContract.EXTRA_EVENT_ALL_DAY, false);
        intent.putExtra(Events.CALENDAR_ID, 1);
```

```
        intent.putExtra(Events.TITLE, "SMITH-party of 4");
        intent.putExtra(Events.DESCRIPTION, "booth requested");
        intent.putExtra(Events.ACCESS_LEVEL, Events.ACCESS_PUBLIC);
        startActivity(intent);

        // end intent style

    }

    @Override
    public boolean onCreateOptionsMenu(Menu menu) {
        getMenuInflater().inflate(R.menu.activity_main, menu);
        return true;
    }

}
```

The dates to be used for the event are based on the Java `Calendar` class object, which you may have used in the past. You can probably guess that the parameters sent to the constructor are the year, month, day, hour, and minute, and an entry is made for both the beginning time and the ending time. Make a note that the month is a zero-based value. (In other words, the month of January is represented by zero, and December is represented by 11, and so on.) Also note that the hours are in military time (for example, 13 is 1:00 p.m.).

The calendar dates and times are converted to milliseconds before they are sent to the events table.

Many more fields are available in the events table than we are using here. You can find them by searching Google for `android CalendarContract.Events`. The fields we are using, however, are recognizable as all caps preceded by `Events`. We use the `.putExtra( )` method of the `Intent` class to preload the fields on the default calendar entry user interface with the values we specify. Of particular importance is the `CALENDAR_ID` value, because we want to be sure to post to the correct calendar if there are many on the system. Remember, these calendars are synced, and if we want to post to the right server, we must be careful with this. We obtained the calendar's ID from the previous exercise. On the Toshiba Thrive, the calendar posting screen with the data imported from the program looks like Figure 5.1.

Posting the same data to a calendar event without the use of an intent is similar to adding a record to an SQLite table. However, a few extra steps are necessary. First, if the calendar is synchronized with an outside server (it's possible to create a self-contained calendar rather than using one associated with an email account or other server-based calendar), permission to read and write to the calendar must be expressed in the application's manifest file. The following entries will do that.

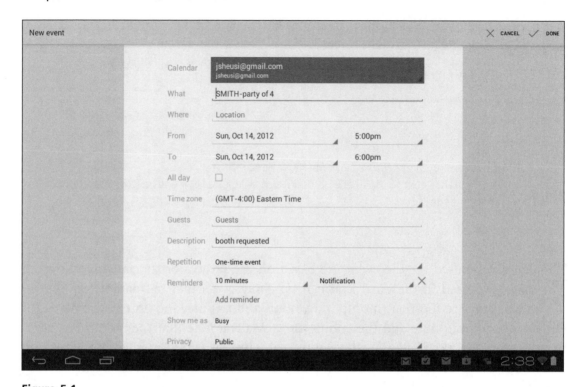

Figure 5.1
Calendar application using an intent with application data and calendar screen running on a Toshiba Thrive tablet.
Source: Google.

```
<uses-permission android:name="android.permission.READ_CALENDAR"/>
<uses-permission android:name="android.permission.WRITE_CALENDAR"/>
```

The permissions can be added just about the closing manifest tag but should be on their own and not enclosed in any other tag pair.

Second, we need not only the database ID as we did for the intent version of the code, but we need the event's time zone, the start time, and unless the item is recurring, the end time. If you go back to the calendar detail-retrieving exercise, you will notice that we retrieved the calendar's time zone. (For my Thrive, it was expressed as America/New_York.) You can retrieve the device's time zone without the use of the content providers by including the java.util.TimeZone class with your include statements and invoking the following in your code.

```
TimeZone.getDefault().toString()
```

Finally, it is recommended that you post calendar events as a separate thread, but for demonstration purposes, you can do it in the main activity. The following code posts a calendar event and returns the event's unique ID, which can be used to edit the event later, just as you might update any table record using its unique ID as a search parameter. The ID appears in the TextView in the center of the screen.

```java
package com.sheusi.calendarapp;

import java.util.Calendar;

import android.os.Bundle;
import android.provider.CalendarContract.Calendars;
import android.provider.CalendarContract;
import android.app.Activity;
import android.view.Menu;
import android.database.Cursor;
import android.content.ContentResolver;
import android.content.ContentValues;
import android.net.Uri;
import android.widget.*;

public class MainActivity extends Activity {
    Cursor cur = null;
    ContentResolver cr = null;
    ContentValues cv = null;
    Uri uri = null;
    EditText et1 = null;
    TextView centertext = null;

    @Override
    public void onCreate(Bundle savedInstanceState) {
        super.onCreate(savedInstanceState);
        setContentView(R.layout.activity_main);
        et1 = (EditText) findViewById(R.id.et1);
        centertext = (TextView) findViewById(R.id.centertext);
        cr = getContentResolver();
        uri = Calendars.CONTENT_URI;

        Calendar begintime = Calendar.getInstance();
        Calendar endtime = Calendar.getInstance();
        begintime.set(2012, 9, 13, 17, 0);
        endtime.set(2012, 9, 13, 17, 30);
        long startMillis = begintime.getTimeInMillis();
        long endMillis = endtime.getTimeInMillis();
        cr = getContentResolver();
        cv = new ContentValues();
        cv.put(CalendarContract.Events.DTSTART, startMillis);
        cv.put(CalendarContract.Events.DTEND, endMillis);
        cv.put(CalendarContract.Events.TITLE, "Jones-party of 6");
```

```
            cv.put(CalendarContract.Events.DESCRIPTION, "Requests window seat.");
            cv.put(CalendarContract.Events.CALENDAR_ID, 1);
            cv.put(CalendarContract.Events.EVENT_TIMEZONE, "America/New_York");
            Uri eventUri = cr.insert(
                    Uri.parse("content://com.android.calendar/events"), cv);
            long eventId = Long.parseLong(eventUri.getLastPathSegment());
            centertext.setText(String.valueOf(eventId) + "   ");

    }

    @Override
    public boolean onCreateOptionsMenu(Menu menu) {
        getMenuInflater().inflate(R.menu.activity_main, menu);
        return true;
    }

}
```

Using the Contacts

One of the most useful features in smart phones that actually began in cell phones before what we consider smart phones even existed was the contact list. Originally, this was a convenience that allowed the user to "speed dial" a given contact, saving many strokes on the phone's keypad. As cell phones evolved into what we consider smart phones, such as the iPhone and the many Android phones, multiple phone numbers, email addresses, photographs, and other details could be added for a given contact. Contacts can even be included in groups.

Tablets, of course, continue to allow the maintenance of a contact list and give the applications programmer access to it through a content provider. Unfortunately, the rich configuration of data that can be stored to a given contact is a double-edged sword for the programmer because the features come with a relatively complex collection of related tables. The tables share some data that maintains their relationship and contain many unique pieces of data that build the complete contact's profile. Contacts can be synchronized with many services. Probably the most common for the Android user is the user's Google mailing list.

At the top level is a Contacts table represented by the class ContactsContract.Contacts. It has two essential fields that have a one-to-one relationship: one set (and record) for each contact in the system. These are the Contact ID and the Display Name. There is also an _ID field and a LOOKUP_KEY field; they have no value to the end user, but they are essential to the maintenance of the contact system by the device.

For any given contact with one specific Display Name, there can be multiple occurrences in a table called RawContacts. For instance, if a user posted a contact name and a Gmail address in her mailing list at www.gmail.com and later added a corresponding entry for that person with a mobile phone number on her Android phone, the synchronization process (if the user chose to synchronize the lists) would aggregate the listings to one entry in the Contacts table and two entries in the RawContacts table. The RawContacts table contains a field called CONTACT_ID, which is a foreign key to the CONTACT_ID field in the Contacts table. Finally, for a given RawContact entry, there can be one or more Data table rows that contain the actual details for the RawContact. Because different types of data have different characteristics—for example, phone numbers should behave differently from a thumbnail photo or an email address—their data types and characteristics are maintained in a separate table called CommonDataKinds. Details from this table are stored in the Data table along with the actual values. More details on the table structures and relationships can be found on one of the Android Developer's website pages at http://developer.android.com/guide/topics/providers/contacts-provider.html.

Needless to say, there is a high level of overhead necessary for the Android system to maintain the onboard contact list, including synchronizing the contacts with those of multiple email accounts that can be accessed through the Android device. Any attempt by an applications programmer to access and take advantage of this system would certainly be daunting. Indeed, even with the examples that will be provided in this book and the examples and tutorials that appear elsewhere, and using the tools the API provides, the applications programmer would have to spend a lot of time and effort to build a complete contact management application. My recommendation is for the applications programmer to interact with the contact management system only to the extent that it enhances a given application, and that the bulk of contact management on a given device be done with the user interface that the Android device provides. For example, the People app that came with the Toshiba Thrive manages contacts. Remember that you can work the device's own contact management system into your application through an intent, just as we did with the calendar posting at the beginning of this chapter.

With that in mind, the following paragraphs contain some experiments that illustrate how an application might interact with the contact system and perform the create, read, update, and delete (CRUD) operations commonly carried out by applications involving a database.

First, we need to look at two essential classes needed to carry out operations on the contact management system. The first is the ContentProviderOperation. This class has, among others, the three methods newDelete( ), newInsert( ), and newUpdate( ). As we have seen earlier in the chapter, content providers are addressed as URIs, and each of these methods takes a URI as an argument—more specifically, an instance of the `Uri` class. The `ContentProviderOperation` has a nested class called `ContentProviderOperation.Builder` that provides other methods essential to interaction with the contacts system. The methods of the `ContentProviderOperation` class listed earlier, along with several of the methods of the `ContentProviderOperation.Builder`, return an instance of the `ContentProviderOperation.Builder`. This allows multiple method calls to be "chained" together to perform one operation. An assortment of these methods is assembled to provide instructions for a particular CRUD operation and the tables, data types, and values that are needed to carry it out. Multiple operations can be combined in an `ArrayList` of `ContentProviderOperation` instances to be carried out as one, such as to add an email address and a phone number.

The second essential class is the `ContentResolver`. An instance of the `ContentResolver` class is returned by a call to the application's `Context` method, `getContentResolver( )`, and carries out the batch of instructions provided in the `ArrayList` of `ContentProviderOperations`. The content resolver can return an instance of the `Cursor` class that would contain the results of a query into the contact system.

It sounds very confusing! Hopefully as we go through the following demonstrations, you will see patterns and corresponding outcomes that will help you understand what is happening, allow you to make intuitive modifications, and correctly anticipate the results. Then you can use the patterns in your own applications successfully.

Before we can access and modify the contact records, we must set the permissions in the manifest, just like we did for the calendar postings. Add these two lines to the manifest of your project.

```
<uses-permission android:name="android.permission.READ_CONTACTS"/>
<uses-permission android:name="android.permission.WRITE_CONTACTS"/>
```

In the first application, we are going to browse a few of the essential fields of the `Contacts` table. Again, this is the primary table that contains unique IDs, display names, and look-up keys. Only the `Display Name` field has any user value and is recognizable by the user; the other two fields are used internally. We will display them in our list, however, because later we will see how to eliminate a record using either the ID or the look-up key.

Note

Remember, displaying the fields will use a `Cursor` object returned by the `ContentResolver` object and perform the `Read` operation of the CRUD database operations.

Build a main XML file that at least contains a button and an `EditText` field. The following will do.

```xml
<?xml version="1.0" encoding="utf-8"?>
<LinearLayout xmlns:android="http://schemas.android.com/apk/res/android"
    android:layout_width="fill_parent"
    android:layout_height="fill_parent"
    android:orientation="vertical" >
        <TableRow
            android:layout_width="wrap_content"
            android:layout_height="wrap_content" >

            <Button
                android:id="@+id/records"
                android:layout_width="wrap_content"
                android:layout_height="wrap_content"
                android:text="List My Contacts" />
        </TableRow>

        <TableRow
            android:layout_width="match_parent"
            android:layout_height="wrap_content" >

            <EditText
                android:id="@+id/contactlist"
                android:layout_width="match_parent"
                android:layout_height="wrap_content"
                android:text="" />
        </TableRow>

    </TableLayout>

</LinearLayout>
```

Following is the Java code for the main activity.

```java
package com.sheusi.Membership;

import android.app.Activity;
import android.os.Bundle;
import android.provider.ContactsContract;
import android.database.*;
import android.view.*;
import android.widget.*;
import android.content.*;

public class MembershipActivity extends Activity {
    /** Called when the activity is first created. */
    Button records = null;
    EditText contactlist = null;

    @Override
    public void onCreate(Bundle savedInstanceState) {
```

```
            super.onCreate(savedInstanceState);
            setContentView(R.layout.main);
            this.setRequestedOrientation(android.content.
            pm.ActivityInfo.SCREEN_ORIENTATION_PORTRAIT);
        records = (Button) findViewById(R.id.records);
        contactlist = (EditText) findViewById(R.id.contactlist);
        records.setOnClickListener(new View.OnClickListener() {
            public void onClick(View v) {
                ContentResolver cr = MembershipActivity.this
                        .getContentResolver();
                Cursor cur = cr.query(ContactsContract.Contacts.CONTENT_URI,
                        null, null, null, null);
                // retrieve all fields, all records
                contactlist.setText(String.valueOf(cur.getCount()));
                cur.moveToFirst();
                while (cur.moveToNext()) {
                    String deets = cur.getString(cur
                        .getColumnIndex(ContactsContract.Contacts._ID))
                        + "   "
                        + cur.getString(cur
                        .getColumnIndex(ContactsContract.Contacts.DISPLAY_NAME))
                        + "   "
                        + cur.getString(cur
                        .getColumnIndex(ContactsContract.Contacts.LOOKUP_KEY));
                    contactlist.append(deets + "\n");
                    }
                }
        });
    }// ends onCreate()

    @Override
    public void onStop() {
        super.onStop();

        contactlist.setText(null);
    }
}
```

If you run this code on a device, you will get the list of contacts. Of course, a real device would likely have one or more email accounts installed, so a contact list would be available. Each line displayed will have an ID number, a simple integer, the display name (which may be an email address, a first and last name, or however the record was originally stored by the user), and finally a look-up key. The next part of this exercise will be to add the code necessary to delete a contact either by the ID or the look-up key. If you are running this exercise on a device that is actually displaying records, it would be useful to record the ID of one record you do not mind deleting and the look-up key from another. Jot them down in the margin of the book or on a piece of paper. Obviously, no application should require a user to jot down information, but this is just a demonstration. If such a thing were necessary in a real application, we might create a list with an `OnClickListener` object associated with each row to react to a click or touch on a given contact. To the XML file you have created, add the following `TableRow` and fields.

```xml
<TableRow
        android:layout_width="wrap_content"
        android:layout_height="wrap_content" >

    <TextView
        android:layout_width="match_parent"
        android:layout_height="wrap_content"
        android:text="Enter ID for deletion-->" />

    <EditText
        android:id="@+id/contactid"
        android:layout_width="match_parent"
        android:layout_height="wrap_content"
        android:text="" />

    <Button
        android:id="@+id/delrec"
        android:layout_width="wrap_content"
        android:layout_height="wrap_content"
        android:text="Delete this Contact" />
</TableRow>
```

This will give us a tiny `EditText` field where we can enter the contact ID you jotted down and a button to click that will actually delete the entry. Revise your Java file to match the one listed next. It includes an `import` statement for the Java `ArrayList` class and necessary references to the elements added to the XML file. It also includes the code necessary to delete the contact.

```java
package com.sheusi.Membership;

import android.app.Activity;
import android.os.Bundle;
import android.provider.ContactsContract;
import android.database.*;
import android.view.*;
import android.widget.*;
import android.content.*;
import java.util.ArrayList;
```

```java
public class MembershipActivity extends Activity {
    /** Called when the activity is first created. */
    Button records = null;
    EditText contactlist = null;
    Button delrec = null;
    EditText contactid = null;

    @Override
    public void onCreate(Bundle savedInstanceState) {
        super.onCreate(savedInstanceState);
        setContentView(R.layout.main);

this.setRequestedOrientation(android.content.pm.ActivityInfo.SCREEN_ORIENTATION_
PORTRAIT);
        records = (Button) findViewById(R.id.records);
        contactlist = (EditText) findViewById(R.id.contactlist);
        delrec = (Button) findViewById(R.id.delrec);
        contactid = (EditText) findViewById(R.id.contactid);
        records.setOnClickListener(new View.OnClickListener() {
            public void onClick(View v) {

                ContentResolver cr = MembershipActivity.this
                        .getContentResolver();
                Cursor cur = cr.query(ContactsContract.Contacts.CONTENT_URI,
                        null, null, null, null);
                // retrieve all fields, all records
                contactlist.setText(String.valueOf(cur.getCount()));
                cur.moveToFirst();
                while (cur.moveToNext()) {
                    String deets = cur.getString(cur
                            .getColumnIndex(ContactsContract.Contacts._ID))
                            + " "
                            + cur.getString(cur
.getColumnIndex(ContactsContract.Contacts.DISPLAY_NAME))
                            + " "
                            + cur.getString(cur
.getColumnIndex(ContactsContract.Contacts.LOOKUP_KEY));
                    contactlist.append(deets + "\n");
                }
            }
        });

        delrec.setOnClickListener(new View.OnClickListener() {
            public void onClick(View v) {

                ArrayList<ContentProviderOperation> deleteCPO = new
```

```
                ArrayList<ContentProviderOperation>();
                        deleteCPO
                            .add(ContentProviderOperation
                                .newDelete(
                                        ContactsContract.RawContacts.
                                        CONTENT_URI)
                                .withSelection(
                                        ContactsContract.Data.CONTACT_ID
                                            + " = ? ",
                                        new String[] { contactid.getText()
                                            .toString() }).build());
                try {
                    getContentResolver().applyBatch(ContactsContract.AUTHORITY,
                            deleteCPO);
                    Toast.makeText(
                            getApplicationContext(),
                            "Record with ID: " + contactid.getText()
                                    + " Deleted from Contacts",
                            Toast.LENGTH_LONG).show();
                } catch (Exception e) {
                    Toast.makeText(getApplicationContext(),
                            "Exception: " + e.getMessage(), Toast.LENGTH_LONG)
                            .show();
                }
            }
        });
    }// ends onCreate()

    @Override
    public void onStop() {
        super.onStop();
        contactlist.setText(null);
    }
}
```

If you run the code and delete the record whose ID you jotted down, you will see a confirmation message indicating that you deleted the chosen record. You may then want to list the contacts and confirm for yourself that it is indeed gone.

The next modification is minor, but it shows a different method for deleting records, this time using the look-up key you jotted down. First, add the following import statement to the top of your code.

```
import android.net.Uri;
```

Then, in the onTouch( ) method of the Delete button's listener, substitute the following code for the code segment that immediately follows it next.

Use this

```
Uri uri =        Uri.withAppendedPath(ContactsContract.Contacts.CONTENT_LOOKUP_URI,
        contactid.getText().toString());
cr.delete(uri, null, null);

Toast.makeText(getApplicationContext(),
        "Record with Look-up key: " + contactid.getText()       + " Deleted from Contacts",
        Toast.LENGTH_LONG).show();
```

To replace this

```
ArrayList<ContentProviderOperation> deleteCPO = new ArrayList<ContentProvider
Operation>();
                deleteCPO
                        .add(ContentProviderOperation
                                .newDelete(
                                        ContactsContract.RawContacts.
                                        CONTENT_URI)
                                .withSelection(
                                        ContactsContract.Data.CONTACT_ID
                                                + " = ? ",
                                        new String[] { contactid.getText()
                                                .toString() }).build());

        try {
            getContentResolver().applyBatch(ContactsContract.AUTHORITY,
                    deleteCPO);
            Toast.makeText(
                    getApplicationContext(),
                    "Record with ID: " + contactid.getText()
                            + " Deleted from Contacts",
                    Toast.LENGTH_LONG).show();
        } catch (Exception e) {
            Toast.makeText(getApplicationContext(),
                    "Exception: " + e.getMessage(), Toast.LENGTH_LONG)
                    .show();
        }
```

When you run the program, insert the look-up key you jotted instead of the ID. (Because the XML file wasn't changed, it still requests an ID; just use the look-up key in its place.) Again, if you then list your contacts, you should find that the second record is gone.

So far we have read and deleted contacts, but we have yet to create and update contacts to complete the CRUD operations. To do this, we will borrow some form design work from our Membership application found in the database chapter and add some functionality to it. We will add a button that will take the data from the form and create a contact with it. We will also add a button that will perform a single edit, again for simplicity's sake. In the original exercise, the email address at the top was used as a look-up field for the membership database. This time, using a chosen ID, any entry the user would make in the email field will replace the current email for that ID when the user clicks the update method. The code is long and redundant, but it is important that you can see how the different components connect. Again, if you start this as a new project, be sure to put the appropriate permissions in the manifest file.

First, here's the `main.xml` file.

```xml
<?xml version="1.0" encoding="utf-8"?>
<LinearLayout xmlns:android="http://schemas.android.com/apk/res/android"
    android:layout_width="fill_parent"
    android:layout_height="fill_parent"
    android:orientation="vertical" >
    <TextView
        android:layout_width="fill_parent"
        android:layout_height="wrap_content"
        android:text="Android Developer's Association" />

    <TableLayout
        android:layout_width="fill_parent"
        android:layout_height="wrap_content" >

        <TableRow
            android:layout_width="wrap_content"
            android:layout_height="wrap_content" >

            <TextView
                android:layout_width="wrap_content"
                android:layout_height="wrap_content"
                android:layout_weight=".5"
                android:text="Email Address:" />

            <EditText
                android:id="@+id/et_email"
                android:layout_width="wrap_content"
                android:layout_height="wrap_content"
                android:layout_weight=".5"
                android:background="#808080"
```

```
                android:text="" />
    </TableRow>

    <TableRow
        android:layout_width="wrap_content"
        android:layout_height="wrap_content" >

        <Button
            android:id="@+id/retrievebutton"
            android:layout_width="wrap_content"
            android:layout_height="wrap_content"
            android:layout_weight=".5"
            android:text="Retrieve" />
    </TableRow>

    <TableRow
        android:layout_width="wrap_content"
        android:layout_height="wrap_content" >

        <TextView
            android:layout_width="wrap_content"
            android:layout_height="wrap_content"
            android:layout_weight=".5"
            android:text="First Name:" />

        <EditText
            android:id="@+id/et_fname"
            android:layout_width="wrap_content"
            android:layout_height="wrap_content"
            android:layout_weight=".5"
            android:background="#404040"
            android:text="" />
    </TableRow>

    <TableRow
        android:layout_width="wrap_content"
        android:layout_height="wrap_content" >

        <TextView
            android:layout_width="wrap_content"
            android:layout_height="wrap_content"
            android:layout_weight=".5"
            android:text="Last Name:" />

        <EditText
            android:id="@+id/et_lname"
            android:layout_width="wrap_content"
            android:layout_height="wrap_content"
            android:layout_weight=".5"
```

```xml
            android:background="#606060"
            android:text="" />
    </TableRow>

    <TableRow
        android:layout_width="wrap_content"
        android:layout_height="wrap_content" >

        <TextView
            android:layout_width="wrap_content"
            android:layout_height="wrap_content"
            android:layout_weight=".5"
            android:text="Address:" />

        <EditText
            android:id="@+id/et_address"
            android:layout_width="wrap_content"
            android:layout_height="wrap_content"
            android:layout_weight=".5"
            android:background="#404040"
            android:text="" />
    </TableRow>

    <TableRow
        android:layout_width="wrap_content"
        android:layout_height="wrap_content" >

        <TextView
            android:layout_width="wrap_content"
            android:layout_height="wrap_content"
            android:layout_weight=".5"
            android:text="City:" />

        <EditText
            android:id="@+id/et_city"
            android:layout_width="wrap_content"
            android:layout_height="wrap_content"
            android:layout_weight=".5"
            android:background="#606060"
            android:text="" />
    </TableRow>

    <TableRow
        android:layout_width="wrap_content"
        android:layout_height="wrap_content" >

        <TextView
            android:layout_width="wrap_content"
            android:layout_height="wrap_content"
```

```
                android:layout_weight=".5"
                android:text="State:" />

        <EditText
            android:id="@+id/et_state"
            android:layout_width="wrap_content"
            android:layout_height="wrap_content"
            android:layout_weight=".5"
            android:background="#404040"
            android:text="" />
    </TableRow>

    <TableRow
        android:layout_width="wrap_content"
        android:layout_height="wrap_content" >

        <TextView
            android:layout_width="wrap_content"
            android:layout_height="wrap_content"
            android:layout_weight=".5"
            android:text="Zip:" />

        <EditText
            android:id="@+id/et_zip"
            android:layout_width="wrap_content"
            android:layout_height="wrap_content"
            android:layout_weight=".5"
            android:background="#606060"
            android:text="" />
    </TableRow>

    <TableRow
        android:layout_width="wrap_content"
        android:layout_height="wrap_content" >

        <TextView
            android:layout_width="wrap_content"
            android:layout_height="wrap_content"
            android:layout_weight=".5"
            android:text="Phone:" />

        <EditText
            android:id="@+id/et_phone"
            android:layout_width="wrap_content"
            android:layout_height="wrap_content"
            android:layout_weight=".5"
            android:background="#404040"
            android:text="" />
    </TableRow>
```

```
<TableRow
    android:layout_width="wrap_content"
    android:layout_height="wrap_content" >

    <Button
        android:id="@+id/savebutton"
        android:layout_width="wrap_content"
        android:layout_height="wrap_content"
        android:layout_weight=".5"
        android:text="Save new member" />

    <Button
        android:id="@+id/clearbutton"
        android:layout_width="wrap_content"
        android:layout_height="wrap_content"
        android:layout_weight=".5"
        android:text="Clear fields" />

    <Button
        android:id="@+id/deletebutton"
        android:layout_width="wrap_content"
        android:layout_height="wrap_content"
        android:layout_weight=".5"
        android:text="Delete from Table" />

    <Button
        android:id="@+id/postbutton"
        android:layout_width="wrap_content"
        android:layout_height="wrap_content"
        android:layout_weight=".5"
        android:text="Add to My Contacts" />
</TableRow>

<TableRow
    android:layout_width="wrap_content"
    android:layout_height="wrap_content" >

    <Button
        android:id="@+id/records"
        android:layout_width="wrap_content"
        android:layout_height="wrap_content"
        android:layout_weight=".5"
        android:text="List My Contacts" />

    <Button
        android:id="@+id/closelist"
        android:layout_width="wrap_content"
```

```
                        android:layout_height="wrap_content"
                        android:layout_weight=".5"
                        android:text="Close the List" />
            </TableRow>

            <TableRow
                android:layout_width="wrap_content"
                android:layout_height="wrap_content" >

                <EditText
                    android:id="@+id/contactlist"
                    android:layout_width="200dp"
                    android:layout_height="wrap_content"
                    android:layout_weight=".5"
                    android:text="" />
            </TableRow>

            <TableRow
                android:layout_width="wrap_content"
                android:layout_height="wrap_content" >

                <Button
                    android:id="@+id/editrec"
                    android:layout_width="wrap_content"
                    android:layout_height="wrap_content"
                    android:layout_weight=".5"
                    android:text="Enter new email above and \n ID from list at far right, then
                    click HERE to UPDATE" />

                <Button
                    android:id="@+id/delrec"
                    android:layout_width="wrap_content"
                    android:layout_height="wrap_content"
                    android:layout_weight=".5"
                    android:text="Enter ID from list at right\n, then click HERE to DELETE" />

                <EditText
                    android:id="@+id/contactid"
                    android:layout_width="match_parent"
                    android:layout_height="wrap_content"
                    android:layout_weight=".5"
                    android:text="" />
            </TableRow>
        </TableLayout>

</LinearLayout>
```

Next, here's the Java file.

```java
package com.sheusi.Membership;

import android.app.Activity;
import android.os.Bundle;
import android.provider.ContactsContract;
import android.database.*;
import android.database.sqlite.*;
import android.view.*;
import android.widget.*;
import android.content.*;
import android.database.sqlite.SQLiteQueryBuilder;
import java.util.ArrayList;

public class MembershipActivity extends Activity {
    /** Called when the activity is first created. */
    SQLiteDatabase database = null;
    Button retrieve = null;
    Button save = null;
    Button delete = null;
    Button clear = null;
    EditText email = null;
    EditText fname = null;
    EditText lname = null;
    EditText address = null;
    EditText city = null;
    EditText state = null;
    EditText zip = null;
    EditText phone = null;
    Context myContext = null;
    Button postbutton = null;
    Button records = null;
    EditText contactlist = null;
    Button delrec = null;
    Button editrec = null;
    EditText contactid = null;
    Button closelist = null;

    @Override
    public void onCreate(Bundle savedInstanceState) {
        super.onCreate(savedInstanceState);
        setContentView(R.layout.main);
        myContext = this.getApplicationContext();

this.setRequestedOrientation(android.content.pm.ActivityInfo.SCREEN_ORIENTATION_
PORTRAIT);
```

```
            // build table if it doesn't exist already
            database = openOrCreateDatabase("membership.db",
                    SQLiteDatabase.CREATE_IF_NECESSARY, null);
            database.setLockingEnabled(true);
            if (checkForTable() != true)
                database.execSQL("create table members(_id integer primary key
autoincrement,email text,fname text,lname text, address text,city text, state text, zip
text, phone text)");

            // end build
            retrieve = (Button) findViewById(R.id.retrievebutton);
            save = (Button) findViewById(R.id.savebutton);
            delete = (Button) findViewById(R.id.deletebutton);
            clear = (Button) findViewById(R.id.clearbutton);
            email = (EditText) findViewById(R.id.et_email);
            fname = (EditText) findViewById(R.id.et_fname);
            lname = (EditText) findViewById(R.id.et_lname);
            address = (EditText) findViewById(R.id.et_address);
            city = (EditText) findViewById(R.id.et_city);
            state = (EditText) findViewById(R.id.et_state);
            zip = (EditText) findViewById(R.id.et_zip);
            phone = (EditText) findViewById(R.id.et_phone);
            postbutton = (Button) findViewById(R.id.postbutton);
            records = (Button) findViewById(R.id.records);
            contactlist = (EditText) findViewById(R.id.contactlist);
            delrec = (Button) findViewById(R.id.delrec);
            editrec = (Button) findViewById(R.id.editrec);
            contactid = (EditText) findViewById(R.id.contactid);
            closelist = (Button) findViewById(R.id.closelist);
            email.setText(null);
            fname.setText(null);
            lname.setText(null);
            address.setText(null);
            city.setText(null);
            state.setText(null);
            zip.setText(null);
            phone.setText(null);

            records.setOnClickListener(new View.OnClickListener() {
                public void onClick(View v) {

                    ContentResolver cr = MembershipActivity.this
                            .getContentResolver();
                    Cursor cur = cr.query(ContactsContract.Contacts.CONTENT_URI,
                            null, null, null, null);
                    // all fields no specs
```

```
                    contactlist.setText(String.valueOf(cur.getCount()));
                    cur.moveToFirst();
                    while (cur.moveToNext()) {
                        String deets = cur.getString(cur
                                .getColumnIndex(ContactsContract.Contacts._ID))
                            + "   "
                            + cur.getString(cur
.getColumnIndex(ContactsContract.Contacts.DISPLAY_NAME))
                            + "   "
                            + cur.getString(cur
.getColumnIndex(ContactsContract.Contacts.LOOKUP_KEY));
                        contactlist.append(deets + "\n");

                    }
                }
            });
            // */
            retrieve.setOnClickListener(new View.OnClickListener() {
                public void onClick(View v) {
                    // if record exists, retrieve it; if not, give toast message
                    String key = email.getText().toString();
                    SQLiteQueryBuilder sqlqb = new SQLiteQueryBuilder();
                    sqlqb.setTables("members");
                    Cursor c = sqlqb.query(database, null, "email=?",
                            new String[] { key }, null, null, null);
                    if (c.getCount() == 0)
                        Toast.makeText(myContext, "no record exists",
                                Toast.LENGTH_SHORT).show();
                    else {
                        c.moveToFirst();
                        fname.setText(c.getString(2));
                        lname.setText(c.getString(3));
                        address.setText(c.getString(4));
                        city.setText(c.getString(5));
                        state.setText(c.getString(6));
                        zip.setText(c.getString(7));
                        phone.setText(c.getString(8));
                    }

                }
            });
            save.setOnClickListener(new View.OnClickListener() {
                public void onClick(View v) {
                    // if record exists, update it; if not, insert it
                    String key = email.getText().toString();
```

```
            Cursor c = database.query("members", null, "email=?",
                    new String[] { key }, null, null, null, null);
            if (c.getCount() > 0) { // it exists, so update
                ContentValues cv = new ContentValues();
                cv.put("fname", fname.getText().toString());
                cv.put("lname", lname.getText().toString());
                cv.put("address", address.getText().toString());
                cv.put("city", city.getText().toString());
                cv.put("state", state.getText().toString());
                cv.put("zip", zip.getText().toString());
                cv.put("phone", phone.getText().toString());

                database.update("members", cv, "email=?",
                        new String[] { key });

            } else { // doesn't exist so insert
                ContentValues cv = new ContentValues();
                cv.put("email", key);
                cv.put("fname", fname.getText().toString());
                cv.put("lname", lname.getText().toString());
                cv.put("address", address.getText().toString());
                cv.put("city", city.getText().toString());
                cv.put("state", state.getText().toString());
                cv.put("zip", zip.getText().toString());
                cv.put("phone", phone.getText().toString());
                database.insert("members", null, cv);
            }

        }
    });
    delete.setOnClickListener(new View.OnClickListener() {
        public void onClick(View v) {
            String key = email.getText().toString();
            database.delete("members", "email=?", new String[] { key });
            email.setText(null);
            fname.setText(null);
            lname.setText(null);
            address.setText(null);
            city.setText(null);
            state.setText(null);
            zip.setText(null);
            phone.setText(null);
            Toast.makeText(myContext, "Record was deleted.",
                    Toast.LENGTH_SHORT).show();

        }
    });
```

```java
clear.setOnClickListener(new View.OnClickListener() {
    public void onClick(View v) {
        email.setText(null);
        fname.setText(null);
        lname.setText(null);
        address.setText(null);
        city.setText(null);
        state.setText(null);
        zip.setText(null);
        phone.setText(null);

    }
});

postbutton.setOnClickListener(new View.OnClickListener() {
    public void onClick(View v) {

        ArrayList<ContentProviderOperation> alcpo = new
ArrayList<ContentProviderOperation>();
        alcpo.add(ContentProviderOperation
                .newInsert(ContactsContract.RawContacts.CONTENT_URI)
                .withValue(ContactsContract.RawContacts.ACCOUNT_TYPE,
                    null)
                .withValue(ContactsContract.RawContacts.ACCOUNT_NAME,
                    null).build());

        // Names
        if (lname.getText() != null) {
            alcpo.add(ContentProviderOperation
                .newInsert(ContactsContract.Data.CONTENT_URI)
                .withValueBackReference(
                    ContactsContract.Data.RAW_CONTACT_ID, 0)
                .withValue(
                    ContactsContract.Data.MIMETYPE,
ContactsContract.CommonDataKinds.StructuredName.CONTENT_ITEM_TYPE)
                .withValue(
ContactsContract.CommonDataKinds.StructuredName.DISPLAY_NAME,
                        lname.getText().toString() + ", "
                            + fname.getText().toString())
                .build());
        }
        // Mobile
        // Number
        if (phone.getText() != null) {
```

```
                                    alcpo.add(ContentProviderOperation
                                        .newInsert(ContactsContract.Data.CONTENT_URI)
                                        .withValueBackReference(
                                                ContactsContract.Data.RAW_CONTACT_ID, 0)
                                        .withValue(
                                                ContactsContract.Data.MIMETYPE,
ContactsContract.CommonDataKinds.Phone.CONTENT_ITEM_TYPE)
                                        .withValue(
                                                ContactsContract.CommonDataKinds.
                                                Phone.NUMBER,
                                                phone.getText().toString())
                                        .withValue(
                                                ContactsContract.CommonDataKinds.
                                                Phone.TYPE,
ContactsContract.CommonDataKinds.Phone.TYPE_MOBILE)
                                        .build());
                    }

                    // for now, post same phone number for mobile and home phone
                    if (phone.getText() != null) {
                            alcpo.add(ContentProviderOperation
                                        .newInsert(ContactsContract.Data.CONTENT_URI)
                                        .withValueBackReference(
                                                ContactsContract.Data.RAW_CONTACT_ID, 0)
                                        .withValue(
                                                ContactsContract.Data.MIMETYPE,
ContactsContract.CommonDataKinds.Phone.CONTENT_ITEM_TYPE)
                                        .withValue(
                                                ContactsContract.CommonDataKinds.
                                                Phone.NUMBER,
                                                phone.getText().toString())
                                        .withValue(
                                                ContactsContract.CommonDataKinds.
                                                Phone.TYPE,
                                                ContactsContract.CommonDataKinds.
                                                Phone.TYPE_HOME)
                                        .build());
                    }
                    // Address
                    if (address.getText() != null) {
                            alcpo.add(ContentProviderOperation
                                        .newInsert(ContactsContract.Data.CONTENT_URI)
                                        .withValueBackReference(
```

```
                             ContactsContract.Data.RAW_CONTACT_ID, 0)
                 .withValue(
                         ContactsContract.Data.MIMETYPE,


ContactsContract.CommonDataKinds.StructuredPostal.CONTENT_ITEM_TYPE)
                 .withValue(

ContactsContract.CommonDataKinds.StructuredPostal.STREET,
                             address.getText().toString()).build());
             }
             // City
             if (city.getText() != null) {
                 alcpo.add(ContentProviderOperation
                         .newInsert(ContactsContract.Data.CONTENT_URI)
                         .withValueBackReference(
                             ContactsContract.Data.RAW_CONTACT_ID, 0)
                         .withValue(
                             ContactsContract.Data.MIMETYPE,


ContactsContract.CommonDataKinds.StructuredPostal.CONTENT_ITEM_TYPE)
                 .withValue(

ContactsContract.CommonDataKinds.StructuredPostal.CITY,
                             city.getText().toString()).build());
             }
             // State
             if (state.getText() != null) {
                 alcpo.add(ContentProviderOperation
                         .newInsert(ContactsContract.Data.CONTENT_URI)
                         .withValueBackReference(
                             ContactsContract.Data.RAW_CONTACT_ID, 0)
                         .withValue(
                             ContactsContract.Data.MIMETYPE,


ContactsContract.CommonDataKinds.StructuredPostal.CONTENT_ITEM_TYPE)
                 .withValue(

ContactsContract.CommonDataKinds.StructuredPostal.REGION,
                             state.getText().toString()).build());
             }
             // Zip
             if (zip.getText() != null) {
                 alcpo.add(ContentProviderOperation
                         .newInsert(ContactsContract.Data.CONTENT_URI)
```

```
                                    .withValueBackReference(
                                            ContactsContract.Data.RAW_CONTACT_ID, 0)
                                    .withValue(
                                            ContactsContract.Data.MIMETYPE,

ContactsContract.CommonDataKinds.StructuredPostal.CONTENT_ITEM_TYPE)
                                    .withValue(

ContactsContract.CommonDataKinds.StructuredPostal.POSTCODE,
                                            zip.getText().toString()).build());
                }
                // Email
                if (email.getText() != null) {
                    alcpo.add(ContentProviderOperation
                            .newInsert(ContactsContract.Data.CONTENT_URI)
                            .withValueBackReference(
                                    ContactsContract.Data.RAW_CONTACT_ID, 0)
                            .withValue(
                                    ContactsContract.Data.MIMETYPE,

ContactsContract.CommonDataKinds.Email.CONTENT_ITEM_TYPE)
                            .withValue(
                                    ContactsContract.CommonDataKinds.
                                    Email.DATA,
                                    email.getText().toString())
                            .withValue(
                                    ContactsContract.CommonDataKinds.
                                    Email.TYPE,

ContactsContract.CommonDataKinds.Email.TYPE_WORK)
                            .build());
                }

                // Asking the contact provider to create a new contact
                try {
                    getContentResolver().applyBatch(ContactsContract.
                    AUTHORITY,
                            alcpo);
                } catch (Exception e) {
                    e.printStackTrace();
                    Toast.makeText(getApplicationContext(),
                            "Exception: " + e.getMessage(), Toast.LENGTH_SHORT)
                            .show();
                }

            }
```

```
            });
        delrec.setOnClickListener(new View.OnClickListener() {
            public void onClick(View v) {

                ArrayList<ContentProviderOperation> deleteCPO = new
ArrayList<ContentProviderOperation>();
                deleteCPO
                        .add(ContentProviderOperation
                                .newDelete(
                                        ContactsContract.RawContacts.
                                        CONTENT_URI)
                                .withSelection(
                                        ContactsContract.Data.CONTACT_ID
                                                + " = ? ",
                                        new String[] {
                                        contactid.getText()
                                                .toString() }).build());
                try {
                    getContentResolver().applyBatch(ContactsContract.
                    AUTHORITY,
                            deleteCPO);
                    Toast.makeText(getApplicationContext(),
                            "ID: " + contactid.getText() + " deleted.",
                            Toast.LENGTH_LONG).show();
                } catch (Exception e) {
                    Toast.makeText(getApplicationContext(),
                            "Exception: " + e.getMessage(), Toast.LENGTH_LONG)
                            .show();
                }
            }
        });
        editrec.setOnClickListener(new View.OnClickListener() {
            public void onClick(View v) {

                ArrayList<ContentProviderOperation> updateCPO = new
ArrayList<ContentProviderOperation>();
                updateCPO
                        .add(ContentProviderOperation
                                .newUpdate(ContactsContract.Data.
                                CONTENT_URI)
                                .withSelection(
                                        ContactsContract.Data.CONTACT_ID
                                                + " = ? ",
```

```
                                            new String[] { contactid.getText()
                                                      .toString() })
                                    .withValue(
                                            ContactsContract.Data.MIMETYPE,
ContactsContract.CommonDataKinds.Email.CONTENT_ITEM_TYPE)
                                    .withValue(
ContactsContract.CommonDataKinds.Email.DATA,
                                            email.getText().toString())
                                    .withValue(
ContactsContract.CommonDataKinds.Email.TYPE,
ContactsContract.CommonDataKinds.Email.TYPE_OTHER)
                                    .build());

                try {
                    getContentResolver().applyBatch(ContactsContract.AUTHORITY,
                            updateCPO);
                    Toast.makeText(getApplicationContext(),
                            "ID: " + contactid.getText() + " updated.",
                            Toast.LENGTH_LONG).show();
                } catch (Exception e) {
                    Toast.makeText(getApplicationContext(),
                            "Exception: " + e.getMessage(), Toast.LENGTH_LONG)
                            .show();
                }
            }
        });
        closelist.setOnClickListener(new View.OnClickListener() {
            public void onClick(View v) {
                contactlist.setText("");
            }
        });
    }// ends onCreate

    public boolean checkForTable() {
        Cursor c = database.query("sqlite_master", null, "type=? and name=?",
                new String[] { "table", "members" }, null, null, null);
        if (c.getCount() > 0)
            return true;
        else
            return false;
    }

    @Override
```

```
public void onStop() {
    super.onStop();
    email.setText(null);
    fname.setText(null);
    lname.setText(null);
    address.setText(null);
    city.setText(null);
    state.setText(null);
    zip.setText(null);
    phone.setText(null);
    database.close();
    }
}
```

When running on a tablet in portrait orientation (the code fixes this application in portrait mode), the application would look like Figure 5.2.

A complete list of the content providers that Android offers can be found at http://developer.android.com/reference/android/provider/package-summary.html.

Summary of Key Concepts

- Content providers allow the applications programmer to access data stored by the common services found on typical Android devices such as contact lists and calendars. Data is accessed through queries like those used to access tables created by applications programmers for specific applications. Though not covered in this book, applications programmers can create their own content providers around data tables stored on the device.

- All of the typical operations used on data tables such as creating, reading, updating, and deleting records can be done to records maintained by content providers through third-party applications. However, applications will need specific permissions written into the manifest file to allow the application to make changes to the content provider's records. The manifest entries will alert the installer of applications with these permission requests and allow the user of the device to cancel the installation if he chooses not to allow the permissions.

- While some content providers' record system might have a very simple design, others such as the contact list can be fairly complicated. The applications programmer who chooses to access records of a content provider should do extensive testing of applications to ensure that the integrity of these records remains intact.

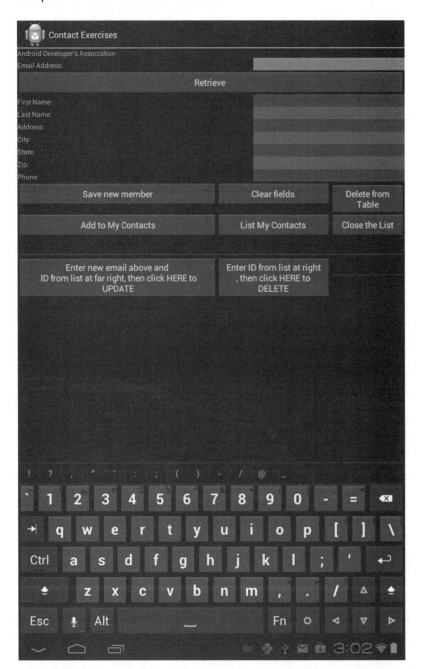

Figure 5.2
Membership application with contact list enhancements running on Toshiba Thrive tablet device.
Source: Google.

REVIEW QUESTIONS

You can find the answers to these review questions in the appendix at the end of the book.

1. The common syntax for the universal resource identifiers (URIs) used by content providers is _____.

2. Objects of the _____ class are used to hold results of queries sent to content providers.

3. When adding events to the system's calendar, which five time values should be added to the start time and end time for an event?

   _____

4. The month of January has the following integer value when used to add an event.

   _____

5. An event that begins at 2:00 p.m. should have what integer value for the hour when used to add an event? _____

6. What permissions should be added to the manifest file for access to the Calendar content provider?

   _____ and _____

7. What permissions should be added to the manifest file for access to the Contacts content provider?

   _____ and _____

8. Objects of which class return Cursor objects when content providers are queried?

   _____

9. Multiple email accounts added to the same device share the same Contacts content provider, true or false? _____

10. For convenience sake, an applications programmer might choose to access a content provider's built-in interface through an _____.

SUGGESTED PROJECTS

- In Chapters 4 and 5, we used the ListView object to present data in a structured form. Rewrite the application that lists the device's calendars using ListView objects instead of displaying the data in a text field.

- Build a simple appointment booking system or reservation system using the Calendar content provider.

- Develop a query that retrieves your contacts that have email addresses from your contact list. Then, using email through an intent, send them all a greeting through the application.

- Do some research on your own to discover which other services on your Android device can be accessed as content providers. Then build an application to retrieve records from one or more of them.

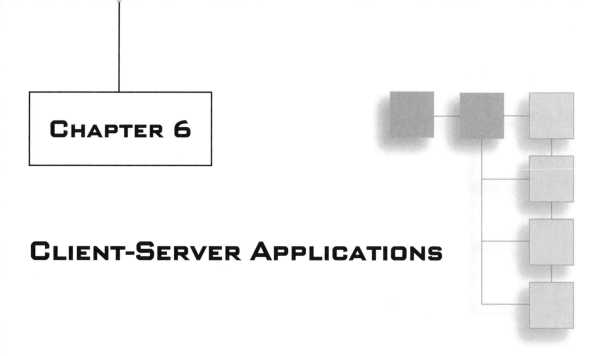

CHAPTER 6

CLIENT-SERVER APPLICATIONS

CONNECTIONLESS COMMUNICATIONS ON THE INTERNET

As rich in processing power and resources as the typical handset or tablet is, any business application will likely rely or at least benefit from access to outside data, whether it is from the Internet or a local area network (LAN). Data can come in and go out of the device in many formats, from plain text to images and everything in between. Access can be of a connectionless nature, such as a web page, for example, or through connection-oriented data streams connected to a server-side application. For those unfamiliar with networking, *connection-oriented communications* are those in which the communicating devices establish a connection through an exchange of messages before passing useful information. In this type of communication, the parties send acknowledgements when data is received. This type of communication is more reliable, but more data must be passed between the parties. This extra data is referred to as *overhead*. Connectionless communications, on the other hand, use no such acknowledgements, and neither side has an obligation to keep track of the state of the communications. These connections are inherently less reliable but require less overhead. Web page requests, for example, are connectionless because each request requires a new connection. In this chapter, we will look at several options and leave it to the application developer to choose the best method for a given application.

Probably the easiest to incorporate into an application and certainly the easiest to demonstrate is simple access to a web page using a WebView widget. The newer application programming interfaces (APIs) give a rich set of capabilities to the WebView object, such as zoom control. However, even the most basic settings render a usable platform to allow for quick access to the World Wide Web. Possible uses for web access might be access to an online or internal company directory, access to company products, and so on. The application programmer need not redevelop any web design work and information already developed by the enterprise specifically for the tablet. Essentially, anything available to a browser can be made available to the application.

In the first demonstration, we will cover two ways to use a `WebView` widget. The first is to include a `WebView` in the main XML file and set a specific size in pixels to it. This allows the browser window to share space on the screen with the rest of an application. By the example, the reader can see how easily the `WebView` can be located on the screen. The second option is to display the `WebView` on its own screen through the use of a separate intent with its own XML file. This method allows the maximum size for the `WebView` and preserves the entire main screen for the application's balance.

Before we do anything with the Internet, however, we must enter the appropriate permission in our manifest file. Add the following line to your project's manifest.

```
<uses-permission android:name="android.permission.INTERNET"/>
```

As always, be sure that it is an outermost element, and don't include it in any other tag pair. Also, because this demonstration uses two `Activity` classes, the second must be added to the manifest file. This time, however, the entry belongs between the `<application>` and `</application>` tags.

```
<activity android:name=".WebIntent"/>
```

If you have never written a multiscreen application, here is a quick tutorial. First, the various activities are written as separate classes with separate source code files. In Eclipse, you can do this by right-clicking your package in the Package Explorer panel and choosing New, Class. Be sure you have the package name at the top and the necessary imports, and be sure that your class extends the `Activity` class. Override the `onCreate( )` method with your own code, but be sure to call the "super" constructor before anything else in the method. You also need to create an XML file for this activity and refer to it in your new class with a line like this.

```
setContentView(R.layout.browse);
```

The actual name of your XML file without the XML extension will replace the word `browse` above. You start the XML file for your additional activity by right-clicking the `layout` folder under the `res` folder in the Package Explorer and choosing Android XML File as the file type. (See Figures 6.1 and 6.2.)

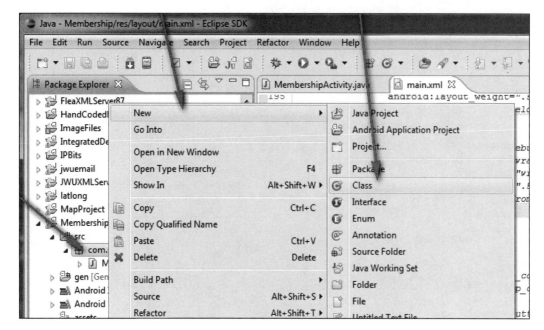

Figure 6.1
Starting a new class file from the Package Explorer.
Source: The Eclipse Foundation.

From your main activity, you call another activity by invoking an intent with code similar to the following:

```
Intent  myIntent=new  Intent(MainActivity.this.getApplicationContext(),WebIntent.
class);
startActivity(myIntent);
```

Many of the device's services, such as phone (if the device is a smart phone, of course), email, and so on, have built-in symbolic constants in the Intent class. To use one of these, you call it with code similar to the following, which would start the phone service.

```
Uri uri=Uri.parse("tel:888-555-1212");
Intent myIntent=new Intent(Intent.CALL,uri);
startActivity(myIntent);
```

In our example, notice that we need to pass the website URL from the main screen to the second screen containing the web browser. We do this by passing a bundle with the call to the second intent. The bundle is populated by using the .putExtra( ) method of the Intent class and using a name-value pair as the argument. You can make as many entries to the bundle as necessary. On the second activities side, you pull values from the bundle by using the matching name in the name-value pair.

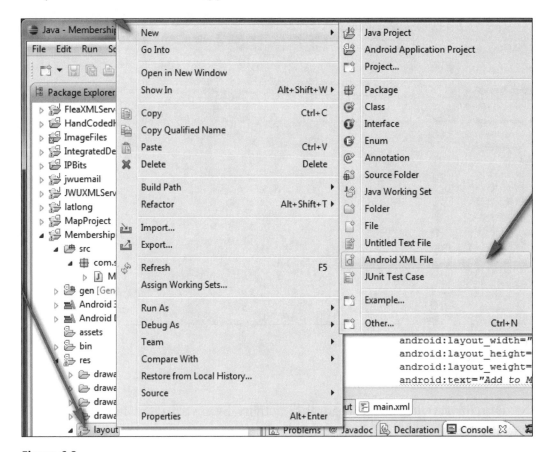

Figure 6.2
Starting a new XML file from the Package Explorer.
Source: The Eclipse Foundation.

If you want to send values back to the original activity from the called activity, be sure to use the `startActivityForResult( )` method of the calling activity instead of `startActivity( )`. To prevent the system from confusing which bundles go with which activities, a unique identifying integer is added as a second argument to the `startActivityForResult( )` method, for instance.

```
startActivityForResult(myIntent, 2);
```

To return to the original activity from the called activity, you can do it in code by adding the `finish( )` method call in the appropriate place or just clicking the hardware or firmware Back button on the device. You will notice all these techniques in the example to follow. First, here are the two XML files: the first for the main activity, and the second for the full-screen browser activity.

```
<RelativeLayout xmlns:android="http://schemas.android.com/apk/res/android"
    xmlns:tools="http://schemas.android.com/tools"
    android:layout_width="match_parent"
    android:layout_height="match_parent" >

    <TextView
        android:id="@+id/greeting"
        android:layout_width="wrap_content"
        android:layout_height="wrap_content"
        android:layout_alignParentTop="true"
        android:layout_centerHorizontal="true"
        android:padding="@dimen/padding_medium"
        android:text="@string/hello_world"
        tools:context=".MainActivity" />

    <EditText
        android:id="@+id/urlrequest"
        android:layout_width="wrap_content"
        android:layout_height="wrap_content"
        android:layout_below="@+id/greeting"
        android:layout_centerHorizontal="true"
        android:hint="Enter website here:"
        android:padding="@dimen/padding_medium"
        android:text=""
        tools:context=".MainActivity" />

    <Button
        android:id="@+id/getpage"
        android:layout_width="wrap_content"
        android:layout_height="wrap_content"
        android:layout_below="@+id/urlrequest"
        android:layout_centerHorizontal="true"
        android:padding="@dimen/padding_medium"
        android:text="Click to retrieve webpage and display below."
        tools:context=".MainActivity" />

    <Button
        android:id="@+id/getpageforintent"
        android:layout_width="wrap_content"
        android:layout_height="wrap_content"
        android:layout_below="@+id/getpage"
        android:layout_centerHorizontal="true"
        android:padding="@dimen/padding_medium"
        android:text="Click to retrieve webpage and display on separate screen."
        tools:context=".MainActivity" />
```

```
    <WebView
        android:id="@+id/website"
        android:layout_width="500dp"
        android:layout_height="500dp"
        android:layout_below="@+id/getpageforintent"
        android:layout_centerHorizontal="true"
        android:padding="@dimen/padding_medium"
        android:text="@string/hello_world"
        tools:context=".MainActivity" />
```

```
</RelativeLayout>
```

What follows is the XML file for the browser screen. It contains nothing but the format for the single WebView object.

```
<?xml version="1.0" encoding="utf-8"?>
<LinearLayout xmlns:android="http://schemas.android.com/apk/res/android"
    android:layout_width="match_parent"
    android:layout_height="match_parent"
    android:orientation="vertical" >

    <WebView
        android:id="@+id/fullpagewebsite"
        android:layout_width="match_parent"
        android:layout_height="match_parent" />
```

```
</LinearLayout>
```

Next, you will find the source code for the main activity and the full-screen browser activity. Remember to look for the bundling and unbundling of the web page uniform resource locator (URL).

```
package com.sheusi.clientserver;

import android.os.Bundle;
import android.app.Activity;
import android.view.Menu;
import android.view.MenuItem;
import android.view.View;
import android.support.v4.app.NavUtils;
import android.webkit.*;
import android.widget.*;
import android.content.Intent;

public class MainActivity extends Activity {
    WebView website = null;
    Button getpage = null;
    Button getpageforintent = null;
    EditText urlrequest = null;
```

```java
@Override
public void onCreate(Bundle savedInstanceState) {
    super.onCreate(savedInstanceState);
    setContentView(R.layout.activity_main);
    website = (WebView) findViewById(R.id.website);
    getpage = (Button) findViewById(R.id.getpage);
    getpageforintent = (Button) findViewById(R.id.getpageforintent);
    urlrequest = (EditText) findViewById(R.id.urlrequest);
    getpage.setOnClickListener(new View.OnClickListener() {
        public void onClick(View v) {
            website.getSettings().setJavaScriptEnabled(true);
            String myurl = urlrequest.getText().toString();
            if (!myurl.contains("http://"))
                myurl = "http://" + myurl;
            website.loadUrl(myurl);
        }
    });
    getpageforintent.setOnClickListener(new View.OnClickListener() {
        public void onClick(View v) {
            String myurl = urlrequest.getText().toString();
            if (!myurl.contains("http://"))
                myurl = "http://" + myurl;
            Intent myIntent = new Intent(MainActivity.this
                    .getApplicationContext(), WebIntent.class);
            myIntent.putExtra("payload", myurl);
            startActivity(myIntent);
        }
    });
}// ends onCreate
public void onStop(){
super.onStop();
this.finish();
}

@Override
public boolean onCreateOptionsMenu(Menu menu) {
    getMenuInflater().inflate(R.menu.activity_main, menu);
    return true;
}

}
```

Following is the brief code for the second activity. It pulls the web page URL from the bundle and uses it to load the WebView object.

```
package com.sheusi.clientserver;

import android.app.Activity;
import android.os.Bundle;
import android.webkit.*;

public class WebIntent extends Activity{
WebView fullpagewebsite=null;
public void onCreate(Bundle savedInstanceState){
    super.onCreate(savedInstanceState);
        setContentView(R.layout.browse);
    Bundle tobedisplayed=this.getIntent().getExtras();
    String pageaddress=tobedisplayed.getString("payload");
    fullpagewebsite=(WebView)findViewById(R.id.fullpagewebsite);
    fullpagewebsite.getSettings().setJavaScriptEnabled(true);
    fullpagewebsite.loadUrl(pageaddress);
}
}
```

The running application using the in-screen browser should look like Figure 6.3.

Figure 6.3
Running client-server application using the in-screen browser on the Toshiba Thrive tablet.
Source: Google.

Recall that a web page is essentially a text file with specific content, namely HTML, and that it only appears as a web page when it is interpreted and rendered in a browser. The fact that a web page is formatted as such has nothing to do with the way it is transported. There is no reason that a text file, XML file, or image file cannot be transported using the same techniques. For the following modification of the application we just covered, I loaded the basic Miranda Rights from Wikipedia.org on my web server at Fleamobile.com. The file is plain text and is appropriately called `miranda.txt`. I chose the Rights because they have meaning as plain text (a web page usually doesn't mean much as plain text), they are brief, and they can be useful, although one hopes to never need them. We will modify the previous application by substituting the in-screen `WebView` with an `EditText` field and use it to display the downloaded text.

Replace the `WebView` in your main XML file with the following element.

```
<EditText
        android:id="@+id/website"
        android:layout_width="match_parent"
        android:layout_height="500dp"
        android:layout_below="@+id/getpageforintent"
        android:layout_centerHorizontal="true"
        android:padding="@dimen/padding_medium"
        tools:context=".MainActivity" />
```

To download a file using a URL connection, we must run the process in a separate thread. To do this, I created an inner class that extends the Java `Thread` class to deal with the download. The constructor for the thread takes the target URL (the web address combined with the name of the file to be downloaded) as its sole argument. As the text is downloaded, it fills a `StringBuffer` object that is later returned to the button's `onClick( )` method. Once the download is complete and the `StringBuffer` is returned to the `onClick( )` method, it can be displayed in any widget capable of displaying text, saved to a file, or both.

There are occasions when conditions warrant that the application be patient about downloading from a URL, such as if the connection is weak or the server is busy. If the programmer assesses that such a thing is possible, he may want to set an allowed timeout period for the connection before the application attempts to move on without the download. To do this, he would use the `setConnectTimeout( )` method of the `URLConnection` class with an allowable number of milliseconds as the argument. If the connection is not made in the allowable time, however, the method will fail and cause a `SocketTimeoutException`, which must be handled by the application in some elegant fashion.

Another timing issue to address is that the code in the onClick( ) method must wait for the downloading thread to finish before it can carry on with the business of retrieving the StringBuffer and using it. To do this, we use the join( ) method of the thread we created and instantiated to do the download.

One thing to note is that for convenience sake, I hard-coded the actual filename of the download (miranda.txt) and appended it to the URL to keep the user interface consistent and allow the full-screen browser choice to continue to function properly. The programmer would have to address how the filename should be specified in his adaptation of the application. The revised code for the main activity appears here.

```java
package com.sheusi.clientserver;

import android.os.Bundle;
import android.app.Activity;
import android.view.Menu;
import android.view.MenuItem;
import android.view.View;
import android.support.v4.app.NavUtils;
import android.widget.*;
import android.content.Intent;
import java.net.*;
import java.io.*;
import android.util.Log;

public class MainActivity extends Activity {
    EditText website = null;
    Button getpage = null;
    Button getpageforintent = null;
    EditText urlrequest = null;

    @Override
    public void onCreate(Bundle savedInstanceState) {
        super.onCreate(savedInstanceState);
        setContentView(R.layout.activity_main);
        website = (EditText) findViewById(R.id.website);
        getpage = (Button) findViewById(R.id.getpage);
        getpageforintent = (Button) findViewById(R.id.getpageforintent);
        urlrequest = (EditText) findViewById(R.id.urlrequest);

        getpage.setOnClickListener(new View.OnClickListener() {
            public void onClick(View v) {

                Object lock = new Object();
                String myurl = urlrequest.getText().toString();
                if (!myurl.contains("http://"))
                    myurl = "http://" + myurl;
```

```
                    myurl = myurl + "/miranda.txt";
                    Background b = new Background(myurl);
                    b.start();
                    // the following waits for download to finish
                    try {
                           b.join();
                    } catch (InterruptedException ie) {
                    }
                    StringBuffer sb = b.retrieveBuffer();
                    website.setText(sb.toString());
              }// ends onClick( )
        });

        getpageforintent.setOnClickListener(new View.OnClickListener() {
              public void onClick(View v) {

                    String myurl = urlrequest.getText().toString();
                    if (!myurl.contains("http://"))
                          myurl = "http://" + myurl;

                    Intent myIntent = new Intent(MainActivity.this
                                .getApplicationContext(), WebIntent.class);
                    myIntent.putExtra("payload", myurl);
                    startActivity(myIntent);
              }
        });
}// ends onCreate

private class Background extends Thread {
      String theurl = "";
      StringBuffer localsb;

      public Background(String myurl) {

            theurl = myurl;

      }

      public StringBuffer retrieveBuffer() {

            return localsb;
      }

      public void run() {

            try {

                  localsb = new StringBuffer();
                  URL docsource = new URL(theurl);
                  URLConnection con = docsource.openConnection();
                  //con.setConnectTimeout(1000); //optional
```

```
                    BufferedReader br = new BufferedReader(new InputStreamReader(
                            con.getInputStream()));
                    String line = "";
                    while ((line = br.readLine()) != null) {
                        localsb.append(line + "\n");
                    }
                    br.close();
                } catch (MalformedURLException murle) {
                    Log.e("error", "bad url");
                } catch (IOException ioe) {
                    Log.e("error", "bad i/o");
                } catch (Exception e) {
                    Log.e("error", "some other error");
                }
            }// ends run()
        }// ends inner class
        public void onStop(){
super.onStop();
this.finish();
}

    @Override
    public boolean onCreateOptionsMenu(Menu menu) {
        getMenuInflater().inflate(R.menu.activity_main, menu);
        return true;
    }

}
```

The retrieved StringBuffer object containing the text file contents can be stored to a file for later use. This might be valuable, for instance, if the latest version of an updated file is not available from a server at run-time, and a slightly aged version might do. The following code can be used to save it to the application's default storage directory.

```
try{
    File f = new File(MainActivity.this.getApplicationContext()
            .getFilesDir() + "/myrights.txt");   //Target filename hard-coded here
    BufferedWriter bw = new BufferedWriter( new FileWriter(f));
    bw.write(sb.toString());
    bw.close();
}catch(IOException ioe){
    Log.i("info", "couldn't save the file");
}
```

The running application should look like Figure 6.4.

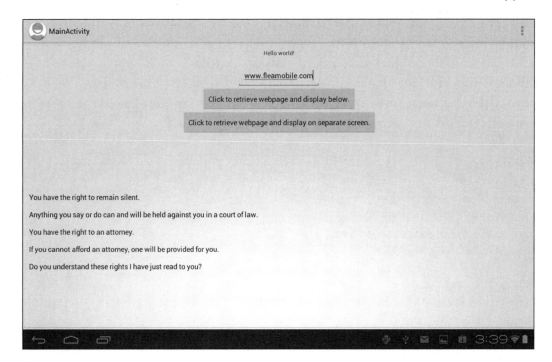

Figure 6.4
Client-server application displaying retrieved text file on Toshiba Thrive tablet.
Source: Google.

CONNECTION-ORIENTED CLIENT-SERVER APPLICATIONS

Sometimes an enterprise application may include running server applications to support devices in the field. Instances include returning data based on a query to an enterprise database and posting data from the device to an enterprise database. Connected-oriented communications are also useful when data has to travel back and forth between the device and the server, connecting with the server-side application to accomplish a useful purpose.

Connection-oriented network communications are conducted with the establishment of a socket between the device and the server, consisting of an IP address and a port number. The port numbers used by in-house applications are normally in the range from 49152 to 65535. The port number is set on the server-side application, so the client application must know the appropriate port number at design time or at least be able to set it at run-time.

Design of connection-oriented applications for the Android device is relatively simple and uses the java.net package classes. The bulk of the work generally falls on the server-side application, because this is where the custom processing normally takes place. Applications on the server side can be written in any number of languages, including Java, and can be run in the background on the server. Just remember that if you intend to run an application in the background on any machine, don't write it in such a way that it writes to the standard output. Following is a simple server-side application written in Java that receives a text string from a remote client (such as an Android device), attaches a trailer to the original message, and sends it back to the device it came from. We will set the port number at 50000.

```java
import java.io.*;
import java.net.*;
import java.util.*;
public class SimpleJavaServer {
    public static final int PORT=50000;
    public static void main(String args[]){
        new SimpleJavaServer().doIt();
    }
    public void doIt(){
        String received="";
        try{
            ServerSocket ss = new ServerSocket( PORT );
            while( true ){
                Socket sock = ss.accept();
                BufferedReader in =
new BufferedReader(new InputStreamReader(
sock.getInputStream() ) );
                received=in.readLine();
                System.out.println(received);
                OutputStreamWriter out =
new OutputStreamWriter(
sock.getOutputStream() );
                BufferedWriter bw=new BufferedWriter(out);
                bw.write(received +" received by server \n");
                    bw.flush();
            }
        } catch( Exception e ){
                e.printStackTrace();
        }
    }
}
```

Our application on the Android tablet just needs an EditText field to enter text to be sent to the server, a button to send the data, and another EditText field to receive the response. Again, the Android system starting with 3.0 requires that network connections be done in a separate thread, so we will use a class structure similar to the previous application example. You will notice in the Background Class definition that a two-second (2000 millisecond) timeout is allowed for contacting the server, done on this line.

```
s.connect(sa, 2000);
```

The full source code for the client-server application using a socket follows.

```java
package com.sheusi.statefulapp;

import android.app.Activity;
import android.os.Bundle;
import android.widget.*;
import android.view.*;
import java.net.*;
import java.io.*;

public class MainActivity extends Activity {
    /** Called when the activity is first created. */
    EditText stringout = null;
    EditText stringback = null;
    Button send = null;

    @Override
    public void onCreate(Bundle savedInstanceState) {
        super.onCreate(savedInstanceState);
        setContentView(R.layout.activity_main);
        stringout = (EditText) findViewById(R.id.stringout);
        stringback = (EditText) findViewById(R.id.stringback);
        send = (Button) findViewById(R.id.send);
        send.setOnClickListener(new View.OnClickListener() {
            public void onClick(View v) {
                Background b = new Background(stringout.getText().toString());
                b.start();
                // the following waits for download to finish
                try {
                    b.join();
                } catch (InterruptedException ie) {
                }
                stringback.setText(b.retrieveResponse());
            }
        });
    }// ends onCreate()

    private class Background extends Thread {
        String textout;
        StringBuffer sb = null;

        public Background(String textout) {
            this.textout = textout;
```

```
        }
        public String retrieveResponse() {
            return sb.toString();
        }
        public void run() {
            try {
                sb = new StringBuffer();
                InetSocketAddress sa = new InetSocketAddress("184.106.98.114",
                    50000);
                Socket s = new Socket();
                s.connect(sa, 2000);
                OutputStreamWriter osw = new OutputStreamWriter(
                    s.getOutputStream());
                osw.write(textout + "\n");
                osw.flush();
                InputStreamReader isr = new InputStreamReader(
                    s.getInputStream());
                BufferedReader br = new BufferedReader(isr);
                sb.append(br.readLine());
                br.close();
                s.close();
            } catch (SocketTimeoutException ste) {
                sb.append("attempt to connect timed out");
            } catch (IOException ioe) {
                sb.append("Couldn't connect with server");
            }
        }// ends run()
    }// ends inner class
}
```

The running application will look like Figure 6.5.

The next chapter concentrates on sending and receiving data from a server through a variety of methods and formats, some of which we touched on in this chapter. To round out this chapter, we will do an exercise that utilizes the principles and methods we covered here. The exercise is entertaining, if not especially useful. We will construct a client-server application, both client side and server side, in which a tablet client will transmit a block of text to the server and retrieve a QR code representing the text. To cover both styles we have seen—stateful and stateless—we will send the text through a socketed connection and retrieve the QR image through the web server. The application on the server side will receive the text, convert it, and place the image in the server's web page directory. The server-side application, like the last

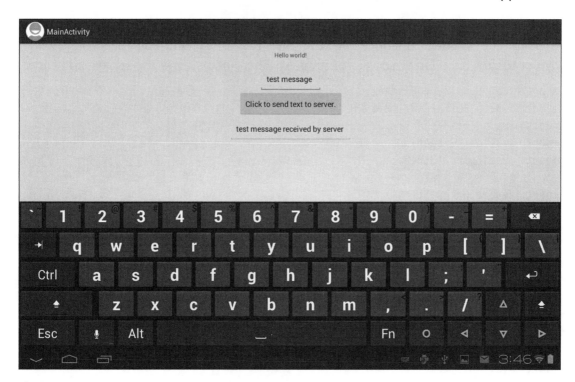

Figure 6.5
Client-server application on Toshiba Thrive sending and receiving text through a socket.
Source: Google.

one, is written in Java. The source code is included in this text for your curiosity and is not intended for use on a handheld Android device; it is strictly server side. The code for the construction of the QR symbol is done with the Zebra Crossing open source library. You can find details on this at http://code.google.com/p/zxing/. To build this server, you must download the libraries and add them to the build path of the project.

Other than the actual processing of the symbol, the rest of the server side is basically a lot of file handling and storing. The server waits for a message to arrive on the assigned port and parses the message, looking for "qr" as the first two characters. If those characters are present, the server uses the balance of the text string to produce a 500-pixel-by-500-pixel QR code. Instead of sending the code back down the socket's data stream, it stores the symbol in the web page directory and waits for a request from the Android device that submitted the text in the first place. A single name is used repeatedly to store the QR image because the server side was originally written as a demonstration that never would see much traffic; hence, there was no likelihood that two users would cross messages and symbols. You might notice the use of a `StringBuilder` object instead of a `StringBuffer`; I used it because it is more efficient. You might also notice that the path names are unusual; the program was written to run on a Linux server running Apache. Following is the server-side code.

```java
import java.io.BufferedReader;
import java.io.BufferedWriter;
import java.io.FileReader;
import java.io.IOException;
import java.io.InputStream;
import java.io.InputStreamReader;
import java.io.OutputStream;
import java.io.OutputStreamWriter;
import java.io.File;
import java.io.FileWriter;
import java.io.StringWriter;
import java.io.UnsupportedEncodingException;
import java.net.ServerSocket;
import java.net.Socket;
import com.google.zxing.qrcode.*;
import java.nio.charset.*;
import java.nio.ByteBuffer;
import java.nio.CharBuffer;
import java.io.*;
import com.google.zxing.common.BitMatrix;
import javax.imageio.ImageIO;
import java.awt.image.BufferedImage;

public class QRServer {
    ServerSocket ss;
    Socket s1 = null;

    public void startUp() {
        try {
            ss = new ServerSocket(50000);
        } catch (IOException ioe) {
            ioe.printStackTrace();
        }
        while (true) {
            try {
                s1 = ss.accept();
                InputStream is = s1.getInputStream();
                InputStreamReader isr = new InputStreamReader(is);
                OutputStream os = s1.getOutputStream();
                OutputStreamWriter osr = new OutputStreamWriter(os);
                BufferedWriter bw = new BufferedWriter(osr);
```

```
                BufferedReader br = new BufferedReader(isr);
                String greeting = br.readLine();
                String[] newrecord;
                newrecord = greeting.split(":");
                // just look for the greeting here; if first word is QR, make
                // the pic and send it.
                if (newrecord[0].equals("qr")) {
                    try {
                        File f = new File("/var/www/html/qr.txt");
                        FileWriter fr = new FileWriter(f);
                        BufferedWriter bwriter = new BufferedWriter(fr);
                        newrecord[1] = newrecord[1].replace("~", "\n");
                        newrecord[1] = newrecord[1].replace(";", ",");
                        bwriter.write(newrecord[1]);
                        bwriter.close();
                        storeTheImage();
                    } catch (IOException ioe) {
                    }
                } // ends if
            } catch (Exception e) {
            }
        }// ends while
    }// ends method

    public void storeTheImage() {
        Charset charset = Charset.forName("UTF-8");
        CharsetEncoder encoder = charset.newEncoder();
        byte[] b = null;
        ByteBuffer bbuf = null;
        File f = new File("/var/www/html/qr.txt");
        String thetext = null;
        try {
            FileReader fr = new FileReader(f);
            BufferedReader br = new BufferedReader(fr);
            String line = null;
            char[] myarray = null;
            StringBuilder stringBuilder = new StringBuilder((int) f.length());
            while ((line = br.readLine()) != null) {
                stringBuilder.append(line);
                stringBuilder.append("\n");
            }
            thetext = stringBuilder.toString();
            br.close();

            myarray = thetext.toCharArray();
```

```
            bbuf = encoder.encode(CharBuffer.wrap(myarray, 0, myarray.length));
            b = new byte[bbuf.remaining()];
            bbuf.get(b);

        } catch (CharacterCodingException cce) {

        } catch (Exception e) {

        }

        String data = null;
        try {
            data = new String(b, "UTF-8");
        } catch (UnsupportedEncodingException e) {

        }

        // get a byte matrix for the data
        BitMatrix matrix = null;
        int h = 500;
        int w = 500;
        QRCodeWriter writer = new QRCodeWriter();
        try {
            matrix = writer.encode(data,
                        com.google.zxing.BarcodeFormat.QR_CODE, w, h);
        } catch (com.google.zxing.WriterException e) {

        }

        String filePath = "/var/www/html/qr_png.png";
        File file = new File(filePath);
        try {
            MatrixToImageWriter.writeToFile(matrix, "PNG", file);
        } catch (IOException e) {

        }
    }

    public static void main(String[] args) {
        // TODO Auto-generated method stub
        QRServer f = new QRServer();
        f.startUp();
    }
}

final class MatrixToImageWriter {

    private static final int BLACK = 0xFF000000;
    private static final int WHITE = 0xFFFFFFFF;

    private MatrixToImageWriter() {
    }
```

```java
/**
 * Renders a {@link BitMatrix} as an image, where "false" bits are rendered
 * as white, and "true" bits are rendered as black.
 */
public static BufferedImage toBufferedImage(BitMatrix matrix) {
    int width = matrix.getWidth();
    int height = matrix.getHeight();
    BufferedImage image = new BufferedImage(width, height,
            BufferedImage.TYPE_INT_ARGB);
    for (int x = 0; x < width; x++) {
        for (int y = 0; y < height; y++) {
            image.setRGB(x, y, matrix.get(x, y) ? BLACK : WHITE);
        }
    }
    return image;
}

public static void writeToFile(BitMatrix matrix, String format, File file)
        throws IOException {
    BufferedImage image = toBufferedImage(matrix);
    ImageIO.write(image, format, file);
}

public static void writeToStream(BitMatrix matrix, String format,
        OutputStream stream) throws IOException {
    BufferedImage image = toBufferedImage(matrix);
    ImageIO.write(image, format, stream);
}
}
```

If you don't have access to an outside server, you could run both the client side and the server side on the same machine with a little bit of work. Because you are already using Eclipse, you need only to create a Java project instead of an Android project. You would use the loopback IP address 127.0.0.1 on both the client and the server sides. To create a standalone Java application in Eclipse, you would right-click on the project title in the Package Explorer, choose Export from the menu, and then choose Runnable JAR File from the panel that follows. Once you have done that, the server application can run on its own without Eclipse. If you are developing on a Windows machine, be sure to replace the file path and name with the correct Windows syntax, such as c:\\mypath\\myfilename.ext. The application we are working on requires a web server. Windows comes with its own, called IIS (Internet Information Services). Although it's not industrial grade, it is certainly sufficient for testing applications such as this. You can find details on how to configure and start IIS on a Windows machine at http://support.microsoft.com/kb/323972.

On the client side, we continue to use a separate thread to contact the server and submit text for conversion. In the listing of the code, the server IP address is expressed as 111.222.333.444 and would have to be replaced with a legitimate server IP. No special management of QR codes is necessary on the client side because the code is just retrieved as an image to be displayed in a WebView. Remember to add the Internet permission to your manifest file. The code listing for the client side appears next.

```java
package com.example.qrretreiver;

import android.app.Activity;
import android.content.Context;
import java.io.*;
import java.net.*;
import android.util.*;
import android.os.Bundle;
import android.widget.*;
import android.view.*;

import android.webkit.*;

public class MainActivity extends Activity {
    WebView iv = null;
    Button qrb = null;
    EditText et = null;
    Context myContext = null;

    public void onCreate(Bundle savedInstanceState) {
        super.onCreate(savedInstanceState);
        setContentView(R.layout.activity_main);
        myContext = this.getApplicationContext();
        iv = (WebView) findViewById(R.id.qrview);
        et = (EditText) findViewById(R.id.et);
        qrb = (Button) findViewById(R.id.qrb);

        qrb.setOnClickListener(new View.OnClickListener() {

            @Override
            public void onClick(View v) {
                Background b = new Background(et.getText().toString());
                b.start();
                // the following waits for download to finish
                try {
                    b.join();
                    Thread.sleep(500); // give server a chance to create QR
                } catch (InterruptedException ie) {
                }
```

```
                    iv.loadUrl("http://184.106.98.114/qr_png.png");
                }
            });
    }// ends onCreate

    private class Background extends Thread {
        String datastring = null;

        public Background(String message) {
            datastring = message;

        }

        public void run() {
            try {
                Socket client = new Socket("184.106.98.114", 6600);
                OutputStreamWriter osw = new OutputStreamWriter(
                        client.getOutputStream());
                BufferedWriter bw = new BufferedWriter(osw);
                // the character replacements below will be reversed on the
                // server side
                datastring = datastring.replace(",", ";");
                datastring = datastring.replace("\n", "~");
                Log.i("qr", datastring);
                bw.write("qr:" + datastring + "\n");
                bw.flush();
                client.close();
            } catch (IOException ioe) {

                Log.i("info", "connection refused");

            }
        }// ends run
    }// ends inner class

}// ends class
```

You can save the QR code to a file for use later instead of simply displaying it as a web page. Once you have saved it as a file, you can view the code in an ImageView object at a later time, transfer it to another device, or use it any way you might want to use a QR file. The method listed next could be added to a thread class of its own or shared with another I/O transfer. In the example given, a timeout allowance of 3000 milliseconds is given; this is probably too liberal and could be shortened. The URL for the web address and the image filename is supplied as the argument to the method, so it doesn't appear literally anywhere in the code. The openFileOutput( ) method of the Context class manages the file path for the file storage, so only the chosen filename is necessary. The method also manages the visibility for the file. The possibilities are as follows. Of course, MODE_APPEND would not be an appropriate alternative here.

Here are the possible modes for opening files.

1. MODE_APPEND

2. MODE_PRIVATE

3. MODE_WORLD_READABLE

4. MODE_WORLD_WRITEABLE

The code listed next takes the QR image straight from the input stream and sends it directly to the file specified in the code. Assuming that no exception has occurred and the image file was successfully downloaded and stored, the file can then be opened and displayed in an ImageView object.

```java
public void storeLogoToFile(String u) {

        try {
                URL source = new URL(u);
                URLConnection ucon = source.openConnection();
                ucon.setConnectTimeout(3000);
                ucon.setReadTimeout(3000);
                InputStream is = (InputStream) source.getContent();

                int bytesRead;
                ByteArrayOutputStream output = new ByteArrayOutputStream();

                while ((bytesRead = is.read()) != -1) {
                    output.write(bytesRead);
                }
                FileOutputStream fos = this.getApplicationContext().openFileOutput(
                        "qr_png.png", MODE_WORLD_READABLE);

                output.writeTo(fos);
                fos.close();
        } catch (SocketTimeoutException stoe) {
                Log.i("info", stoe.getMessage());
        } catch (MalformedURLException male) {
                Log.i("info", male.getMessage());
        } catch (UnknownHostException e) {
                Log.i("info", e.getMessage());
        } catch (IOException ioe) {
                Log.i("info", ioe.getMessage());
```

```
    } catch (Exception e) {
            Log.i("info", "some other error");
    }


}
```

The running application should look like Figure 6.6.

Figure 6.6
Application receiving a QR code running on a Toshiba Thrive tablet.
Source: Google.

SUMMARY OF KEY CONCEPTS

■ Android devices allow some type of connectivity, via either wireless networking or a data plan through a cell network provider. Connections can be stateless or stateful. A stateless connection waits for a request, sends a response, and waits for the next request. It doesn't wait for an acknowledgement that the response was received. A stateful connection, on the other hand, maintains communication between the two parties through a system of requests, responses, and acknowledgements as long as the connection is not cancelled by one side or the other.

■ Stateful connections are done through a socket, which is a combination of an IP address and a port number. The port number distinguishes one connection from others that may be in place. Using a stateful connection, two-way traffic can be conducted, such as might be necessary for a database query and response.

■ Port numbers are 16-bit values, meaning there are 2 to the power of 16, or 65,536, possible values. Some port numbers are reserved for specific common purposes; port 80, for example, is reserved for web traffic. Values from 49,152 to 65,535 are commonly used for in-house applications.

■ Web page requests are done through stateless connections. The Android system and software development toolkit allows us to receive and display data through the web in two ways: using the web browser through an intent, or displaying data within the application using a WebView widget. The WebView is a convenient way to display data from a stateless source where no interaction is required, such as an image or a static web page.

REVIEW QUESTIONS

You can find the answers to these review questions in the appendix at the end of the book.

1. For networking applications, the following permission must be included in the manifest file.

   _____

2. The WebView widget requires which package to be included in the import statements?

   _____

3. When using the setConnectTimeout( ) method of the URLConnection class, we must manage the following checked exception.

   _____

4. Port numbers used by in-house applications should be between _____ and _____.

5. The port number is set in code on the _____ side of a client-server application.

6. Connection timeouts are set using what unit of time?

   _____

7. Only files with the extension HTML or HTM can be viewed in a `WebView` object, true or false?

   _____

8. URI is an acronym for _____.

9. Only Android services and other installed applications can be used by an application through intents, true or false?

   _____

10. If a server-side application is to be used by an Android device, it must be written specifically for Android clients, true or false?

    _____

SUGGESTED PROJECTS

- Write an application that allows a user to enter a search parameter in a text field. Then combine the contents of the text field with the URL for a search engine such as Google and return the results to a `WebView` object.

- Discover your development computer's inside address. It will likely begin with 127 or 10. Write and execute a server-side program on your development computer, similar to the example in the chapter. Next, write and execute a simple client-side application for your Android device that targets the server device using its internal IP address. See if the two devices connect.

- If your development machine is so equipped, start its web service. Enter and deploy one of the web service examples in this chapter on your Android device (or emulator) and target the internal IP address of your development machine. See if your device displays a web page from the development machine.

- Research, compare, and contrast stateful and stateless connections. Determine where they are commonly used and what their advantages and disadvantages are. Discover and record the port numbers used for common Internet services such as the World Wide Web, email, and FTP.

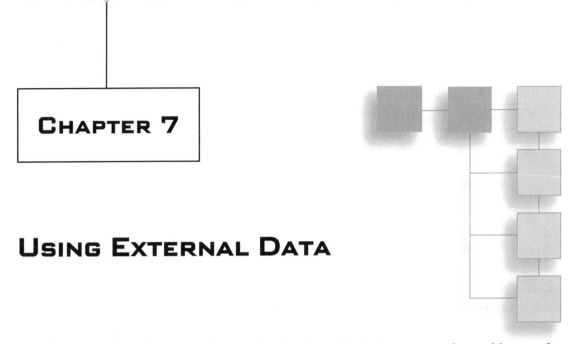

CHAPTER 7

USING EXTERNAL DATA

In Chapter 3, "Databases in the Application," we looked at using data tables on the tablet or device itself, but it is likely that any useful application will need to use information that an outside source provides. This could be data on a company or enterprise server most likely managed by its own DBMS or data provided by a multitude of external sources such as the Google application programming interfaces (APIs). One current limitation in the Android operating system is the lack of availability of drivers for various server-based database management systems such as MySQL. To provide data to a client device in the field, handset, tablet, or otherwise, we can run a dedicated application on the server that exists solely to respond to queries (I do this quite often), or we can do essentially the same job with a PHP or similar script on a web server. We covered connection to the server by the client device in the previous chapter. Now we will look at the data formatting.

Data can be returned to the device using various plain text encodings such as CSV (comma-separated values), XML, and JSON (JavaScript Object Notation). CSV has its disadvantages. One such disadvantage is that it does not support hierarchical data. We will see an example of hierarchical data later in this chapter in the address data we will retrieve from Google. Another disadvantage is the use of double quotes, which are used to enclose data fields but might be found in the text of the field. This requires special handling. Yet another disadvantage is handling of fields with missing data.

To avoid these difficulties and ambiguities, a standardized structured format is preferred when transferring data. Two popular methods that have packages included in the standard Android development toolkit are XML and JSON.

Just briefly, XML, or Extensible Markup Language, is visibly similar to HTML (Hypertext Markup Language). However, while XML uses a system of opening and closing tags to define elements like HTML, XML element names and structures are defined by the programmer. XML is versatile; just about any structured data—such as records from a relational database, a document, an email, and even a vector graphic—can be structured in XML. However, to serve as a universal data transfer structure whose content is expected to be read by any program coded to anticipate a certain structure, the XML data must be correctly structured according to the specifications. In other words, the document must be "well formed." A document consists of a prologue and a single root element. The root element has an opening and a closing tag. Each logical record has an opening and a closing tag, and there can be multiples of these pairs inside the root element. Tag pairs cannot overlap, though. Inside the logical record's tags, the logical fields are defined as elements with their own opening and closing tag pairs with the actual data placed between the tags. The data is all plain text and numeric values needed to be converted on the receiving side. For fields having composite data, such as a name field with separate entries for first and last, "nested" elements can be used. Comments can also be included, using an XML-defined syntax. What follows is a sample of an XML file.

```
<?xml version="1.0"?>                          prolog
                                               space left on purpose
<person>                                       begin root element
<name>
<first>Jim</first>
<last>Sheusi</last>
</name>
<occupation>College Professor</occupation>
<position>Dept. Chair</position>
</person>                                       end root element
```

Comments are enclosed with the following tag pair:

```
<!--        -->
```

Attributes, which provide additional information about a particular element aside from its actual data, are presented as a name-value pair with the value enclosed in double quotation marks or single quotation marks and included in the opening tag. For example

```
<book  binding="paperback">The Title</book>
```

Of course, XML should come as no surprise to an Android programmer because screen layouts and manifest files are laid out in XML format!

Although the XML document must be formed perfectly, the burden for the layout is managed by the classes that are included in the application's packages. The programmer is responsible for assembling its content correctly if the data is going out in XML format, or interpreting the content correctly if the data is coming in.

The first application we will look at is a simple one that uses a PHP script on the server side to send an XML listing of member information based on the submission of an email address. You will recall from our exercise in Chapter 3 that we built an internal database and screen that we could use to maintain a club membership, and we used the email address as our unique identifier. On the device side, we will use the basic screen layout from that application, but we will change the mechanics in the program to poll a remote server for the member data based on submission of the unique identifier. Because we are concentrating on the device side of this "client-server" application, the server side will "simulate" the database search and just return a set of fixed values in response to the submission of *any* value for an email address. In fact, we can use the same PHP server-side script for the upcoming JSON version of the application. The server-side PHP script follows.

```php
<?php


//static data used in response
$response_data = array(
     "firstname"=>"John",
     "lastname"=>"Doe",
     "address"=>"101 Main Street",
     "city"=>"Springfield",
     "state"=>"MA",
     "zip"=>"12345",
     "phone"=>"508-867-5309"
     );


if ($_REQUEST["encoding"] == "json") {
     echo json_encode($response_data); //requires PHP 5.2 or above
} else {
     $xml = new SimpleXMLElement('<person/>');
     foreach ($response_data as $key=>$value) //loop over all elements, add to SimpleXML
     object
          $xml->addChild($key,$value);
     echo $xml->asXML();
}
?>
```

Of course, use of this code on the server assumes that the server is properly configured, but it is easy to figure out what is happening. As stated, the client side on the
device is configured similarly to our membership database. The main.xml file is only
slightly changed, because some of the buttons will now be unused. I also added an
EditText field at the bottom of the screen to display the raw data as either XML or
JSON, depending on which version of the program we are running. The file listing
follows.

```xml
<?xml version="1.0" encoding="utf-8"?>
<LinearLayout xmlns:android="http://schemas.android.com/apk/res/android"
    android:layout_width="fill_parent"
    android:layout_height="fill_parent"
    android:orientation="vertical" >

    <TextView
        android:layout_width="fill_parent"
        android:layout_height="wrap_content"
        android:text="Android Developer's Association" />

    <TableLayout
        android:layout_width="fill_parent"
        android:layout_height="wrap_content" >

        <TableRow
            android:layout_width="wrap_content"
            android:layout_height="wrap_content" >

            <TextView
                android:layout_width="wrap_content"
                android:layout_height="wrap_content"
                android:layout_weight=".5"
                android:text="Email Address:" />

            <EditText
                android:id="@+id/et_email"
                android:layout_width="wrap_content"
                android:layout_height="wrap_content"
                android:layout_weight=".5"
                android:background="#808080"
                android:text="" />
        </TableRow>

        <TableRow
            android:layout_width="wrap_content"
            android:layout_height="wrap_content" >
```

```
        <Button
            android:id="@+id/retrievebutton"
            android:layout_width="wrap_content"
            android:layout_height="wrap_content"
            android:layout_weight=".5"
            android:text="Retrieve" />
</TableRow>

<TableRow
    android:layout_width="wrap_content"
    android:layout_height="wrap_content" >

    <TextView
        android:layout_width="wrap_content"
        android:layout_height="wrap_content"
        android:layout_weight=".5"
        android:text="First Name:" />

    <EditText
        android:id="@+id/et_fname"
        android:layout_width="wrap_content"
        android:layout_height="wrap_content"
        android:layout_weight=".5"
        android:background="#404040"
        android:text="" />
</TableRow>

<TableRow
    android:layout_width="wrap_content"
    android:layout_height="wrap_content" >

    <TextView
        android:layout_width="wrap_content"
        android:layout_height="wrap_content"
        android:layout_weight=".5"
        android:text="Last Name:" />

    <EditText
        android:id="@+id/et_lname"
        android:layout_width="wrap_content"
        android:layout_height="wrap_content"
        android:layout_weight=".5"
        android:background="#606060"
        android:text="" />
</TableRow>
```

```xml
<TableRow
    android:layout_width="wrap_content"
    android:layout_height="wrap_content" >

    <TextView
        android:layout_width="wrap_content"
        android:layout_height="wrap_content"
        android:layout_weight=".5"
        android:text="Address:" />

    <EditText
        android:id="@+id/et_address"
        android:layout_width="wrap_content"
        android:layout_height="wrap_content"
        android:layout_weight=".5"
        android:background="#404040"
        android:text="" />
</TableRow>

<TableRow
    android:layout_width="wrap_content"
    android:layout_height="wrap_content" >

    <TextView
        android:layout_width="wrap_content"
        android:layout_height="wrap_content"
        android:layout_weight=".5"
        android:text="City:" />

    <EditText
        android:id="@+id/et_city"
        android:layout_width="wrap_content"
        android:layout_height="wrap_content"
        android:layout_weight=".5"
        android:background="#606060"
        android:text="" />
</TableRow>

<TableRow
    android:layout_width="wrap_content"
    android:layout_height="wrap_content" >

    <TextView
        android:layout_width="wrap_content"
        android:layout_height="wrap_content"
        android:layout_weight=".5"
        android:text="State:" />
```

```
        <EditText
            android:id="@+id/et_state"
            android:layout_width="wrap_content"
            android:layout_height="wrap_content"
            android:layout_weight=".5"
            android:background="#404040"
            android:text="" />
    </TableRow>

    <TableRow
        android:layout_width="wrap_content"
        android:layout_height="wrap_content" >

        <TextView
            android:layout_width="wrap_content"
            android:layout_height="wrap_content"
            android:layout_weight=".5"
            android:text="Zip:" />

        <EditText
            android:id="@+id/et_zip"
            android:layout_width="wrap_content"
            android:layout_height="wrap_content"
            android:layout_weight=".5"
            android:background="#606060"
            android:text="" />
    </TableRow>

    <TableRow
        android:layout_width="wrap_content"
        android:layout_height="wrap_content" >

        <TextView
            android:layout_width="wrap_content"
            android:layout_height="wrap_content"
            android:layout_weight=".5"
            android:text="Phone:" />

        <EditText
            android:id="@+id/et_phone"
            android:layout_width="wrap_content"
            android:layout_height="wrap_content"
            android:layout_weight=".5"
            android:background="#404040"
            android:text="" />
    </TableRow>
```

```
<TableRow
    android:layout_width="wrap_content"
    android:layout_height="wrap_content" >

    <Button
        android:id="@+id/savebutton"
        android:layout_width="wrap_content"
        android:layout_height="wrap_content"
        android:layout_weight=".5"
        android:text="Unused" />

    <Button
        android:id="@+id/clearbutton"
        android:layout_width="wrap_content"
        android:layout_height="wrap_content"
        android:layout_weight=".5"
        android:text="Unused" />

    <Button
        android:id="@+id/deletebutton"
        android:layout_width="wrap_content"
        android:layout_height="wrap_content"
        android:layout_weight=".5"
        android:text="Unused" />

    </TableRow>
</TableLayout>

<EditText
    android:id="@+id/incoming_display"
    android:layout_width="match_parent"
    android:layout_height="wrap_content"
    android:text="" />

</LinearLayout>
```

Note

_____

You need to give Internet permission in your manifest file as usual.

━━━

In the source code for the application, we need to run a separate thread for network input/output (I/O), as we have been doing all along. Also, we will use a StringReader object because the XMLPullParser object can only use a Reader class object as its input. We could use the StreamReader as the XMLPullParser's argument, but then we wouldn't have the opportunity, in this example anyway, to build the display of the actual XML code in the EditText at the bottom of the screen.

At the heart of the application are the `XMLPullParser` and `XMLPullParserFactory` objects that appear in the `Thread` class. They are found in the `org.xmlpull.v1` package that is included in the Android toolkit. This is one of several packages you can use to manage XML files. Another is SAX, which can be found at the website sax.sourceforge.net. I happen to like `XMLPullParser` because it is reasonably easy to use, and it doesn't have to be downloaded separately and added to the application build as an outside package. To add outside packages, incidentally, you would choose Properties under Eclipse's Project menu, choose Java Build Path in the properties, and choose the Libraries tab. In that panel, you would choose Add External JARs on the right side and specify the path to the JAR containing packages you want to use on your development machine.

For convenience, I specified the URL for the data as a literal string. This data may or may not be available when you are reading this, but at least you can see where it could go and what it looks like. If you are writing an application for use for your company or for yourself, this address will likely be within your control or influence, so you could manage it in the same fashion should you choose. If some kind of account authentication is necessary, you can check with your network administrator on how to handle that.

As you can surmise from the code, the `XMLPullParser` class is able to recognize the element tags in the XML file as opening or closing tags and is able to spot the data between the tags. The code has multiple checked exceptions, and you can handle them as you wish: logging messages, controlling the program flow, or whatever you want.

The source code for the XML version appears next. Because the PHP script will handle both XML and JSON returns, you will notice that the script looks for a parameter that specifies either XML or JSON. The parameter is supplied with the URL.

```
package com.sheusi.xmlviaphp;

import android.os.Bundle;
import android.app.Activity;
import android.view.Menu;
import android.view.MenuItem;
import android.support.v4.app.NavUtils;
import org.xmlpull.v1.*;
import java.util.HashMap;
import java.io.*;
import java.net.*;
import android.widget.*;
import android.view.View;
import android.util.Log;
```

```java
public class MainActivity extends Activity {
    EditText email = null;
    EditText lname = null;
    EditText fname = null;
    EditText address = null;
    EditText city = null;
    EditText state = null;
    EditText zip = null;
    EditText phone = null;
    Button retrieve = null;
    EditText icd=null;
    @Override
    public void onCreate(Bundle savedInstanceState) {
        super.onCreate(savedInstanceState);
        setContentView(R.layout.activity_main);
        email = (EditText) findViewById(R.id.et_email);
        lname = (EditText) findViewById(R.id.et_lname);
        fname = (EditText) findViewById(R.id.et_fname);
        address = (EditText) findViewById(R.id.et_address);
        city = (EditText) findViewById(R.id.et_city);
        state = (EditText) findViewById(R.id.et_state);
        zip = (EditText) findViewById(R.id.et_zip);
        phone = (EditText) findViewById(R.id.et_phone);
        retrieve = (Button) findViewById(R.id.retrievebutton);
            icd=(EditText)findViewById(R.id.incoming_display);
        retrieve.setOnClickListener(new View.OnClickListener() {
            public void onClick(View v) {
                Background b = new Background(email.getText().toString());
                b.start();
                // the following waits for download to finish
                try {
                    b.join();
                } catch (InterruptedException ie) {
                }
                HashMap<String, String> hmresponse = b.retrieveResponse();
                Iterator i = hmresponse.keySet().iterator();
                while (i.hasNext()) {
                    String keyvalue = (String) i.next();
                    if (keyvalue.equals("firstname"))
                        fname.setText(hmresponse.get(keyvalue));
                    if (keyvalue.equals("lastname"))
                        lname.setText(hmresponse.get(keyvalue));
```

```
                        if (keyvalue.equals("address"))
                            address.setText(hmresponse.get(keyvalue));
                        if (keyvalue.equals("city"))
                            city.setText(hmresponse.get(keyvalue));
                        if (keyvalue.equals("state"))
                            state.setText(hmresponse.get(keyvalue));
                        // if (keyvalue.equals("zip"))
                        // zip.setText(hmresponse.get(keyvalue));
                        if (keyvalue.equals("phone"))
                            phone.setText(hmresponse.get(keyvalue));
                    }// ends while
                icd.setText(b.retrieveRawData()); //display the raw XML file
                }
        });

    }

    private class Background extends Thread {
        String textout;
        String rawdata="";
        HashMap<String, String> hm = new HashMap<String, String>();

        public Background(String textout) {
            this.textout = textout;
        }

        public HashMap<String, String> retrieveResponse() {
            return hm;
        }
        public String retrieveRawData(){
            return rawdata;
        }

        public void run() {
            getXMLData();
        //     getJSONData();
        }

        public void getJSONData() {
            String querystring =
"http://somewebaddress.com/client/somepath/data.php?encoding=json&"
                    + textout;
            try {
                URL myUrl = new URL(querystring);
                HttpURLConnection myConnection = (HttpURLConnection) myUrl
                    .openConnection();
```

```
            InputStreamReader isr = new InputStreamReader(
                    myConnection.getInputStream(), "UTF-8");
            BufferedReader reader = new BufferedReader(isr);
            StringBuilder sb = new StringBuilder();

            for (String line = null; (line = reader.readLine()) != null;) {
                sb.append(line).append("\n");
            }
            rawdata=sb.toString();
            JSONObject data = new JSONObject(sb.toString()); //outer object
            Iterator keys = data.keys();
            while (keys.hasNext()) {
                while (keys.hasNext()) {
                    String key = (String) keys.next();
                    String value = data.getString(key);
                    hm.put(key, value);
                }
            }
        } catch (JSONException jsone) {
      Log.i("info","json error");
        } catch (MalformedURLException male) {
            Log.i("info","bad URL");
        }

      catch (IOException ioe) {
            Log.i("info","some other error");
        }
    }

    public void getXMLData() {

        String querystring =
"http://tageninformatics.com/client/sheusi/data.php?encoding=xml&"
                + textout;
        try {
            URL myUrl = new URL(querystring);
            HttpURLConnection myConnection = (HttpURLConnection) myUrl
                    .openConnection();
            InputStreamReader isr = new InputStreamReader(
                    myConnection.getInputStream(), "UTF-8");
        BufferedReader br=new BufferedReader(isr);
        String s="";
        StringBuffer sb=new StringBuffer();
        while((s=br.readLine())!=null)
            sb.append(s);
```

```
            rawdata=sb.toString();
                try {

                    XmlPullParserFactory factory = XmlPullParserFactory
                            .newInstance();
                    factory.setNamespaceAware(true);
                    XmlPullParser xpp = factory.newPullParser();
                    StringReader sr=new StringReader(rawdata);
                    xpp.setInput(sr);
                    String currenttag = "";
                    xpp.next(); // skips over the descriptor line in the XML
                            // input
                    int eventType = xpp.getEventType(); // all these ints will
                                                        // appear as symbolic
                                                        // constants
                    while (eventType != XmlPullParser.END_DOCUMENT) {
                        if (eventType == XmlPullParser.START_DOCUMENT) {
                            // do nothing;
                        }
                        if (eventType == XmlPullParser.START_TAG)
                            currenttag = xpp.getName();

                        if (eventType == XmlPullParser.TEXT) {
                            hm.put(currenttag, xpp.getText());

                        }
                        if (eventType == XmlPullParser.END_TAG) {
                            // do nothing
                        }
                        eventType = xpp.next(); // keep going
                    }// ends while

                } catch (XmlPullParserException mppe) {
                }
            } catch (MalformedURLException male) {
            }
            catch (IOException ioe) {
            }

        }// ends run()

    }// ends inner class

    @Override
    public void onStop() {
        super.onStop();
        this.finish();
    }
```

```
    @Override
    public boolean onCreateOptionsMenu(Menu menu) {
        getMenuInflater().inflate(R.menu.activity_main, menu);
        return true;
    }

}
```

When the application is running, you should see a display like the one shown in Figure 7.1.

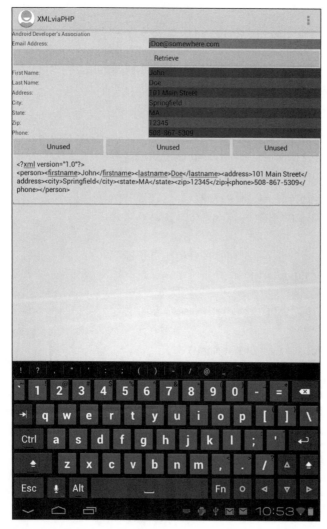

Figure 7.1
Screenshot of Toshiba Thrive running XML from PHP application in portrait orientation.
Source: Google.

The second format used to transmit data, which is becoming increasingly popular, is JSON (JavaScript Object Notation). JSON is an open standard for data exchange. Many consider its advantage over XML to be the fact that there is less overhead to transfer than there is with XML. For instance, a pair of tags might take 20 bytes, whereas the same demarcation can be done in JSON with much less. Instead of using a single root element as XML does, JSON uses a pair of curly braces. Instead of using tags with a value between them to specify a field, JSON uses a name-value pair separated by a colon. The name and value are enclosed in their own quotation marks. What is enclosed in a single pair of curly braces is referred to as an *object*, analogous to what we might refer to as a "record" in a data table.

An array, or series of similar name-value pairs, is demarcated by a pair of square brackets. As an example, let us take the XML example we used earlier and restate it in JSON notation. First, here is the original XML notation.

```xml
<?xml version="1.0"?>

<person>
<name>
    <first>Jim</first>
    <last>Sheusi</last>
</name>
<occupation>College Professor</occupation>
<position>Dept. Chair</position>
</person>
```

Next, here's the same thing using JSON.

```json
{
"name":{
    "first":"Jim",
    "last":"Sheusi
},
 "occupation":"College Professor" ,
 "position":"Dept. Chair"
}
```

Right off the bat, the character count for the JSON version without spaces is 95, versus 159 for the same data in XML. This makes JSON about 50 percent more efficient compared to XML.

To perform the same exercise that we did before only using JSON as our format for receiving the results from the server, we first have to add the following package and class to the source code: `org.json.*` and `java.util.Iterator`.

Next, revise your internal thread class to look like the following.

```java
private class Background extends Thread {
        String textout;
        String rawdata="";
        HashMap<String, String> hm = new HashMap<String, String>();

        public Background(String textout) {
            this.textout = textout;
        }

        public HashMap<String, String> retrieveResponse() {
            return hm;
        }
        public String retrieveRawData(){
            return rawdata;
        }

        public void run() {
           // getXMLData();
        getJSONData();
        }

        public void getJSONData() {
            String querystring =
"http://tageninformatics.com/client/sheusi/data.php?encoding=json&"
                    + textout;
            try {
                URL myUrl = new URL(querystring);
                HttpURLConnection myConnection = (HttpURLConnection) myUrl
                        .openConnection();
                InputStreamReader isr = new InputStreamReader(
                        myConnection.getInputStream(), "UTF-8");
                BufferedReader reader = new BufferedReader(isr);
                StringBuilder sb = new StringBuilder();

                for (String line = null; (line = reader.readLine()) != null;) {
                    sb.append(line).append("\n");
                }
                rawdata=sb.toString();
                JSONObject data = new JSONObject(sb.toString()); //outer object
                Iterator keys = data.keys();
                while (keys.hasNext()) {
                    while (keys.hasNext()) {
                        String key = (String) keys.next();
                        String value = data.getString(key);
```

```
                        hm.put(key, value);
                    }
                }
        } catch (JSONException jsone) {
      Log.i("info","json error");
        } catch (MalformedURLException male) {
            Log.i("info","bad URL");
        }
        catch (IOException ioe) {
            Log.i("info","some other error");
        }
    }
    public void getXMLData() {
        String querystring =
"http://somewebaddress.com/client/somepath/data.php?encoding=xml&"
                + textout;
        try {
            URL myUrl = new URL(querystring);
            HttpURLConnection myConnection = (HttpURLConnection) myUrl
                    .openConnection();
            InputStreamReader isr = new InputStreamReader(
                    myConnection.getInputStream(), "UTF-8");
        BufferedReader br=new BufferedReader(isr);
        String s="";
        StringBuffer sb=new StringBuffer();
        while((s=br.readLine())!=null)
            sb.append(s);
        rawdata=sb.toString();
            try {
                XmlPullParserFactory factory = XmlPullParserFactory
                        .newInstance();
                factory.setNamespaceAware(true);
                XmlPullParser xpp = factory.newPullParser();
                StringReader sr=new StringReader(rawdata); //set stream
                back to beginning
                xpp.setInput(sr);
                //xpp.setInput(isr);
                String currenttag = "";
                xpp.next(); // skips over the descriptor line in the XML
                            // input
```

```
                        int eventType = xpp.getEventType(); // all these ints will
                                                            // appear as symbolic
                                                            // constants
                    while (eventType != XmlPullParser.END_DOCUMENT) {
                        if (eventType == XmlPullParser.START_DOCUMENT) {
                            // do nothing;
                        }
                        if (eventType == XmlPullParser.START_TAG)
                            currenttag = xpp.getName();

                        if (eventType == XmlPullParser.TEXT) {
                            hm.put(currenttag, xpp.getText());

                        }
                        if (eventType == XmlPullParser.END_TAG) {
                            // do nothing
                        }
                        eventType = xpp.next(); // keep going
                    }// ends while
                } catch (XmlPullParserException mppe) {
                }

            } catch (MalformedURLException male) {
            }

            catch (IOException ioe) {
            }

        }// ends run()

    }// ends inner class
```

Note that in the run( ) method of the threading inner class, there is a specification for running either the XML version or the JSON version. This isn't the greatest code construct, but as an application developer, you would probably code for either JSON or XML, and this choice wouldn't be necessary. When you run the JSON version of the application, the results will look essentially the same in the data section, but the raw JSON file at the bottom will, of course, be different. The JSON version running on the Toshiba Thrive tablet will look like Figure 7.2.

Some other JSON libraries that can be used are Gson from Google, which can be found at http://code.google.com/p/google-gson/, and Jackson, which can be found at http://jackson.codehaus.org/.

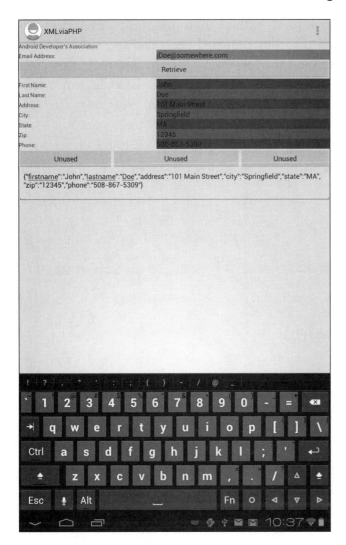

Figure 7.2
Screenshot of Toshiba Thrive running JSON from PHP application in portrait orientation.
Source: Google.

USING XML AND JSON WITH EXTERNAL SOURCES

Using the networking skills we have covered up to this point, along with the ability to deal with both JSON and XML, many doors can be opened for bringing data into an application from external sources. RSS feeds are formatted as XML files, the photo-sharing site Flickr uses JSON for feeds, and Google delivers data in both formats. In the next exercise, we will use both XML and JSON to collect geographic data from Google. In the first part of the exercise, we will use JSON format to retrieve the geo-codes (latitude and longitude positions) for a specific address from Google. These values will be returned in decimal format rather than the traditional degrees-minutes-seconds format. We will then take our returned geocodes and submit them to retrieve a static map with a pin marking the location. You can find details on how to retrieve and use Google's static maps at http://developers.google.com/maps/documentation/staticmaps/#quick_example. For documentation on how to use Google Maps in general, see http://developers.google.com/maps/.

What follows is a copy of the data from Google after a request for information on a given address to be returned in JSON format. The address happens to be that of the Rhode Island State House.

```
{
    "results" : [
        {
            "address_components" : [
                {
                    "long_name" : "90",
                    "short_name" : "90",
                    "types" : [ "street_number" ]
                },
                {
                    "long_name" : "Smith St",
                    "short_name" : "Smith St",
                    "types" : [ "route" ]
                },
                {
                    "long_name" : "Providence",
                    "short_name" : "Providence",
                    "types" : [ "locality", "political" ]
                },
                {
                    "long_name" : "Providence",
                    "short_name" : "Providence",
                    "types" : [ "administrative_area_level_2", "political" ]
                },
                {
                    "long_name" : "Rhode Island",
                    "short_name" : "RI",
                    "types" : [ "administrative_area_level_1", "political" ]
                },
                {
                    "long_name" : "United States",
                    "short_name" : "US",
                    "types" : [ "country", "political" ]
```

```
            },
            {
                "long_name" : "02904",
                "short_name" : "02904",
                "types" : [ "postal_code" ]
            }
        ],
        "formatted_address" : "90 Smith St, Providence, RI 02904, USA",
        "geometry" : {
            "bounds" : {
                "northeast" : {
                    "lat" : 41.83145190,
                    "lng" : -71.41205339999999
                },
                "southwest" : {
                    "lat" : 41.83145120,
                    "lng" : -71.41205350
                }
            },
            "location" : {
                "lat" : 41.83145120,
                "lng" : -71.41205350
            },
            "location_type" : "RANGE_INTERPOLATED",
            "viewport" : {
                "northeast" : {
                    "lat" : 41.83280053029149,
                    "lng" : -71.41070446970849
                },
                "southwest" : {
                    "lat" : 41.83010256970849,
                    "lng" : -71.41340243029151
                }
            }
        },
        "types" : [ "street_address" ]
    }
],
"status" : "OK"
}
```

For comparison sake, here is the same data in XML format.

```xml
<GeocodeResponse>
   <status>OK</status>
   <result>
      <type>street_address</type>
      <formatted_address>90 Smith St, Providence, RI 02904, USA</formatted_address>
      <address_component>
         <long_name>90</long_name>
         <short_name>90</short_name>
         <type>street_number</type>
      </address_component>
      <address_component>
         <long_name>Smith St</long_name>
         <short_name>Smith St</short_name>
         <type>route</type>
      </address_component>
      <address_component>
         <long_name>Providence</long_name>
         <short_name>Providence</short_name>
         <type>locality</type>
         <type>political</type>
      </address_component>
      <address_component>
         <long_name>Providence</long_name>
         <short_name>Providence</short_name>
         <type>administrative_area_level_2</type>
         <type>political</type>
      </address_component>
      <address_component>
         <long_name>Rhode Island</long_name>
         <short_name>RI</short_name>
         <type>administrative_area_level_1</type>
         <type>political</type>
      </address_component>
      <address_component>
         <long_name>United States</long_name>
         <short_name>US</short_name>
         <type>country</type>
         <type>political</type>
      </address_component>
      <address_component>
         <long_name>02904</long_name>
```

```
        <short_name>02904</short_name>
        <type>postal_code</type>
    </address_component>
    <geometry>
        <location>
            <lat>41.8314512</lat>
            <lng>-71.4120535</lng>
        </location>
        <location_type>RANGE_INTERPOLATED</location_type>
        <viewport>
            <southwest>
                <lat>41.8301026</lat>
                <lng>-71.4134024</lng>
            </southwest>
            <northeast>
                <lat>41.8328005</lat>
                <lng>-71.4107045</lng>
            </northeast>
        </viewport>
        <bounds>
            <southwest>
                <lat>41.8314512</lat>
                <lng>-71.4120535</lng>
            </southwest>
            <northeast>
                <lat>41.8314519</lat>
                <lng>-71.4120534</lng>
            </northeast>
        </bounds>
    </geometry>
  </result>
</GeocodeResponse>
```

Notice how the listings adhere to the standards we went through earlier. Also, notice the many pairs of latitude and longitude codes and the many data groups embedded in other data groups. On the XML side, you can see tag pairs between other tag pairs, between still other tag pairs. The pair of geocodes that we want for our application is the pair surrounded by the <location></location> pair in the XML listing, and the pair below the location name in the JSON listing. The pair we are targeting is in bold print in the listings displayed earlier.

This application is a little more complicated than the others because we have to parse through the JSON and XML files to get the data items needed.

If you are parsing a JSON file, there are two data structures to be concerned with: the objects that are demarcated by curly braces, and the arrays that are demarcated by square brackets. If you have any programming experience at all, you know that array elements are specified by their index values. The same is true with JSON structures. Any given array structure in the main structure can be specified by its name value and an object method, which requests an index value as its argument. Likewise, JSON objects are separated by curly braces and are specified by their name values. Unlike arrays, though, their elements are specified by names. Both arrays can be nested several levels deep, which is where the challenge lies. The applications programmer needs to "map" the input to determine on which level the desired data appears and drill down to it. There seems to be no easy way to parse a JSON object before the application is written. I find that the best way is to count through the layers of curly brace pairs and square bracket pairs until you get to the data items you want and build the code accordingly. You can find more information on using the JSON format at www.json.org. The process is similar when you're working with XML, although in code the parsing is a little different.

The application is bare boned and only needs two lines for user data entry: one for the street address of the target location and the other for the city and state, separated by commas. Google does not require a zip code to resolve an address and return the data listed earlier. In fact, the zip code is returned with the plethora of data that Google supplies. A single button sets the balance of the application in motion. The XML file for the application follows.

```xml
<LinearLayout xmlns:android="http://schemas.android.com/apk/res/android"
    xmlns:tools="http://schemas.android.com/tools"
    android:layout_width="fill_parent"
    android:layout_height="fill_parent"
    android:orientation="vertical" >

    <TextView
        android:layout_width="fill_parent"
        android:layout_height="wrap_content"
        android:text="Street Address" />

    <EditText
        android:id="@+id/requestAddress"
        android:layout_width="fill_parent"
        android:layout_height="wrap_content"
        android:text=""
        android:textSize="15pt" />

    <TextView
        android:layout_width="fill_parent"
```

```
        android:layout_height="wrap_content"
        android:text="City, State" />
    <EditText
        android:id="@+id/requestCityState"
        android:layout_width="fill_parent"
        android:layout_height="wrap_content"
        android:text=""
        android:textSize="15pt" />
    <Button
        android:id="@+id/makeRequest"
        android:layout_width="fill_parent"
        android:layout_height="wrap_content"
        android:text="Click to send request"
        android:textSize="15pt" />
    <EditText
        android:id="@+id/responseInfo"
        android:layout_width="fill_parent"
        android:layout_height="wrap_content"
        android:text=""
        android:textSize="15pt" />
    <WebView
        android:id="@+id/wv"
        android:layout_width="600dp"
        android:layout_height="300dp" />

</LinearLayout>
```

The structure of the main activity's Java file is similar to that of the exercises we have been doing. Again, it contains an internal class that runs a separate thread for networking and has methods for returning data to the main activity in response to button clicks. I am supplying code for both the JSON and the XML methods for parsing data returned from Google, so you will notice that there are packages in the import statements at the top of the program for both org.json.* and org.xmlpull.v1.* respectively. Also, notice that you switch between the two in the run( ) method of the thread class. Choosing either of those doesn't affect anything else in the program. If you look carefully, you will notice that Google knows which format to return based on the XML and JSON specifications in the URL.

On the XML side, the code is set to match the depth of the XML input through the getDepth( ) method of the XmlPullParser object. On the JSON side, we just keep assigning the objects within objects to new variables—for example, j2, j3, and j4— using the names from the input stream to select them. You can look back at the Google output listings at the top of this section to match them up visually. Each retrieval method in the code includes a multitude of exception handling, with messages that are sent to Eclipse's logger, LogCat. It is helpful to use the logger to see which values you are getting as you fine-tune the parser in your own applications.

If the streams in and out of the application are not encoded with UTF-8 encoding, your third-party website or data source may not respond correctly.

The code for the application, including both the JSON and XML parsing methods, is listed here.

```
package com.sheusi.addressdata;

import android.app.Activity;
import android.os.Bundle;
import java.io.*;
import android.view.*;
import android.widget.*;
import android.util.Log;
import org.xmlpull.v1.*;
import java.net.*;
import android.webkit.*;
import org.json.*;

public class MainActivity extends Activity {
    Button send = null;
    EditText addr = null;
    EditText citst = null;
    EditText info = null;
    WebView wv = null;

    /** Called when the activity is first created. */
    @Override
    public void onCreate(Bundle savedInstanceState) {
        super.onCreate(savedInstanceState);
        setContentView(R.layout.activity_main);
        send = (Button) findViewById(R.id.makeRequest);
        addr = (EditText) findViewById(R.id.requestAddress);
        citst = (EditText) findViewById(R.id.requestCityState);
        info = (EditText) findViewById(R.id.responseInfo);
        wv = (WebView) findViewById(R.id.wv);
            send.setOnClickListener(new View.OnClickListener() {
            public void onClick(View v) {
                String maddr = addr.getText().toString().replace(" ", "+");
                String mcitst = citst.getText().toString().replace(" ", "+");
                Background b = new Background(maddr + " + " + mcitst);
                b.start();
                // the following waits for download to finish
```

```
                try {
                    b.join();
                } catch (InterruptedException ie) {
                }
                String coords= b.retrieveResponse();
                //info.setText(coords);
                String[] latlong=coords.split(":");
                info.setText("Latitude: "+latlong[0]+"      Longitude: "+latlong[1]);
wv.loadUrl("http://maps.googleapis.com/maps/api/staticmap?center="+latlong[0]
+","+latlong
[1]+"&zoom=13&size=600x300&sensor=true&markers=color:green%7c"+latlong[0]+","+
latlong[1]);
                wv.refreshDrawableState();
            }
        });
    }

    private class Background extends Thread {
        String textout;
        String geocodes;

        public Background(String textout) {
            this.textout = textout;
        }

        public void run() {
            // geocodes = googleIt(textout);
            geocodes = googleItJSON(textout);
        }

        public String retrieveResponse() {
            return geocodes;
        }

        public String googleIt(String tout) {
            XmlPullParserFactory factory = null;
            StringBuffer info = new StringBuffer();
            try {
                tout = URLEncoder.encode(tout, "UTF-8");
                final String querystring =
"http://maps.googleapis.com/maps/api/geocode/xml?address="
                        + tout + "&sensor=true";
                Log.i("info",querystring);
                URL myUrl = new URL(querystring);
                HttpURLConnection myConnection = (HttpURLConnection) myUrl
                        .openConnection();
                InputStreamReader isr = new InputStreamReader(
                        myConnection.getInputStream()(), "utf-8");
```

```
                    BufferedReader br = new BufferedReader(isr);
                    try {
                        factory = XmlPullParserFactory.newInstance();
                        factory.setNamespaceAware(true);
                        XmlPullParser xpp = factory.newPullParser();
                        xpp.setInput(isr);
                        String curtag = "";
                        xpp.next();// skips descriptor line in XML file
                        int eventType = xpp.getEventType();
                        while (eventType != XmlPullParser.END_DOCUMENT) {
                            // while we haven't reached the end of the xml file
                            if (eventType == XmlPullParser.START_DOCUMENT) {
                                // do nothing for start document tag
                            }
                            if (eventType == XmlPullParser.START_TAG
                                    & xpp.getDepth() == 5) {
                                if (xpp.getName().equals("lng"))
                                    curtag = "lng";
                                if (xpp.getName().equals("lat"))
                                    curtag = "lat";
                            }
                            if (eventType == XmlPullParser.END_TAG) {
                                // do nothing for end tags
                            }
                            if (eventType == XmlPullParser.TEXT) {
                                if (curtag == "lat")
                                    info.append(xpp.getText()+":");
                                if (curtag == "lng")
                                    info.append(xpp.getText());
                                curtag = "";
                            }
                            eventType = xpp.next();
                        }// end while loop when end is reached
                        br.close();
                    } catch (XmlPullParserException xppe) {
                        Log.e("Code Error", xppe.getMessage());
                    }
                } catch (IOException ioe) {
                    Log.e("Code Error", ioe.getMessage());
                } finally {
                    return info.toString();
                }
            } // ends googleIt
```

```java
        public String googleItJSON(String tout) {
            JSONObject jobject = null;
            JSONArray jarray = null;
            StringBuilder jbuffer = new StringBuilder();
            String codestring = null;

            try {
                tout = URLEncoder.encode(tout, "UTF-8");
                final String querystring =
"http://maps.googleapis.com/maps/api/geocode/json?address="
                        + tout + "&sensor=true";
                Log.i("info",querystring);
                URL myUrl = new URL(querystring);
                URLConnection myConnection = myUrl.openConnection();
                myConnection.setConnectTimeout(2000);
                InputStreamReader is = new InputStreamReader(
                        myConnection.getInputStream(), "utf-8");
                BufferedReader bis = new BufferedReader(is);
                String frag = "";
                while ((frag = bis.readLine()) != null)
                    jbuffer.append(frag + "\n");
                bis.close();
                jobject = new JSONObject(jbuffer.toString());
                Log.i("info", jobject.getString("status"));
                jarray = jobject.getJSONArray("results"); // first level down
                JSONObject j2 = jarray.getJSONObject(0);
                JSONObject j3 = j2.getJSONObject("geometry");
                JSONObject j4 = j3.getJSONObject("location");
                Log.i("info",j4.toString());
                codestring =
String.valueOf(j4.getDouble("lat"))+":"+String.valueOf(j4.getDouble("lng"));
            } catch (SocketTimeoutException stoe) {
                Log.i("info", "Socket timed out");
            } catch (MalformedURLException male) {
                Log.i("info", "bad url");
            } catch (JSONException jsone) {
                Log.i("info", "JSON Exception");
            } catch (IOException ioe) {
            } finally {
                return codestring;
            }
        } // ends googleItJSON
    } // ends inner class

    @Override
```

```
public void onStop() {
    super.onStop();
    this.finish();
}
}
```

The running application in portrait orientation should look like Figure 7.3. Google encourages users to apply for a key to use Google Map services, although it is not required, and sets a limit on daily usage. Remember to set the Internet permissions in the manifest file for this application.

Figure 7.3
AddressData application running on Toshiba Thrive tablet in portrait mode.
Source: Google.

Any application using these formats will likely be on the receiving end of data, but occasionally it might be necessary to send data in either JSON or XML format. The following exercise takes data from two text fields, converts them to both XML and JSON format, and displays them in two `EditText` fields. The basic process could be applied to a record pulled from an SQLite table on the device or, as this exercise demonstrates, from a form in the application. The only thing to note about using a form as a data source is that if you use the text from a form label as an element label, as I do in this exercise, you need to adhere to the naming rules for JSON or XML. For example, I used an underscore to connect the two words in the field labels to replace the space. Of course, you could parse the label text and correct it in code, or you could use hard-coded element labels instead of the actual form label text.

The exercise uses only two data fields for convenience, but the process would be the same for any number of fields. The XML file for the screen appears here.

```xml
<?xml version="1.0" encoding="utf-8"?>
<LinearLayout xmlns:android="http://schemas.android.com/apk/res/android"
    android:layout_width="match_parent"
    android:layout_height="match_parent"
    android:orientation="vertical" >
    <TableLayout
        android:layout_width="fill_parent"
        android:layout_height="wrap_content" >
        <TableRow>
            <TextView
                android:id="@+id/name"
                android:layout_weight=".5"
                android:text="Your_Name" />

            <EditText
                android:id="@+id/etname"
                android:layout_weight=".5"
                android:inputType="text"
                android:width="200dp" />
        </TableRow>

        <TableRow>
            <TextView
                android:id="@+id/phone"
                android:layout_weight=".5"
                android:text="Phone_Number" />

            <EditText
                android:id="@+id/etphone"
```

```
                android:layout_weight=".5"
                android:inputType="text"
                android:width="200dp" />
        </TableRow>

        <TableRow>

            <Button
                android:id="@+id/convertbutton"
                android:layout_weight=".5"
                android:text="Produce JSON and XML output" />
        </TableRow>

        <TableRow>

            <EditText
                android:id="@+id/XMLout"
                android:width="300dp" />
        </TableRow>

        <TableRow>

            <EditText
                android:id="@+id/JSONout"
                android:layout_width="fill_parent" />
        </TableRow>
    </TableLayout>
</LinearLayout>
```

The Java code and XML file include only one button to do both conversions. Remember that both XML and JSON formats appear as plain text, so no special considerations need to be made to display them once the data is formatted in their respective formats. Likewise, no special considerations need to be made to transfer the JSON or XML listing that we create; a simple text stream is fine. Both conversion processes involve some checked exceptions, and the applications programmer may want to put some logging in the catch-blocks or some other code to respond to possible exceptions. I haven't done so here because the application is so simple and controlled. The Java code appears here.

```
package com.sheusi.MakeJSONXML;

import javax.xml.parsers.DocumentBuilderFactory;

import android.app.Activity;
import android.os.Bundle;
import android.widget.*;
import org.json.JSONObject;
import org.json.JSONException;
import org.w3c.dom.*;
```

```java
import javax.xml.parsers.*;
import javax.xml.transform.*;
import javax.xml.transform.stream.*;
import javax.xml.transform.dom.*;
import android.view.*;
import java.io.StringWriter;

public class MakeJSONXMLActivity extends Activity {
    /** Called when the activity is first created. */
    TextView name = null;
    EditText etname = null;
    TextView phone = null;
    EditText etphone = null;
    Button convert = null;
    EditText XMLoutput = null;
    EditText JSONoutput = null;

    @Override
    public void onCreate(Bundle savedInstanceState) {
        super.onCreate(savedInstanceState);
        setContentView(R.layout.main);
        name = (TextView) findViewById(R.id.name);
        etname = (EditText) findViewById(R.id.etname);
        phone = (TextView) findViewById(R.id.phone);
        etphone = (EditText) findViewById(R.id.etphone);
        convert = (Button) findViewById(R.id.convertbutton);
        XMLoutput = (EditText) findViewById(R.id.XMLout);
        JSONoutput = (EditText) findViewById(R.id.JSONout);
        convert.setOnClickListener(new View.OnClickListener() {
            public void onClick(View v) {
                // XML output first
                Document doc = null;
                try {
                    Element root = null;
                    Element node1 = null;
                    Element node2 = null;
                    Element row = null;
                    DocumentBuilderFactory myFactory = DocumentBuilderFactory
                            .newInstance();
                    DocumentBuilder myDocBuilder = myFactory
                            .newDocumentBuilder();
                    doc = myDocBuilder.newDocument();
                    root = doc.createElement("RootElement");
                    doc.appendChild(root);
                    row = doc.createElement("Row");
```

```
                            root.appendChild(row);
                            node1 = doc.createElement(name.getText().toString());
                            node1.appendChild(doc.createTextNode(etname.getText()
                                    .toString()));
                            row.appendChild(node1);
                            node2 = doc.createElement(phone.getText().toString());
                            node2.appendChild(doc.createTextNode(etphone.getText()
                                    .toString()));
                            row.appendChild(node2);
                    } catch (ParserConfigurationException pce) {
                    }
                    // convert the document to a text string
                    try {
                            DOMSource domsource = new DOMSource(doc);
                            TransformerFactory myFactory = TransformerFactory
                                    .newInstance();
                            Transformer transformer = myFactory.newTransformer();
                            transformer.setOutputProperty(OutputKeys.METHOD, "xml");
                            transformer.setOutputProperty(OutputKeys.ENCODING, "UTF-8");
                            transformer.setOutputProperty(OutputKeys.INDENT, "yes");
                            StringWriter sw = new StringWriter();
                            StreamResult sr = new StreamResult(sw);
                            transformer.transform(domsource, sr);
                            XMLoutput.setText(sw.toString());
                    } catch (TransformerConfigurationException tce) {
                    } catch (TransformerException te) {
                    }

                    // now, the JSON output
                    try {
                            JSONObject jsonblock = new JSONObject();

                            jsonblock.put(name.getText().toString(), etname.getText()
                                    .toString());
                            jsonblock.put(phone.getText().toString(),
        etphone.getText()
                                            .toString());
                            JSONoutput.setText(jsonblock.toString(4));
        // the argument, 4, sets indents to 4 spaces deep
                    } catch (JSONException je) {
                    }
                }
            });
        }
    }
```

A screenshot of the running application on the Toshiba Thrive tablet in portrait mode is displayed in Figure 7.4.

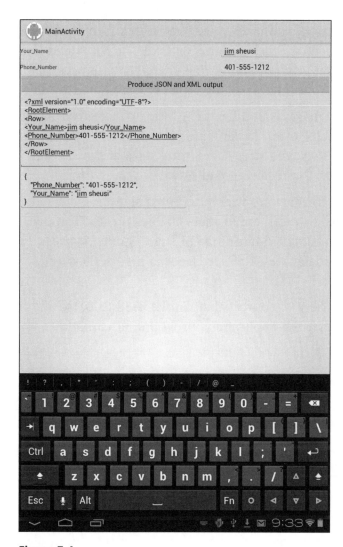

Figure 7.4
AddressData application running on Toshiba Thrive tablet in portrait mode.
Source: Google.

SUMMARY OF KEY CONCEPTS

- It is likely that any mobile application that is an extension of applications used in business will need to transfer data. Although text is sent in simple formats such as CSV, problems can arise from missing fields, separating characters used as punctuation in a given field, hierarchical data, and similar anomalies in the text stream. Also, groups of data embedded in other groups of data, such as line items on an invoice, can cause problems when they are being parsed at the receiving end. A more robust format for transferring text data is desirable.

■ JSON, or JavaScript Object Notation, is one such format. In this format, data is sent in group key-value pairs called objects. Similar objects can be combined in a series called arrays. Although relatively few formatting characters are necessary (overhead), the strict formatting rules make parsing at the receiving end reliable.

■ XML, or Extensible Markup Language, is another such format. Instead of using punctuated key-value pairs as JSON uses, the keys are presented as tags surrounding the data values. Like JSON, the strict formatting rules at the sending end ensure accurate translation at the receiving end.

■ Because of their reliability, both formats are widely accepted standards for data transmittal. Therefore, the ability to use these formats enables the applications programmer to take advantage of data from a range of sources outside the enterprise, such as public-access databases, RSS feeds, social media sites, and government sources.

■ Packages are available from a variety of sources that can be used to parse and assemble data in these formats that the applications programmer can add to an application.

Review Questions

You can find the answers to these review questions in the appendix at the end of the book.

1. The acronym CSV stands for _____.

2. The outermost element in an XML document is called the _____ element.

3. Data included in the opening tag of an XML element is called _____.

4. JSON is an acronym that stands for _____.

5. JSON presents individual data items in _____ - _____ pairs.

6. An advantage of the JSON format over XML is that it requires fewer _____, or lower _____.

7. The only JSON and XML parser libraries that can be used in an Android application are the ones included in the Android SDK, true or false? _____.

8. The information area at the top of an XML document that contains the version number is called the _____.

9. In JSON formatting, the key and value in a pair are separated by a _____.

10. Comments in XML files are surrounded by the following characters: _____ and _____.

SUGGESTED PROJECTS

■ Write an application that allows a user to enter a simple XML-formatted set of data. Let the application parse the text and return it to the text field as JSON.

■ Research, compare, and contrast JSON, XML, and CSV formats. Identify the advantages and disadvantages of each.

■ Using the example presented in this chapter that retrieves geocodes from Google based on an address, try to extract other data on the address that interests you.

■ Using the server-side PHP code supplied in the example, write a simple client- and server-side pair of applications that transfers some simple data such as the server's IP or time of day to the mobile client application.

CHAPTER 8

THE CAMERA AS A DATA SOURCE

BAR CODES AND QR CODES

An Android handheld or tablet's mobility and its camera feature make it a great device for scanning and interpreting bar codes and QR codes. The bar code is certainly nothing new; it was patented in the 1950s and was used in grocery stores as early as the 1970s. Almost every grocery and retail store currently uses bar codes. The quick response (QR) code was invented in the 1990s in Japan and was used by Toyota to track vehicles during their manufacture. Today, handheld devices are used in the field to track inventory in warehouses, track items on their way to delivery, check off pick-lists as orders are prepared to be shipped, and so on. However, until recently, devices for these purposes were proprietary, custom built (often around platforms based on PalmOS or similar), narrowly purposed, and expensive. But now just about any handheld device with a camera, networking capabilities, and a built-in database management system can be adapted for the purpose. Android devices are no exception.

In fact, programming an application for scanning, interpreting, storing, and displaying results for an Android device is one of the easier tasks for the applications programmer. This is because of the resources available from Google under the name ZXing, or Zebra Crossing. For trivia sake, a zebra crossing, shown in Figure 8.1, is actually a pedestrian path across an intersection that is marked by alternating white lines on the road surface. It's similar in appearance to the alternating black-and-white stripes on a zebra. One might observe that the black-and-white alternating stripes on a barcode are similar to the stripes on a zebra.

Figure 8.1
A zebra crossing in downtown Providence, Rhode Island.
Source: © 2013 Cengage Learning®, All Rights Reserved.

For Android programmers, however, Zebra Crossing is an open-source multiformat image processing library implemented in Java. Perfect! The resources are located at the following web address: http://code.google.com/p/zxing/ (zxing is short for Zebra Crossing). At this address, you can find documentation, downloads (both source code and actual installable Android application files), and the Apache license under which the resources can be used. I mentioned earlier that building a scanning application is one of the simpler tasks. That's because instead of building a complete application from scratch, we can build around available tools.

The first step is to install the scanning application from the Zebra Crossing website and install it on the target device or devices. Look for the APK file in the Downloads section. You can also find it free of charge at the Google Play Store. If you have had some experience with Android application programming or if you read my first book, *Android Application Development for Java Programmers*, or a similar text, you might know something about starting other activities or applications through intents. An intent, which is actually implemented as a class called Intent, enables communication on the device between applications at run-time. We can use this vehicle to provide communication between a specific-purpose application written by a programmer and the application downloaded from the Google website named earlier.

Let's begin to put such an application together. From here on I will assume that you were able to find and download the actual scanning application either from the Download section of the website I mentioned (the latest version at the time of this writing was called BarcodeScanner4.3b1.apk) or from the Google Play Store. You can find it by searching the Play Store using Zebra Crossing as the search parameter.

To prepare, start a new project and set the permissions in the manifest file to allow for use of the Internet and the camera. The application specification begins with a simple screen layout, consisting of an initial application banner, a button to begin the scanning process, and an EditText to hold the interpreted code. The XML listing follows.

```
<RelativeLayout xmlns:android="http://schemas.android.com/apk/res/android"
    xmlns:tools="http://schemas.android.com/tools"
    android:layout_width="match_parent"
    android:layout_height="match_parent" >

    <TextView
        android:layout_width="wrap_content"
        android:layout_height="wrap_content"
        android:layout_centerHorizontal="true"
        android:padding="@dimen/padding_medium"
        android:text="Scanner application based on Google's Zebra Crossing utilities."
        android:id="@+id/tv1"
        tools:context=".CodeReader" />
    <Button
        android:layout_width="wrap_content"
        android:layout_height="wrap_content"
        android:layout_centerHorizontal="true"
        android:layout_below="@+id/tv1"
        android:id="@+id/startscan"
        android:text="Start Scan"
        />
    <EditText
        android:layout_width="wrap_content"
        android:layout_height="wrap_content"
        android:layout_centerHorizontal="true"
        android:layout_below="@+id/startscan"
        android:id="@+id/et1"
        android:text=""
        />

</RelativeLayout>
```

For the application code, we again will rely, to some extent, on the Zebra Crossing utilities found on the website. This time we want to download the ZIP file containing source code we will use to call the previously described application and retrieve usable results. The file to download at the time of this writing is ZXing-2.0.zip, which you can find in the Download section.

On the website in the Wiki section, you will find a short article titled "Scanning-ViaIntent" (http://code.google.com/p/zxing/wiki/ScanningViaIntent) that mentions a file called IntentIntegrator.java. This file is included in the ZIP file we downloaded. Once you download the file and unzip it, you will see that there is a directory called android-integration. In that folder is another folder called src, in that one another called com, then google, then zxing, then integration, and then android. Finally, in the android folder are four Java source codes, one of which is the IntentIntegrator.java file. These are four classes we need to add to our project. At the top of each of these source codes is a notice that they are covered by the Apache license, which you can find at www.apache.org/licenses/LICENSE-2.0, as well as on the Zebra Crossing website. If you intend to use these source codes, as we will in this exercise, please read and comply with the license. Once you have read the license, copy these files to the src folder of your project. Change the package name in each of these to match the package name of your project, or you will see errors in the listings. Your Package Explorer with the added code should look like Figure 8.2.

Figure 8.2
Eclipse Package Explorer with added class files.
Source: The Eclipse Foundation.

Once you have reviewed the license, copied the files into your source code directory, and modified the package name, enter the following as your main activity file.

```java
package com.sheusi.codereader;

import android.os.Bundle;
import android.app.Activity;
import android.content.Intent;
import android.view.Menu;
import android.view.MenuItem;
import android.support.v4.app.NavUtils;
import android.widget.*;
import android.view.*;

public class CodeReader extends Activity {
    Button startscan=null;
    EditText et1=null;
    @Override
    public void onCreate(Bundle savedInstanceState) {
        super.onCreate(savedInstanceState);
        setContentView(R.layout.activity_code_reader);
        startscan=(Button)findViewById(R.id.startscan);
        et1=(EditText)findViewById(R.id.et1);
        startscan.setOnClickListener(new View.OnClickListener(){
            public void onClick(View v){
            IntentIntegrator ii= new IntentIntegrator(CodeReader.this);
             //CodeReader.this represents the main activity
             //IntentIntegrator's constructor requires the activity as an argument
             ii.initiateScan();
             }
             });
    }
    public void onActivityResult(int requestCode, int resultCode, Intent intent){
        IntentResult  scanResult=IntentIntegrator.parseActivityResult(requestCode,
resultCode, intent);
        if(scanResult!=null){
            et1.setText(scanResult.getContents());
        }
    }
    @Override
    public boolean onCreateOptionsMenu(Menu menu) {
        getMenuInflater().inflate(R.menu.activity_code_reader, menu);
        return true;
    }


}
```

It is surprising how little this takes, with the help of some licensed code. Once the application is running, if the user touches the button, the application switches to the downloaded scanning application. If you can find a bar code to scan, the application will perform the scan and switch back to the original application to display the code in the EditText field. In Chapter 3, "Databases in the Application," we covered how to create a data table in an application. For some purposes, retrieving the bar code number and saving it with a quantity, date, price, or any other additional data and adding it to a table may be enough. For others, we may need to get product information based on the code. Some businesses subscribe to product databases, and through methods we covered in Chapter 3 and Chapter 7, "Using External Data," we could retrieve and store more information on a product based on the scan. For now, let's take advantage of what we learned in Chapter 6, "Client-Server Applications," and use the Internet to provide some product data. We will add a WebView object to the application, submit our retrieved code to a URL, and display the results. Add the following code to your main XML file.

```
<WebView
        android:layout_width="400dp"
        android:layout_height="400dp"
        android:layout_centerHorizontal="true"
        android:layout_below="@+id/et1"
        android:id="@+id/wv1"
/>
```

Then revise your main activity to match the following listing. You need to make an additional entry to the import statements for the WebView object, declare the object variable for it, and so on. Remember, if you haven't done so, add permission to the manifest to use the Internet.

```
package com.sheusi.codereader;

import android.os.Bundle;
import android.app.Activity;
import android.content.Intent;
import android.view.Menu;
import android.view.MenuItem;
import android.support.v4.app.NavUtils;
import android.widget.*;
import android.view.*;
import android.webkit.WebView;

public class CodeReader extends Activity {
     Button startscan = null;
     EditText et1 = null;
     WebView wv1 = null;
```

```
@Override
public void onCreate(Bundle savedInstanceState) {
    super.onCreate(savedInstanceState);
    setContentView(R.layout.activity_code_reader);
    startscan = (Button) findViewById(R.id.startscan);
    et1 = (EditText) findViewById(R.id.et1);

    startscan.setOnClickListener(new View.OnClickListener() {
        public void onClick(View v) {
            IntentIntegrator ii = new IntentIntegrator(CodeReader.this);
            // CodeReader.this represents the main activity
            // IntentIntegrator's constructor requires the activity
            // as an argument
            ii.initiateScan();
        }
    });
}

public void onActivityResult(int requestCode, int resultCode, Intent intent) {
    IntentResult scanResult = IntentIntegrator.parseActivityResult(
            requestCode, resultCode, intent);
    if (scanResult != null) {
        et1.setText(scanResult.getContents());
        wv1 = (WebView) findViewById(R.id.wv1);
        wv1.getSettings().setJavaScriptEnabled(true);
        wv1.loadUrl("http://www.upcindex.com/" + et1.getText().toString());
    }
}

@Override
public boolean onCreateOptionsMenu(Menu menu) {
    getMenuInflater().inflate(R.menu.activity_code_reader, menu);
    return true;
}
}
```

The running application should look like Figure 8.3.

The website www.upcindex.com is one of many websites that will return a description for a given UPC bar code. Some sites, especially subscriber sites, will return data in JSON or XML format; we covered that in Chapter 7. As you might have guessed, the application works equally well for interpreting QR codes, but you need to change this line of code

```
wv1.loadUrl("http://www.upcindex.com/" + et1.getText().toString());
```

to include just the contents of the text field. In other words, just leave out http://www.upcindex.com/.

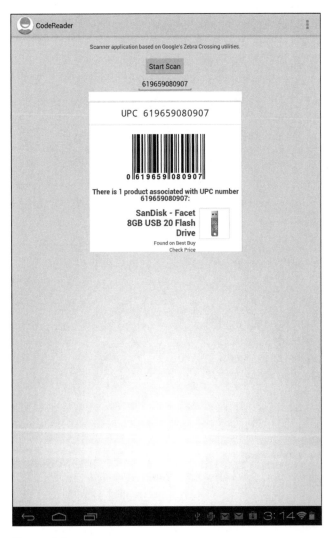

Figure 8.3
Bar code/QR scanner application running on Toshiba Thrive tablet.
Source: Google.

PHOTOGRAPHS IN APPLICATIONS

The need for and use of photographs by professionals in the field is nothing new. For years now, real estate agents and appraisers, law enforcement professionals, insurance adjusters, and health care professionals have been using photographs to support claims and documentation and record significant events, among other things.

However, traditionally the integration of photography in the field involved instant cameras, staples, and paper clips. The advent of digital photography allowed a smoother integration of documents and images but required the images to be transferred to a processing machine, probably a desktop computer, so they could be embedded with the appropriate documents. The process still requires the digital photos to be indexed and properly matched to the documentation, sized properly, and so on.

The high quality of digital cameras in modern handhelds and tablets, the availability of motion photography (videos), the screen size of tablet devices in particular, and the ability to write custom applications tailored to a particular need bring the integration of images and text to a new level. The device itself can take the picture, transfer it, catalog it, and in some cases edit it, resize it, and integrate it into a document all on its own. In this section, we will look at a couple of exercises that focus on using and tracking digital photographs in applications.

Our first exercise involves building an application that will take a photograph and immediately display a bitmap representation of it onscreen. This particular application allows the user to save the date, a specific name for the image (what the Android system calls the image's *title*), and a brief description of the image to a text file on the system. Should the user choose to transfer the images later, a document matching the actual image filenames to their descriptions can accompany them and prevent mix-up later. The application's code is surprisingly brief because it uses the device's built-in camera application as an intent. There is no need to reinvent the wheel when implementing a feature of the Android handheld or tablet; we simply take advantage of built-in software. The screen design is simple. On the left side are a few text fields to display the system date, which will be included in the description text file, to allow the user to enter a descriptive filename and to allow the user to type a brief description of the photo. There are also buttons to save the image, update the description file (called archive.txt in the application's code), and close the application. On the right side, the screen includes a button to start the camera activity and an ImageView object to hold the newly snapped image. The screen is locked in horizontal position in the code. The XML file for the screen appears as follows.

```
<?xml version="1.0" encoding="utf-8"?>
<LinearLayout xmlns:android="http://schemas.android.com/apk/res/android"
    android:layout_width="match_parent"
    android:layout_height="match_parent"
    android:orientation="horizontal" >

    <LinearLayout
        android:id="@+layout/leftside"
        android:layout_width="wrap_content"
```

```
        android:layout_height="match_parent"
        android:layout_weight=".5"
        android:orientation="vertical" >

    <TextView
        android:layout_width="fill_parent"
        android:layout_height="wrap_content"
        android:text="Photo Capture Application" />

    <EditText
        android:id="@+id/pic_date"
        android:layout_width="match_parent"
        android:layout_height="wrap_content"
        android:text="" />

    <EditText
        android:id="@+id/pic_title"
        android:layout_width="match_parent"
        android:layout_height="wrap_content"
        android:hint="Enter title for picture here"
        android:text="" />

    <EditText
        android:id="@+id/pic_desc"
        android:layout_width="match_parent"
        android:layout_height="wrap_content"
        android:hint="Enter brief description here"
        android:text="" />

    <Button
        android:id="@+id/archive"
        android:layout_width="wrap_content"
        android:layout_height="wrap_content"
        android:text="Add these details to archive.txt" />

    <Button
        android:id="@+id/close_app"
        android:layout_width="wrap_content"
        android:layout_height="wrap_content"
        android:padding="20dp"
        android:text="Close application" />

</LinearLayout>

<LinearLayout
        android:id="@+layout/leftside"
        android:layout_width="wrap_content"
        android:layout_height="match_parent"
        android:layout_weight=".5"
        android:orientation="vertical" >
```

```
    <Button
        android:id="@+id/shutter"
        android:layout_width="wrap_content"
        android:layout_height="wrap_content"
        android:text="Take Picture" />

    <ImageView
        android:id="@+id/pic"
        android:layout_width="600dp"
        android:layout_height="600dp" />
    </LinearLayout>

</LinearLayout>
```

As I mentioned, the Java code for the application is brief. It appears here.

```
package com.sheusi.photocapture;

import java.io.*;
import android.app.Activity;
import android.content.Intent;
import android.content.pm.ActivityInfo;
import android.graphics.Bitmap;
import android.graphics.Matrix;
import android.os.Bundle;
import android.os.Environment;
import android.view.View;
import android.widget.Button;
import android.widget.ImageView;
import android.widget.*;
import android.content.Context;
import java.util.Date;
import android.hardware.Camera;

public class PhotoCapture extends Activity {
    Button shutter = null;
    ImageView pic = null;
    EditText picdate = null;
    EditText pictitle = null;
    EditText picdesc = null;
    Button rotate = null;
    Button archive = null;
    Button closeapp = null;
    Matrix tempMatrix = null;
    Context myContext = null;
    Camera camera = null;

    @Override
```

```java
public void onCreate(Bundle savedInstanceState) {
    super.onCreate(savedInstanceState);
    setContentView(R.layout.activity_photo_capture);
            setRequestedOrientation(ActivityInfo.SCREEN_ORIENTATION_LANDSCAPE);
    myContext = this.getApplicationContext();
    pic = (ImageView) findViewById(R.id.pic);
    picdate = (EditText) findViewById(R.id.pic_date);
    pictitle = (EditText) findViewById(R.id.pic_title);
    picdesc = (EditText) findViewById(R.id.pic_desc);
    shutter = (Button) findViewById(R.id.shutter);
    archive = (Button) findViewById(R.id.archive);
    closeapp = (Button) findViewById(R.id.close_app);
    pic.setDrawingCacheEnabled(true);
    picdate.setText(new Date().toString());
    shutter.setOnClickListener(new View.OnClickListener() {
        public void  onClick(View v) {
        Intent intent = new Intent(
        android.provider.MediaStore.ACTION_IMAGE_CAPTURE);
        startActivityForResult(intent, 1);
        }
    });

    archive.setOnClickListener(new View.OnClickListener() {
        public void onClick(View v) {
            addArchive();
        }
    });

    closeapp.setOnClickListener(new View.OnClickListener() {
        public void onClick(View v) {
            if (camera != null) {
                camera.release();
                camera = null;
            }
            PhotoCapture.this.finish();
        }
    });
}// ends onCreate


@Override
protected void onActivityResult(int requestCode,
int resultCode, Intent intent) {
super.onActivityResult(requestCode, resultCode, intent);
if (resultCode == RESULT_OK) {
    Bitmap photo =
```

```
            (Bitmap) intent.getExtras().get("data"); pic.setImageBitmap(photo);
        }
    }

    @Override
    protected void onRestoreInstanceState(Bundle savedInstanceState) {

    }

@Override
protected void onSaveInstanceState(Bundle outState) {

}

public void addArchive() {
    try {
        // if no picture name, toast then return
        if (pictitle.getText().toString() == null) {

            Toast toast = Toast.makeText(getApplicationContext(),
                    "You must enter a name for the picture",
                    Toast.LENGTH_LONG);
            toast.setGravity(android.view.Gravity.TOP
                    | android.view.Gravity.CENTER_HORIZONTAL, 0, 0);
            toast.show();
            return;

        }
        // first save the image
        File picfile = new File(Environment.getExternalStorageDirectory()
                + "/DCIM/Camera/" + pictitle.getText().toString() + ".jpg");
        FileOutputStream fos = new FileOutputStream(picfile);
        pic.getDrawingCache().compress(Bitmap.CompressFormat.JPEG, 100, fos);
        fos.close();
        // next, append these photo details to text file stored with
        // pictures
        File archive = new File(Environment.getExternalStorageDirectory()
                + "/DCIM/Camera/" + "archive.txt");
        fos = new FileOutputStream(archive, true);
        // true argument for append mode
        OutputStreamWriter osw = new OutputStreamWriter(fos);
        BufferedWriter bw = new BufferedWriter(osw);
        bw.write("Date: " + picdate.getText().toString() + "\n");
        bw.write("Title: " + pictitle.getText().toString() + "\n");
        bw.write("Description: " + picdesc.getText().toString() + "\n\n");
        bw.close();

    } catch (IOException ioe) {
    }
}
```

```
        public void onClose() {
        if (camera != null) {
            camera.release();
            camera = null;
        }
        PhotoCapture.this.finish();
    }
}
```

In the manifest file, we need to add the following permission elements.

```
<uses-permission android:name="android.permission.CAMERA"/>
<uses-permission android:name="android.permission.WRITE_EXTERNAL_STORAGE" />
```

The methods `startActivityForResult( )` and `onActivityResult( )` work in tandem. The former starts the device's camera application, and the latter returns the results to the calling activity. The few lines of code in this method extract a bitmap from the returned values and display it in the `ImageView` object. The archive method takes the bitmap image from the screen, converts it to a JPEG image, and stores it where the device stores its images, using the name the user enters into the screen. If the user has neglected to enter a filename for the image, a toast message appears, and the method is ended. Both the archive file and the image file are stored where the device stores its images by default. Figure 8.4 is a screenshot of Eclipse's DDMS (Dalvik Debug Monitor Server) perspective from which we can view the attached device's file tree. In the figure, you can see the entries for the archive file and the image files created by the application.

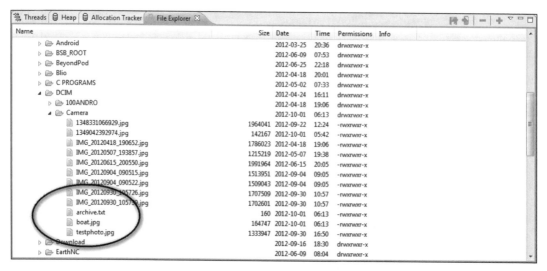

Figure 8.4
DDMS perspective showing device file tree and image files.
Source: The Eclipse Foundation.

The archive text file can be placed anywhere in the system the programmer chooses, assuming the chosen location is accessible. I put it with the images for convenience sake. The running application looks like Figure 8.5.

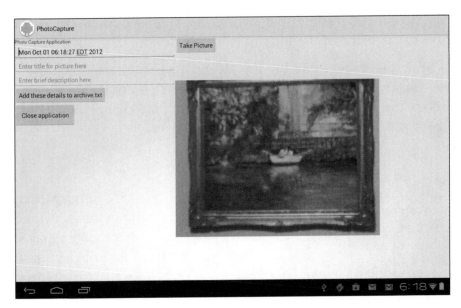

Figure 8.5
Running photo capture and archive application on Toshiba Thrive.
Source: Google.

In this application, the single description file continues to grow as the application is used; should the reader decide to create a variation of this application, he may want to provide functionality to start the archive file from scratch on a given occasion or create multiple archive files.

Some adaptations for the techniques used in this application are to redesign the screen by including a company logo and description, information on the subject to be photographed, a signature field to create a quick photo ID, a sample print ad for a given subject, and a catalog of possessions for insurance records.

The only shortcoming of the application is the quality of the bitmap displayed in the ImageView object. These objects are not meant to display a given image with the best resolution obtainable from the camera. To work around this shortcoming, consider the variation offered in the next example. Instead of shooting pictures from within the application, the next version uses the device's gallery content provider to allow the user to scan the gallery of photos that currently exist on the device and choose one to catalog. Enough information is retrieved when the photo is chosen for the application to go back to the gallery, retrieve the filename, and produce a bitmap rendering of the actual high-quality photo in the ImageView. The only difference in the appearance of the application would be to change the label on the button that was used to start the camera, which will now be used to start the gallery preview. There is no need to change the name that the device gave the image when it was taken, because when the entry is made to the archive file, the name will serve as the link from the archive to the name of the image file on the device.

The XML file will be virtually the same for the second version of the application, except for the label change on the button I mentioned earlier, so there is no name to reprint it. However, the Java file does have some significant changes, including some additional import statements, so it is being reprinted here.

```java
package com.sheusi.photocapture;

import java.io.*;
import android.app.Activity;
import android.content.Intent;
import android.content.pm.ActivityInfo;
import android.graphics.Bitmap;
import android.graphics.Matrix;
import android.os.Bundle;
import android.os.Environment;
import android.view.View;
import android.widget.Button;
import android.widget.ImageView;
import android.widget.*;
import android.content.Context;
import java.util.Date;
import android.hardware.Camera;
// new import statements below
import android.provider.MediaStore;
import android.net.Uri;
import android.database.Cursor;
import android.graphics.BitmapFactory;

public class PhotoCapture extends Activity {
    Button shutter = null;
    ImageView pic = null;
    EditText picdate = null;
    EditText pictitle = null;
    EditText picdesc = null;
    Button rotate = null;
    Button archive = null;
    Button closeapp = null;
    Matrix tempMatrix = null;
```

```java
Context myContext = null;
Camera camera = null;

@Override
public void onCreate(Bundle savedInstanceState) {
    super.onCreate(savedInstanceState);
    setContentView(R.layout.activity_photo_capture);
    setRequestedOrientation(ActivityInfo.SCREEN_ORIENTATION_LANDSCAPE);
    myContext = this.getApplicationContext();
    pic = (ImageView) findViewById(R.id.pic);
    picdate = (EditText) findViewById(R.id.pic_date);
    pictitle = (EditText) findViewById(R.id.pic_title);
    picdesc = (EditText) findViewById(R.id.pic_desc);
    shutter = (Button) findViewById(R.id.shutter);
    archive = (Button) findViewById(R.id.archive);
    closeapp = (Button) findViewById(R.id.close_app);
    pic.setDrawingCacheEnabled(true);
    picdate.setText(new Date().toString());
    shutter.setOnClickListener(new View.OnClickListener() {
        public void onClick(View v) {

            Intent myIntent = new Intent(
                    Intent.ACTION_PICK,
                    android.provider.MediaStore.Images.Media.EXTERNAL_
                    CONTENT_URI);
            startActivityForResult(myIntent, 2);
        }
    });


    archive.setOnClickListener(new View.OnClickListener() {
        public void onClick(View v) {
            addArchive();
        }
    });
    closeapp.setOnClickListener(new View.OnClickListener() {
        public void onClick(View v) {
            if (camera != null) {
                camera.release();
                camera = null;
            }
            PhotoCapture.this.finish();
        }
    });
}// ends onCreate
```

```
        @Override
        protected void onActivityResult(int requestCode, int resultCode,
                Intent intent) {
            super.onActivityResult(requestCode, resultCode, intent);
            String imagefilename = "";
            Cursor cursor = null;
            if (resultCode == Activity.RESULT_OK) {
                Uri selectedImage = intent.getData();
                String[] pathFrags = selectedImage.getPath().split("/");
                String pictureID = pathFrags[pathFrags.length - 1];
// gets last string in the array
// which is the file ID (not the title) for the picture
                String[] selectedFields = { MediaStore.Images.Media._ID,
                        MediaStore.Images.Media.TITLE };
                try {
                    cursor = managedQuery(
                            MediaStore.Images.Media.EXTERNAL_CONTENT_URI,
                            selectedFields, MediaStore.Images.Media._ID + "=?",
                            new String[] { pictureID }, null);
                    cursor.moveToFirst();
                    // only one record will be returned on the unique ID
                    pictitle.setText(cursor.getString(1));
                    imagefilename = cursor.getString(1);
                } catch (NullPointerException npe) {
                }
                pic.setImageBitmap(sizePic(imagefilename));
            }// end if

        }


        @Override
        protected void onSaveInstanceState(Bundle outState) {

        }

        public void addArchive() {
            try {
                // if no picture name, toast then return
                if (pictitle.getText().toString() == null) {
                    Toast toast = Toast.makeText(getApplicationContext(),
                            "You must enter a name for the picture",
                            Toast.LENGTH_LONG);
                    toast.setGravity(android.view.Gravity.TOP
                            | android.view.Gravity.CENTER_HORIZONTAL, 0, 0);
                    toast.show();
```

```
                return;
            }

            //append these photo details to text file stored with pictures
            File archive = new File(Environment.getExternalStorageDirectory()
                    + "/DCIM/Camera/" + "archive.txt");
            FileOutputStream fos = new FileOutputStream(archive, true);
            // true argument for append mode
            OutputStreamWriter osw = new OutputStreamWriter(fos);
            BufferedWriter bw = new BufferedWriter(osw);
            bw.write("Date: " + picdate.getText().toString() + "\n");
            bw.write("Title: " + pictitle.getText().toString() + "\n");
            bw.write("Description: " + picdesc.getText().toString() + "\n\n");
            bw.close();

    } catch (IOException ioe) {
    }
}

private Bitmap sizePic(String picfilename) {
    // Source for basis of this method:
    // http://developer.android.com/training/camera/photobasics.html
    // Get the dimensions of the View
    int targetW = 400; // matches manifest specs for ImageView
    int targetH = 400; // same as above

    // Get the dimensions of the bitmap
    BitmapFactory.Options bmOptions = new BitmapFactory.Options();
    bmOptions.inJustDecodeBounds = true;
    BitmapFactory.decodeFile(Environment.getExternalStorageDirectory()
            + "/pictures/newpic.jpg", bmOptions);
    int photoW = bmOptions.outWidth;
    int photoH = bmOptions.outHeight;

    // Determine how much to scale down the image
    int scaleFactor = Math.min(photoW / targetW, photoH / targetH);

    // Decode the image file into a bitmap sized to fill the view
    bmOptions.inJustDecodeBounds = false;
    bmOptions.inSampleSize = scaleFactor;
    bmOptions.inPurgeable = true;
    try {
        Thread.sleep(500); // half second delay to allow for picture
                                    // processing
    } catch (InterruptedException ie) {
    }
    Bitmap bitmap = BitmapFactory.decodeFile(
            Environment.getExternalStorageDirectory() + "/DCIM/Camera/"
                    + picfilename + ".jpg", bmOptions);
```

```
            return bitmap;
    }

    public void onClose() {
        if (camera != null) {
            camera.release();
            camera = null;
        }
        PhotoCapture.this.finish();
    }
}
```

In this version, the onActivityResult( ) method is a little more involved. What is returned from the intent is a URI for the chosen image. From this we can get the full path to the image: the directories, subdirectories, and file ID. Just as we did in Chapter 5, "Content Providers," with the calendar and contact content providers, we can query the gallery content provider for more details on the image file using the file ID as the unique key. We can then retrieve the image title (the image file-name) and use it as the argument for the method that creates a bitmap for viewing named sizePic( ).

In the sizePic( ) method, I hard-coded the dimensions desired to match the dimensions specified for the ImageView object in the XML file.

Because the image previously exists in this version of the application and should be preserved in its high-resolution form, I removed the code in the archiving method, which saves the image from the ImageView. The appearance of the second variation is essentially the same as the first, so there is no need to reprint it.

In both applications, I chose to store details in a text file because it is plain English and readable. The reader may choose to store description records in an SQLite data table or any other format deemed appropriate. Figure 8.6 is sample text from a started archive file read from the Windows 7 WordPad application.

```
Date: Mon Oct 01 05:42:49 EDT 2012
Title: 1349042392974
Description: My workspace at home.

Date: Mon Oct 01 06:12:52 EDT 2012
Title: boat
Description: Painting of scene in Italy.
```

Figure 8.6
Plain text listing from the archive file stored by this application.
Source: Microsoft® Corporation.

SUMMARY OF KEY CONCEPTS

- The ability to use applications included on the Android device, some applications subsequently installed, and content providers available on the Android device allow the applications programmer to provide enhancements to applications without coding from scratch.

- The camera built into current Android devices provides a useful and valuable source of data for applications, both for scanning bar codes and QR codes and taking photographs for specific purposes.

- Google provides utilities under the Apache license for applications programmers. These utilities can be used to scan, interpret, and even produce one- and two-dimensional codes under the name ZXing, pronounced "Zebra Crossing." The main website for ZXing is http://code.google.com/p/zxing/.

REVIEW QUESTIONS

You can find the answers to these review questions in the appendix at the end of the book.

1. Bar codes were invented in the 1980s after the development of the IBM PC, true or false? _____

2. QR codes can only be used to code website URLs, true or false? _____

3. Applications can engage other applications or system services through _____.

4. The applications programmer can use the ZXing source codes through compliance with the _____ license.

5. UPC code databases are only available through paid subscription, true or false? _____

6. The `startActivityForResult( )` method works in tandem with the following method: _____.

7. The file tree on an Android device connected to a development computer is visible using Eclipse's _____ perspective.

8. Data is retrieved from the system's content providers through _____ statements.

9. The gallery content provider's `title` field corresponds to the image file's _____.

10. `Environment.getExternalStorageDirectory( )` refers to the actual `/sdcard/` directory on the device, true or false? _____

SUGGESTED PROJECTS

- Rewrite one of the examples in the section "Photographs in Applications" to use a SQLite data table to hold photo details instead of the plain text file.

- The ZXing website, http://code.google.com/p/zxing/, lists the types of codes other than UPC and QR that its utilities can be used to interpret. Research one or more of these, learn where you might find them, and if possible write an application that displays their interpretation.

- Using the ZXing code downloads, write an application that produces a QR image from text entered in a text field or small text file.

- Learn how to take a screenshot on your Android device. Then, using the first of the camera applications as a basis, design a screen with an embedded `ImageView` object, an `EditText` field to hold a large font, and a company logo. Take pictures of friends or coworkers, enter their names in the `Text` field, and take a screenshot. Export and print the screenshots for mock photo IDs.

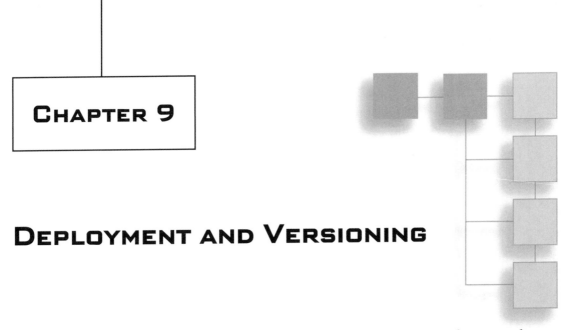

CHAPTER 9

DEPLOYMENT AND VERSIONING

The purpose of this book is not to help you produce applications for general consumption, although I certainly would not discourage it. Instead, the purpose is to extend functionality and productivity to the mobile platform for your specific concern. Even if getting an application to the Android Play Store is not a goal, certain conditions must be met before the application can even be installed on a device.

Many of those conditions start with the manifest file.

The first settings to look at in the manifest file are in the `<uses-sdk>` element. In this element, you specify the application programming interface (API)-level requirements for your application. You will use one or more of the following attributes.

- `android:minSdkVersion`—This attribute specifies the minimum version of the Android platform on which your application will run.

- `android:targetSdkVersion`—This attribute specifies the Android platform version on which the application was meant to run.

- `android:maxSdkVersion`—This is the maximum version of the Android platform on which the application is designed to run. You probably will not need to use this attribute, and you are advised to consult the Android documentation for the `<uses-sdk>` attribute before you use it.

If you are using version 20.0.2 or higher of the Android plug-in for Eclipse, you were prompted for the first two of these settings when you began a new application project. See Figure 9.1.

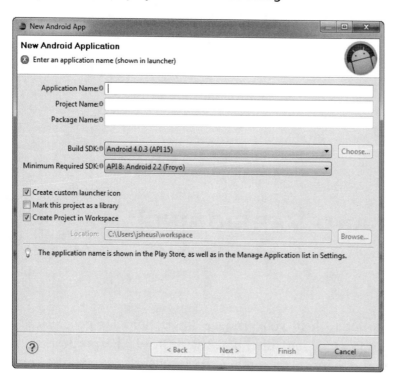

Figure 9.1
API specification settings for a new project in Eclipse.
Source: The Eclipse Foundation.

If you are using an older version of the plug-in that doesn't offer these settings at the beginning of the project (on another development machine, I am using version 16, which doesn't offer the screen in Figure 9.1), you can still set these manually in the manifest file. These attributes can be important if you are in a bring-your-own-device environment and have no control over the devices that will use your application. A device with an Android version less than the minimum you specify will not install the application; therefore, setting the minimum software development toolkit (SDK) version will give you some control over which devices will be installing your application.

The next important settings in your manifest file are attributes of the manifest element itself; in other words, they are attributes found inside the opening manifest tag. They are as follows.

- `android:versionCode`—This is an integer value that represents the version of the application. Newly started projects are set to 1. Successive releases should have a higher number than the previous. You may never intend to put an application on the public markets, but if you do and you plan to replace it at some point with an upgrade, remember to change the version number, or the market will reject the new upload.

- `android:versionName`—This value starts as 1.0 for new projects. The Android system does not pay attention to this number, so the developer can use it at will. The value is stored as a string, so the developer can use multiple decimal points in the name to specify revision levels such as 1.2.1, then 1.2.2, then 1.3.0, and so forth, based on the levels or features added and the bug fixes. Although you do not need to bother with this attribute, I would strongly suggest that, as a developer, you get into the habit of tracking and documenting revisions using this attribute as a reference.

If your application is to use any included files, text files, SQLite tables, or graphics, you should place them in the proper directories of your application at this point. If the application needs no other graphics, it should at least have launch icons. For testing purposes, there are always default launch icons included with the project. Version 20 of the plug-in gives you a range of choices at project start-up time, but these are hardly suitable for deployment. The website http://developer.android.com/guide /practices/ui_guidelines/icon_design.html has the specifics for creating and placing launch icons in the proper directories.

When you are satisfied with your project, and you have determined that it is bug free, you will get your application ready for deployment by condensing it into a single file that will have the extension APK, an abbreviation for Android Package. You can think of the APK file for Android as you would think of a Java JAR file for an application written for a personal computer. You can create the APK file by right-clicking the project name in the Package Explorer and choosing Android Tools from the menu. That choice will bring up another menu, and you can choose either Export Signed Application Package or Export Unsigned Application Package. No Android device will install an unsigned application. Back in Chapter 1, "Installing Eclipse, Java, and the Android SDK," we went through creating a key and saving it to a keystore file. If you choose Export Signed Application Package, you need to know where that keystore file is and what password you gave it when you created it. You will be prompted for these as you move through the screens to create the signed application.

If you held off on creating the key, that is okay for now; just choose Export Unsigned Application Package. You will create the APK file; you just cannot deploy it yet. Once you finally create a key, you can either go back and redo this process choosing Export Signed Application Package from the menus, or you can use a terminal and command line to sign the unsigned APK file you created.

If you choose the latter, you will use the `jarsigner` application to sign your APK file with your key. `jarsigner` is located in the same directory as the `keystore` program. An example of the command-line string follows. Note that the `keystore`'s filename, `myandroid`, and the application's name, `myApplicationName`, are just examples. You would use the `keystore` name you specified when you created the key according to the guide in Chapter 1. The application name, of course, refers to the name you gave in your project.

```
jarsigner -verbose -keystore <path>/myandroid.keystore <path>/myApplicationName.apk
myandroid (enter)
```

You will be prompted for the password you used to create the key (hopefully you saved it), and you will receive several confirmations that components of your application are being signed. We use the `-verbose` switch in the command line to receive these confirmations; they are a visible verification that the signing is taking place.

You can learn about the `keytool` utility, its sister utility, `jarsigner`, and the switches that go with them at http://download.oracle.com/javase/1,5.0/docs/tooldocs/windows/keytool.html.

You may have noticed that when you created the APK file, Eclipse warned you that you still needed to sign it and to zipalign it. The zipalign process aids in the installation of the APK file to a device. The zipalign tool is part of the Android APK. It is in the `/platform-tools` subdirectory of the `android-sdk` directory. A typical command-line string for using zipalign follows.

```
zipalign -v 4  <path>/sourcename.apk   <path>/targetname.apk (enter)
```

The `sourcename.apk` represents your signed APK file, and the `targetname.apk` is the name of your signed and zipaligned APK file. Note that these names should be different, or the target file should be in a different directory. Also, be sure to add the APK extension to these entries, because it isn't automatic.

Your application should now be ready. If you later upgrade or modify your application, you will need to perform these steps again.

Although it's not directly related to preparing the application for deployment, there are some points you should consider for maintaining your application's domain. Should you be fortunate enough to have control over the devices that will run your applications, here are some tips for securing your environment.

The first is keeping the devices you control up to date with the latest operating system (OS) versions. For development sake, this will allow you to narrow your range of SDK versions as we discussed at the beginning of the chapter, and it will give you a better idea of how your application will appear and behave in the field. It will also reduce risks to security.

Another step to take is to ensure that the devices under your control have and use screen-locking, and that they are encrypted. Figure 9.2 shows the Security panel under Settings on my Toshiba Thrive. Visible are choices to lock the screen and to encrypt the entire device.

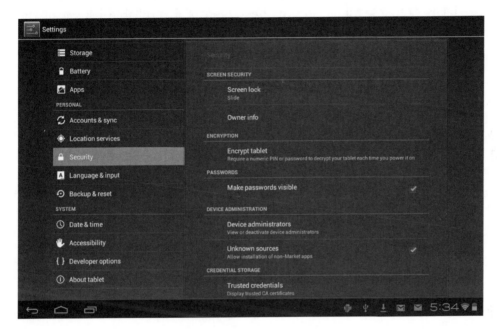

Figure 9.2
Security settings on the Toshiba Thrive tablet.
Source: Google.

Still another security precaution is remote-wipe. This feature wipes out data remotely should the device fall into the wrong hands. Along these lines, you might consider installing a GPS tracking application, or one that detects when a device joins the Internet. Third-party anti-virus software is just as important for mobile devices as it is for desktop and laptop PCs and should be deployed on handheld devices.

It is recommended that device administrators turn off carrier backups while implementing their own backup policy and schedule.

Finally, to the extent possible, try to control the installation of applications from the open market. Malware is a threat to internal networks as long as handheld devices have access to it.

If you cannot control the devices that install and use your application, at least you can learn something about them. The last exercise is an application that draws information about the device itself, including its location, and draws a list of installed applications on the system. The application presents the information in two columns. On the left is some of the information that can be taken from the system. The android.os.Build class provides more system information than I included in the exercise, but you will get the idea. The left side also includes the geocodes for the current location of the device. On the right side of the screen is a scrollable list of all the installed applications.

The application is not intended to be used as such, but it will give you the tools to gain necessary information from an Android device that can be included in part or in whole in any other application. The device information does not necessarily have to be displayed either. It can be stored on the device in a file or transmitted to a server for collection and monitoring.

There are manifest permissions that are necessary for the application to pull device data; the device owner will be notified of these at install time. The specific permissions from the manifest are as follows.

```
<uses-permission android:name="android.permission.READ_SYNC_SETTINGS"/>
<uses-permission android:name="android.permission.READ_PHONE_STATE"/>
<uses-permission android:name="android.permission.ACCESS_COARSE_LOCATION"/>
<uses-permission android:name="android.permission.ACCESS_FINE_LOCATION"/>
```

The screen layout XML file is similar to the one used in the Pareto Chart application. Its listing appears here.

```
<LinearLayout xmlns:android="http://schemas.android.com/apk/res/android"
    xmlns:tools="http://schemas.android.com/tools"
    android:layout_width="match_parent"
    android:layout_height="match_parent"
    android:orientation="horizontal" >

    <LinearLayout
        android:id="@+layout/leftside"
        android:layout_width="wrap_content"
        android:layout_height="match_parent"
        android:layout_weight=".5"
        android:orientation="vertical" >

        <TextView
            android:layout_width="wrap_content"
            android:layout_height="wrap_content"
            android:layout_centerHorizontal="true"
            android:layout_centerVertical="true"
```

```
            android:padding="@dimen/padding_medium"
            android:text="Device Specifications"
            tools:context=".MainActivity" />

        <EditText
            android:id="@+id/sysinfo"
            android:layout_width="wrap_content"
            android:layout_height="wrap_content"
            android:layout_below="@+id/greeting"
            android:layout_centerHorizontal="true"
            android:padding="@dimen/padding_medium"
            tools:context=".MainActivity" />
    </LinearLayout>

    <LinearLayout
        android:id="@+layout/rightside"
        android:layout_width="wrap_content"
        android:layout_height="match_parent"
        android:layout_weight=".5"
        android:orientation="vertical" >

        <TextView
            android:layout_width="wrap_content"
            android:layout_height="wrap_content"
            android:layout_centerHorizontal="true"
            android:layout_centerVertical="true"
            android:padding="@dimen/padding_medium"
            android:text="Installed Applications"
            tools:context=".MainActivity" />

        <EditText
            android:id="@+id/apps"
            android:layout_width="wrap_content"
            android:layout_height="wrap_content"
            android:layout_below="@+id/greeting"
            android:layout_centerHorizontal="true"
            android:padding="@dimen/padding_medium"
            tools:context=".MainActivity" />
    </LinearLayout>
</LinearLayout>
```

Finally, here is the code listing for the main activity.

```
package com.sheusi.deviceinfo;

import android.os.Bundle;
import android.app.Activity;
import android.view.Menu;
```

```java
import android.widget.*;
import android.os.Build;
import java.util.List;
import android.content.Context;
import android.content.pm.PackageManager;
import android.content.pm.ApplicationInfo;
import android.location.*;
public class MainActivity extends Activity {
    EditText info = null;
    EditText apps = null;
    Build build = null;

    @Override
    public void onCreate(Bundle savedInstanceState) {
        super.onCreate(savedInstanceState);
        setContentView(R.layout.activity_main);
        info = (EditText) findViewById(R.id.sysinfo);
        apps = (EditText) findViewById(R.id.apps);
        getSysInfo();
        getPkgInfo();
        getLocation();
    }

    @Override
    public boolean onCreateOptionsMenu(Menu menu) {
        getMenuInflater().inflate(R.menu.activity_main, menu);
        return true;
    }

    public void getPkgInfo() {
        PackageManager pm = this.getPackageManager();
        List<ApplicationInfo> packages = pm.getInstalledApplications(0);
        for (int x = 0; x < packages.size(); ++x) {
            apps.append(packages.get(x).packageName + "\n");
        }
    }

    public void getSysInfo() {
        build = new Build();
        info.append("Device: " + build.DEVICE + "\n");
        info.append("Manufacturer: " + build.MANUFACTURER + "\n");
        info.append("Model: " + build.MODEL + "\n");
        info.append("Build: " + build.ID + "\n");
        info.append("Host:   " + build.HOST + "\n");
    }
```

```
        public void getLocation() {
            LocationManager lm = (LocationManager)
getSystemService(Context.LOCATION_SERVICE);
            MyLocationListener mLocListener = new MyLocationListener();
            lm.requestLocationUpdates(LocationManager.GPS_PROVIDER, 0, 0,
                    mLocListener);
            Criteria criteria = new Criteria();
            criteria.setAccuracy(Criteria.ACCURACY_FINE);
            String gps = lm.getBestProvider(criteria, true);
            LocationProvider lp = lm.getProvider(gps);
            Location loc = lm.getLastKnownLocation(gps);
            info.append("\n\nLocation Data:\n");
            info.append("Latitude: " + loc.getLatitude() + "\n");
            info.append("Longitude:   " + loc.getLongitude() + "\n");
        }

        class MyLocationListener implements LocationListener {
            public void onLocationChanged(Location l) {
            }

            public void onProviderDisabled(String provider) {
            }

            public void onProviderEnabled(String provider) {
            }

            public void onStatusChanged(String provider, int status, Bundle extras) {
            }
        }

}
```

I chose not to include a screen image of the running application because I did not want to reveal information about my own device and its location. There is a class included that implements the LocationListener interface; there isn't code in the methods, but as an interface, it must be implemented rather than simply instantiated into a variable. The getLocation( ) method specifies a fine accuracy, but a coarse accuracy could be used just as easily. It depends on the developer's needs. On that point, both coarse and fine location permissions are requested in the manifest; the developer can eliminate the one that isn't necessary.

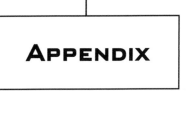

APPENDIX

ANSWERS TO CHAPTER REVIEW QUESTIONS

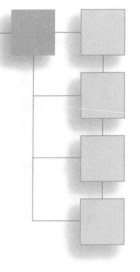

CHAPTER 2

1. In the Eclipse application manager, user-written Java classes are stored in the _____ directory within the project.
   Answer: src or source
   Reference: http://developer.android.com/tools/projects/index.html

2. Three classifications of common errors are _____, _____, and _____.
   Answer: syntax, logic, and run-time
   Reference: http://msdn.microsoft.com/en-us/library/shz02d41(v=vs.80).aspx and many others

3. The onscreen structure that replaces the menu system is the _____.
   Answer: Action Bar
   Reference: http://developer.android.com/guide/topics/ui/actionbar.html

4. Choices that cannot fit on the Action Bar are revealed by touching the _____ button.
   Answer: Overflow Menu
   Reference: http://developer.android.com/guide/topics/ui/actionbar.html

5. The target and minimum versions for the SDK are specified in the application's _____ file.
   Answer: manifest
   Reference: http://developer.android.com/guide/topics/manifest/uses-sdk-element.html

6. To configure their layout at design time, fragments will have their own
_____ file.
Answer: XML
Reference: http://developer.android.com/guide/components/fragments.html

7. All fragments extend the _____ class.
Answer: Fragment
Reference: http://developer.android.com/reference/android/app/Fragment.html

8. Three essential methods of the Fragment class are _____,
_____, and _____.

Answer: onCreate( ), onCreateView( ), and onPause( )
Reference: http://developer.android.com/reference/android/app/Fragment.html

9. To perform a drag-and-drop sequence, the two necessary listeners are the
_____ and the _____.
Answer: OnDragListener and OnLongClickListener
Reference: http://developer.android.com/guide/topics/ui/drag-drop.html

10. The image indicating the transferred item on its drag path is referred to as the
_____.

Answer: drag shadow
Reference: http://developer.android.com/guide/topics/ui/drag-drop.html

CHAPTER 3

1. The database manager used in Android devices as well as other handhelds and
tablets is _____.
Answer: SQLite
Reference: http://developer.android.com/guide/topics/data/data-storage.html#db

2. Middleware that connects the Windows 7 operating system to database man-
agement software running on the computer is _____.
Answer: ODBC
Reference: http://support.microsoft.com/kb/110093

3. A field whose value is unique to every record in a data table is called the
_____.

Answer: primary key
Reference: www.w3schools.com/sql/sql_primarykey.asp

4. A database bundled with an application can be used by the application in its current location at run-time, true or false? _____

Answer: false

Reference: http://developer.android.com/guide/topics/data/data-storage. html#filesInternal

5. Instances of the `HashMap` class are used to maintain data in _____ - _____ pairs.

Answer: key-value

Reference: http://developer.android.com/reference/java/util/HashMap.html

6. The Eclipse perspective that allows access to the directory tree as well as other components of a connected device or an emulator is the _____ perspective.

Answer: DDMS

Reference: http://developer.android.com/tools/debugging/ddms.html

7. The Android class that holds query results is the _____ class.

Answer: `Cursor`

Reference: http://developer.android.com/reference/android/database/Cursor.html

8. The last parameter in `SQLiteDatabase` class's `query( )` method controls the _____ of the returned data.

Answer: order or limit

Reference: http://developer.android.com/reference/android/database/sqlite/ SQLiteDatabase.html

9. The `rawQuery( )` method of the `SQLiteDatabase` class allows the programmer to structure queries using _____ syntax.

Answer: SQL

Reference: http://developer.android.com/reference/android/database/sqlite /SQLiteDatabase.html

10. The UI control or widget used to display a list is the _____.

Answer: `ListView`

Reference: http://developer.android.com/guide/topics/ui/layout/listview.html

CHAPTER 4

1. Layout managers such as the `RelativeLayout` and the `LinearLayout` belong to a group of controls called _____.

Answer: `ViewGroup`

Reference: http://developer.android.com/reference/android/view/ViewGroup .html

2. The proper terms used for the horizontal and vertical orientation of the screen are _____ and _____ modes.

Answer: portrait and landscape

Reference: http://developer.android.com/reference/android/content/pm /ActivityInfo.html#screenOrientation

3. The layout that positions widgets based on their relation to other widgets on the screen is the _____.

Answer: `RelativeLayout`

Reference: http://developer.android.com/guide/topics/ui/layout/relative.html

4. The abbreviations dp and dip are short for _____.

Answer: density-independent pixel

Reference: http://developer.android.com/guide/practices/screens_support.html

5. One `LinearLayout` can be embedded in another on the screen, true or false?

_____

Answer: true

Reference: http://developer.android.com/guide/topics/ui/layout/linear.html

6. Write a single line of code that would lock the screen in portrait mode.

_____

Answer: `this.setRequestedOrientation(ActivityInfo.SCREEN_ORIENTATION_PORTRAIT);` (method of the `Activity` class; when called from an instance of the `Activity` class, the object name `this` refers to the instance)

Reference: http://developer.android.com/reference/android/app/Activity.html and http://developer.android.com/reference/android/content/pm/ActivityInfo. html#screenOrientation

7. A method in all subclasses that refers to its parent class and is often used in a constructor is the _____.

Answer: `super( )`

Reference: http://docs.oracle.com/javase/tutorial/java/IandI/super.html

8. What is the purpose of the modulus operator?_____

Answer: The modulus operator returns the remainder in a division operation.

Reference: http://docs.oracle.com/javase/tutorial/java/nutsandbolts/op1.html

9. Which listener class would a developer use to detect when a user leaves a particular widget on the screen, moving from one EditText to the next in a form, for example? _____

Answer: OnFocusChangeListener (an interface)
Reference: http://developer.android.com/reference/android/view/View. OnFocusChangeListener.html

10. The graph point 0,0 is located in which corner of its container? _____

Answer: upper-left
Reference: http://docs.oracle.com/javase/tutorial/2d/overview/coordinate.html

CHAPTER 5

1. The common syntax for the universal resource identifiers (URIs) used by content providers is _____.
Answer: content://package.and.class.name/tablename (The package and class name are the symbolic name of the provider.)
Reference: http://developer.android.com/guide/topics/providers/content -provider-basics.html

2. Objects of the _____ class are used to hold results of queries sent to content providers.
Answer: Cursor
Reference: http://developer.android.com/reference/android/database/Cursor.html

3. When adding events to the system's calendar, which five time values should be added to the start time and end time for an event?
_____

Answer: year, month, day, hour, and minute
Reference: http://developer.android.com/guide/topics/providers/calendar-provider .html

4. The month of January has the following integer value when used to add an event. _____
Answer: 0 (zero)
Reference: http://docs.oracle.com/javase/1.5.0/docs/api/java/util/Calendar.html

5. An event that begins at 2:00 p.m. should have what integer value for the hour when used to add an event? _____

Answer: 14

Reference: http://docs.oracle.com/javase/1.5.0/docs/api/java/util/Calendar.html (See `HOUR_OF_DAY` constant.)

6. What permissions should be added to the manifest file for access to the Calendar content provider? _____ and _____

   Answer: `android.permission.READ_CALENDAR` and `android.permission.WRITE_CALENDAR`

   Reference: http://developer.android.com/guide/topics/providers/calendar -provider.html and http://developer.android.com/reference/android/Manifest. permission.html

7. What permissions should be added to the manifest file for access to the Contacts content provider? _____ and _____

   Answer: `android.permission.READ_CONTACTS` and `android.permission.WRITE_CONTACTS`

   Reference: http://developer.android.com/guide/topics/providers/contacts -provider.html and http://developer.android.com/reference/android/Manifest. permission.html

8. Objects of which class return `Cursor` objects when content providers are queried? _____

   Answer: `ContentResolver`

   Reference: http://developer.android.com/reference/android/content/ ContentResolver.html

9. Multiple email accounts added to the same device share the same Contacts content provider, true or false? _____

   Answer: true

   Reference: http://developer.android.com/guide/topics/providers/contacts -provider.html

10. For convenience sake, an applications programmer might choose to access a content provider's built-in interface through an _____ .

    Answer: intent

    Reference: http://developer.android.com/guide/topics/providers/contacts -provider.html (See "Batch Modification" on the web page.)

CHAPTER 6

1. For networking applications, the following permission must be included in the manifest file. _____
   Answer: `android.permission.INTERNET`
   Reference: http://developer.android.com/training/basics/network-ops/managing .html and http://developer.android.com/reference/android/Manifest.permission .html

2. The `WebView` widget requires which package to be included in the `import` statements? _____

   Answer: `android.webkit`
   Reference: http://developer.android.com/reference/android/webkit/package -summary.html

3. When using the `setConnectTimeout( )` method of the `URLConnection` class, we must manage the following checked exception. _____

   Answer: `SocketTimeoutException`
   Reference: http://developer.android.com/reference/java/net/URLConnection.html and http://developer.android.com/reference/java/net/SocketTimeoutException .html

4. Port numbers used by in-house applications should be between _____ and _____.
   Answer: 49152 and 65535
   Reference: www.tcpipguide.com/free/t_TCPIPApplicationAssignmentsand ServerPortNumberRang-2.htm

5. The port number is set in code on the _____ side of a client-server application.
   Answer: server
   Reference: http://docs.oracle.com/javase/1.4.2/docs/api/java/net/ServerSocket. html

6. Connection timeouts are set using what unit of time? _____
   Answer: milliseconds
   Reference: http://developer.android.com/reference/java/net/URLConnection.html

7. Only files with the extension HTML or HTM can be viewed in a `WebView` object, true or false? _____

   Answer: false

Reference: http://developer.android.com/reference/android/webkit/WebView .html

8. URI is an acronym for _____ .
   Answer: uniform resource identifier
   Reference: http://developer.android.com/reference/java/net/URI.html

9. Only Android services and other installed applications can be used by an application through intents, true or false? _____
   Answer: false
   Reference: http://developer.android.com/reference/android/content/Intent.html

10. If a server-side application is to be used by an Android device, it must be written specifically for Android clients, true or false? _____
    Answer: false
    Reference: http://developer.android.com/reference/java/net/Socket.html

CHAPTER 7

1. The acronym CSV stands for _____ .
   Answer: comma-separated values
   Reference: www.ietf.org/rfc/rfc4180.txt

2. The outermost element in an XML document is called the _____ element.
   Answer: root
   Reference: www.w3schools.com/xml/xml_tree.asp

3. Data included in the opening tag of an XML element is called _____ .
   Answer: attributes
   Reference: www.w3schools.com/xml/xml_attributes.asp

4. JSON is an acronym that stands for _____ .
   Answer: JavaScript Object Notation
   Reference: www.json.org/

5. JSON presents individual data items in _____ _____ pairs.
   Answer: name – value
   Reference: www.json.org/

6. An advantage of the JSON format over XML is that it requires fewer _____ , or lower _____ .
   Answer: characters, overhead

Reference: www.json.org/xml.html

(Note: The reference lists several other advantages of JSON over XML, but a simple character count on the same data formatted in both JSON and XML will prove the answer to question 6.)

7. The only JSON and XML parser libraries that can be used in an Android application are the ones included in the Android SDK, true or false?

_____.

Answer: false

Reference: http://code.google.com/p/google-gson/, http://sax.sourceforge.net, and others

8. The information area at the top of an XML document that contains the version number is called the _____.

Answer: prolog or declaration

Reference: www.w3schools.com/xml/xml_whatis.asp

9. In JSON formatting, the key and value in a pair are separated by a

_____.

Answer: colon

Reference: www.json.org/example.html

10. Comments in XML files are surrounded by the following characters: _____ and _____.

Answer: <!-- and -->

Reference: www.w3schools.com/xml/xml_syntax.asp

CHAPTER 8

1. Bar codes were invented in the 1980s after the development of the IBM PC, true or false? _____

Answer: false

Reference: www.ehow.com/info_8423248_patents-1950s-bar-code-technology.html

2. QR codes can only be used to code website URLs, true or false?

_____.

Answer: false

Reference: http://qrbcn.com/imatgesbloc/Three_QR_Code.pdf

3. Applications can engage other applications or system services through

_____.

Answer: intents

Reference: http://developer.android.com/reference/android/content/Intent.html

4. The applications programmer can use the ZXing source codes through compliance with the _____ license.
Answer: Apache
Reference: http://code.google.com/p/zxing/ and www.apache.org/licenses/LICENSE-2.0

5. UPC code databases are only available through paid subscription, true or false? _____

Answer: false
Reference: www.upcdatabase.org/ or http://eandata.com/

6. The `startActivityForResult( )` method works in tandem with the following method: _____.

Answer: `onActivityResult( )` (a protected method)
Reference: http://developer.android.com/reference/android/app/Activity.html

7. The file tree on an Android device connected to a development computer is visible using Eclipse's _____ perspective.
Answer: DDMS
Reference: http://developer.android.com/tools/debugging/ddms.html

8. Data is retrieved from the system's content providers through _____ statements.
Answer: `query`

Reference: http://developer.android.com/guide/topics/providers/content-provider-basics.html

9. The gallery content provider's `title` field corresponds to the image file _____.

Answer: name
Reference: http://developer.android.com/reference/android/provider/MediaStore.MediaColumns.html

10. `Environment.getExternalStorageDirectory( )` refers to the actual `/sdcard/` directory on the device, true or false? _____

Answer: true
Reference: http://developer.android.com/reference/android/os/Environment.html#getExternalStorageDirectory() and http://developer.android.com/tools/help/emulator.html

INDEX

????? (command line values), 11

A

Action Bar
    backward compatibility, 25–32
        Context menu, 26
        Options menu, 26–32
    hardware buttons, 25
    help, 31
    viewing, 31
activities, passing bundles, 169–179
adding. *See* **creating**
Android
    Action Bar. *See* Action Bar
    AndroidManifest.xml file, 19
    API levels, 15
    code names, 15
    fragments. *See* fragments
    help, 6
    SDKs
        installing, 4–6
        manifests, 26–29
        versions, 26–29
    versions, 15
AndroidManifest.xml file, 19
APIs (application programming interfaces), 14–15
APK files, creating, 257–258
applications (programs). *See also* **projects**
    APIs (application programming interfaces), 14–15
    APK files, 257–258
    backward compatibility (Action Bar), 25–32
    connectionless client-server applications
        creating multiscreen applications, 168
        downloading files from URLs, 175–176

        intents, 169
        manifests, 168
        overview, 167–168
        passing bundles between activities,
            169–179
        services, 169
        storing data, 178–179
    connection-oriented client-server applications
        opening files, 189–190
        overview, 179–182
        ports, 179–182
        QR codes, 182–191
        scanning applications, 182–191
        sockets, 179–182
        viewing files, 189–190
    keytool, 10–11
    legacy applications. *See* backward compatibility
    multiscreen applications, 168
    naming, 13
    scanning
        classes, 236–237
        connection-oriented client-server applications,
            182–191
        descriptions, 239–240
        errors, 236
        intents, 234–236
        layout, 235
        overview, 233–234
        packages, 236–237
        viewing, 238–240
        Zebra Crossing, 233–236
    SDKs. *See* SDKs
    security, 258–260
    testing, tablets/emulators comparison, 130
    tracking geocode locations, 260–263

applications (programs) *Continued*
 versions (manifests), 255–257
 zipaligning, 258

B
Back button, 25
backward compatibility
 Action Bar, 25–32
  Context menu, 26
  Options menu, 26–32
 Back button, 25
 Home button, 25
 Overflow button, 26
bar codes
 classes, 236–237
 descriptions, 239–240
 errors, 236
 intents, 234–236
 layout, 235
 overview, 233–234
 packages, 236–237
 viewing, 238–240
 Zebra Crossing, 233–236
bitmaps, displaying, 241–247
browsers (SQL Database Browser), 56
build SDKs, 14–15
building. *See* creating
bundles
 connectionless client-server applications, 169–179
 databases, 55–65
  checking database locations, 60–62
  converting tables, 56
  copying databases, 60–62
  creating databases, 56–57
  creating ODBC data sources, 57–59
  downloading SQL Database Browser, 56
  installing SQLite driver, 57
  primary key field IDs, 59–60
  transferring data from flash drives, 63–65
buttons, 25–26

C
calendars
 creating, 130–138
  linear layout, 131
  posting events, 133–138
  querying tables, 131–133
 permissions (manifest), 135–136
cameras
 bar codes
  classes, 236–237
  descriptions, 239–240

 errors, 236
 intents, 234–236
 layout, 235
 overview, 233–234
 packages, 236–237
 viewing, 238–240
 Zebra Crossing, 233–236
 photos
  displaying bitmaps, 241–247
  displaying from galleries, 247–252
  overview, 240–241
  shooting, 241–247
 QR codes
  classes, 236–237
  descriptions, 239–240
  errors, 236
  intents, 234–236
  layout, 235
  overview, 233–234
  packages, 236–237
  viewing, 238–240
  Zebra Crossing, 233–236
charts, creating, 118–126
checking database locations, 60–62
classes
 packages. *See* packages
 scanning applications, 236–237
 subclassing
  overview, 104–105
  text fields, 105–112
  validating data entry, 108–112
client-server applications
 connectionless client-server applications
  creating multiscreen applications, 168
  downloading files from URLs, 175–176
  intents, 169
  manifests, 168
  overview, 167–168
  passing bundles between activities,
   169–179
  services, 169
  storing data, 178–179
 connection-oriented client-server applications
  opening files, 189–190
  overview, 179–182
  ports, 179–182
  QR codes, 182–191
  scanning applications, 182–191
  sockets, 179–182
  viewing files, 189–190
client-side JSON code (data transfer),
 209–213

client-side XML code (data transfer), 198–208

code. *See* JSON; XML

code names (Android), 15

command lines (?????), 11

communications

    connectionless, 167

    connection-oriented, 167

    fragments (hosting activity), 48

    overhead, 167

compatibility. *See* backward compatibility

computers used in this book, 7

configuring

    devices, 7–11

    Eclipse, 5–6

    emulators, 6–8

    IDEs, 7–11

    signatures, 10–11

connectionless client-server applications

    creating multiscreen applications, 168

    downloading files from URLs, 175–176

    intents, 169

    manifests, 168

    overview, 167–168

    passing bundles between activities,
        169–179

    services, 169

    storing data, 178–179

connectionless communications, 167

connection-oriented client-server applications

    opening files, 189–190

    overview, 179–182

    ports, 179–182

    QR codes, 182–191

    scanning applications, 182–191

    sockets, 179–182

    viewing files, 189–190

connection-oriented communications, 167

contacts

    content provider operations, 139–140

    content resolvers, 140

    creating, 147–163

    CRUD, 139

    deleting, 142–146

    lists, displaying, 140–142

    overview, 138–139

    permissions (manifest), 140

    reading, 140–142

    updating, 147–163

content providers

    calendars

        creating, 130–138

        linear layout, 131

        permissions (manifest), 135–136

        posting events, 133–138

        querying tables, 131–133

    contacts

        content provider operations, 139–140

        content resolvers, 140

        creating, 147–163

        CRUD, 139

        deleting, 142–146

        lists, displaying, 140–142

        overview, 138–139

        permissions (manifest), 140

        reading, 140–142

        updating, 147–163

    overview, 129–130

    URIs, 129

content resolvers (contacts), 140

context (tables), 69

Context menu (Action Bar), 26

controls, subclassing

    overview, 104–105

    text fields, 105–112

    validating data entry, 108–112

converting tables, 56

copying databases, 60–62

create, read, update, delete (CRUD), 138

    contacts, 139

    tables, 75

creating

    APK files, 257–258

    calendars, 130–138

        linear layout, 131

        posting events, 133–138

        querying tables, 131–133

    charts, 118–126

    contacts, 147–163

    databases, 56–57

    forms (pick-lists), 94–104

    fragments

        dynamically, 43–47

        placeholders, 34–43

    multiscreen applications, 168

    ODBC data sources, 57–59

    signature fields, 113–118

    tables, run-time, 75–87

CRUD (create, read, update, delete),
    138

    contacts, 139

    tables, 75

CSV (comma-separated values), 195

D

data

data entry, validating, 108–112

data sources (ODBC), creating, 57–59

data transfer. *See* data transfer

storing (connectionless client-server applications), 178–179

data entry, validating, 108–112

data sources (ODBC), creating, 57–59

data transfer

CSV, 195

flash drives, 63–65

JSON

client-side code, 209–213

Google Maps, 213–215, 218–229

overview, 195

XML

client-side code, 198–208

Google Maps, 216–229

overview, 195–196

server-side PHP script, 196–197

well formed, 195–196

databases. *See also* **tables**

bundling, 55–65

checking database locations, 60–62

converting tables, 56

copying databases, 60–62

creating databases, 56–57

creating ODBC data sources, 57–59

downloading SQL Database Browser, 56

installing SQLite driver, 57

primary key field IDs, 59–60

transferring data from flash drives, 63–65

copying, 60–62

creating, 56–57

locations, checking, 60–62

SQLite database management system, 55

Debug perspective, 21–24

debugging devices, 9–10

deleting

contacts, 142–146

tables, 75, 77

descriptions, scanning applications, 239–240

devices

configuring, 7–11

drivers, installing, 8–9

IDEs, viewing, 9–10

manifests, debugging, 10

settings, debugging, 9

used in this book, 7–8

digital signatures

configuring, 10–11

signature fields, creating, 113–118

directories. *See also* **files**

gen, 18–19

layout, 18–19

projects, 17–19

res, 18–19

src, 17–19

values, 18–19

displaying. *See also* **viewing**

bitmaps, 241–247

lists (contacts), 140–142

photos from galleries, 247–252

tables (ListView), 65–75

downloading

files from URLs (connectionless client-server applications), 175–176

SQL Database Browser, 56

SQLite driver, 57

drag and drop (fragments), 48–51

drivers, installing, 8–9

dynamically adding fragments, 43–47

E

Eclipse

configuring, 5–6

Debug perspective, 21–24

editor, 16–18

help, 6

IDE, installing, 3–4

LogCat tab, 22–24

Package Explorer, 16–18

projects. *See* projects

viewing, 16–18

editor, viewing, 16–18

emulators

configuring, 6–8

loading speed, 6–8

size, 7–8

testing, 130

errors, 19–24

Debug perspective, 21–24

LogCat tab, 22–24

logic errors, 20

run-time errors, 21–22

scanning applications, 236

syntax errors, 20–22

events, posting, 133–138

F

fields
database primary key fields, 59–60
printing names, 68–70
signature fields, creating, 113–118
text fields, subclassing, 105–112
files. *See also* **directories**
AndroidManifest.xml, 19
APK, creating, 257–258
connectionless client-server applications,
175–176
connection-oriented client-server applications,
189–190
downloading from URLs, 175–176
filenames, 16
keystore, 10–11
opening, 189–190
projects overview, 17–19
signatures
configuring, 10–11
signature fields, creating, 113–118
viewing, 189–190
flash drives, 63–65
folders. *See* **directories**
forms (pick-lists), 94–104
fragments
adding
dynamically, 43–47
placeholders, 34–43
communicating (hosting activity), 48
drag and drop, 48–51
IDs, 48
life cycle, 32–34
onCreate( ) method, 33
onCreateView( ) method, 33
onPause( ) method, 33
overview, 32

G

galleries, displaying photos, 247–252
gen directory, 18–19
geocode locations, 260–263
ghosted hardware buttons, 25–26
Google Maps (data transfer)
JSON, 213–215, 218–229
XML, 216–229
graphics, creating
charts, 118–126
signature fields, 113–118

H

hardware buttons, 25–26
hash maps (tables), 69
help
Action Bar, 31
Android, 6
Eclipse, 6
Java, 6
projects, 19
hiding. *See* **viewing**
Home button, 25
hosting activity, 48

I

icons (launch icons), 15–16
IDEs (integrated development environments)
configuring, 7–11
devices, viewing, 9–10
Eclipse, installing, 3–4
IDs
database primary key fields, 59–60
fragments, 48
tables, 69
installing
Android SDKs, 4–6
drivers (devices), 8–9
Eclipse IDE, 3–4
JDK, 1–3
SQLite driver, 57
integrated development environments. *See* **IDEs**
intents
connectionless client-server applications, 169
scanning applications, 234–236

J

Java
help, 6
JDK, 1–3
JDK (Java development toolkit), 1–3
JSON (data transfer)
client-side code, 209–213
Google Maps, 213–215, 218–229

K

key values (tables), 69
keystore, 10–11
keytool, 10–11

L

landscape mode, 90–94
launch icons, 15–16
layout
    layout directory, 18–19
    linear layout (calendars), 131
    scanning applications, 235
    screens, 89–94
    tables, 69
    XML, 16
layout directory, 18–19
legacy applications. *See* backward compatibility
life cycle (fragments), 32–34
linear layout, 131
lists, displaying contacts, 140–142
List View, displaying tables, 65–75
loading emulators, 6–8
locations
    checking databases, 60–62
    tracking geocode locations, 260–263
LogCat tab, 22–24
logic errors, 20

M

manifests
    Android SDKs, 26–29
    AndroidManifest.xml file, 19
    connectionless client-server applications,
        168
    devices, debugging, 10
    permissions
        calendars, 135–136
        contacts, 140
    versions (applications), 255–257
menu bar. *See* Action Bar
methods (fragments)
    onCreate( ), 33
    onCreateView( ), 33
    onPause( ), 33
minimum required SDKs, 14–15
multiscreen applications, creating, 168

N

names/naming
    applications, 13
    fields, printing, 68–70
    filenames, 16
    packages, 13–14
    projects, 13

O

ODBC (Open Database Connectivity), 57–59
onCreate( ) method, 33
onCreateView( ) method, 33
onPause( ) method, 33
Open Database Connectivity (ODBC), 57–59
opening files (connection-oriented client-server
        applications), 189–190
Options menu (Action Bar), 26–32
Overflow button, 26
overhead (communications), 167

P

Package Explorer, 16–18
packages
    AndroidManifest.xml, 19
    classes. *See* classes
    directories
        gen, 18–19
        layout, 18–19
        res, 18–19
        src, 17–19
        values, 18–19
    naming, 13–14
    Package Explorer, 16–18
    scanning applications, 236–237
Pareto charts, 118–126
permissions (manifests)
    calendars, 135–136
    contacts, 140
photos
    displaying bitmaps, 241–247
    displaying from galleries, 247–252
    overview, 240–241
    shooting, 241–247
PHP, data transfer, 196–197
pick-lists (forms), 94–104
placeholders (fragments), 34–43
portrait mode, 90–94
ports (connection-oriented client-server applications),
        179–182
posting events (calendars), 133–138
primary key fields, 59–60
printing
    field names, 68–70
    records, 68–71
programs. *See* applications
projects. *See also* applications
    APIs, 14–15
    applications, naming, 13
    directories. *See* directories

errors. *See* errors
filenames, 16
files. *See* files
help, 19
launch icons, 15–16
layout. *See* layout
manifests. *See* manifests
naming, 13
packages, naming, 13–14
SDKs. *See* SDKs
starting overview, 13

Q

QR codes
    classes, 236–237
    connection-oriented client-server applications,
        182–191
    descriptions, 239–240
    errors, 236
    intents, 234–236
    layout, 235
    overview, 233–234
    packages, 236–237
    viewing, 238–240
    Zebra Crossing, 233–236
querying tables, 131–133
question marks (command line values), 11

R

reading
    contacts, 140–142
    tables, 75–76
records, printing, 68–71
res directory, 18–19
resources, 18–19
run-time
    errors, 21–22
    tables, creating, 75–87

S

scanning applications
    classes, 236–237
    connection-oriented client-server applications,
        182–191
    descriptions, 239–240
    errors, 236
    intents, 234–236
    layout, 235
    overview, 233–234
    packages, 236–237
    viewing, 238–240
    Zebra Crossing, 233–236
screens
    landscape mode, 90–94
    layout, 89–94
    portrait mode, 90–94
    size, 89–94
scripts (PHP), 196–197
SDKs (software development toolkits)
    build SDKs, 14–15
    installing, 4–6
    manifests, 26–29
    minimum required SDKs, 14–15
    versions, 26–29
security, 258–260
server-side PHP script, 196–197
**services (connectionless client-server
        applications), 169**
settings, debugging, 9
shooting photos, 241–247
signature fields, creating, 113–118
signatures
    configuring, 10–11
    signature fields, creating, 113–118
signing (APK files), 257–258
size
    emulators, 7–8
    screens, 89–94
**sockets (connection-oriented client-server
        applications), 179–182**
software development toolkits. *See* SDKs
source (src directory), 17–19
speed, loading emulators, 6–8
SQL Database Browser, downloading, 56
SQLite
    database management system, 55
    databases. *See* databases
    driver, installing, 57
src directory, 17–19
starting projects, 13
**storing data (connectionless client-server
        applications), 178–179**
subclassing controls
    overview, 104–105
    text fields, 105–112
    validating data entry, 108–112
subdirectories. *See* directories
support. *See* help
syntax errors, 20–22

T

tables. *See also* **databases**
  context, 69
  converting, 56
  creating, run-time, 75–87
  CRUD, 75
  deleting, 75, 77
  displaying (ListView), 65–75
  field names, printing, 68–70
  hash maps, 69
  IDs, 69
  key values, 69
  layout, 69
  querying (calendars), 131–133
  reading, 75–76
  records, printing, 68, 70–71
  SQLite database management system, 55
  updating, 75–77
tablets, testing, 130
testing applications, 130
text fields
  signature fields, 113–118
  subclassing, 105–112
tracking geocode locations, 260–263
transferring data. *See* **data transfer**
troubleshooting. *See* **errors; help**

U

updating
  contacts, 147–163
  tables, 75–77
URIs (uniform resource identifiers), 129
URLs (connectionless client-server applications),
  175–176

V

validating (data entry), 108–112
values
  ?????, 11
  CSV, 195

  key values (tables), 69
  values directory, 18–19
values directory, 18–19
versions
  Android, 15
  Android SDKs, 26–29
  applications, 255–257
viewing. *See also* **displaying**
  Action Bar, 31
  devices, IDEs, 9–10
  Eclipse, 16–18
  editor, 16–18
  files (connection-oriented client-server applications),
    189–190
  Package Explorer, 16–18
  scanning applications, 238–240

W

well-formed XML, 195–196
widgets, subclassing
  overview, 104–105
  text fields, 105–112
  validating data entry, 108–112

X–Z

XML
  data transfer
    client-side code, 198–208
    Google Maps, 216–229
    overview, 195–196
    server-side PHP script, 196–197
    well formed, 195–196
  layout, 16

Zebra Crossing, 233–236
zipaligning applications, 258

Like the Book?

Let us know on Facebook or Twitter!

facebook.com/courseptr

twitter.com/courseptr